Peace in Piccadilly

THE STORY OF ALBANY

ALBANY, 1958
A drawing by Dennis Flanders

Peace in Piccadilly

THE STORY OF ALBANY

BY

SHEILA BIRKENHEAD

Illustrated

REYNAL & COMPANY

NEW YORK

To
THE MEMORY OF MY FATHER

CONTENTS

ILLUSTRATIONS

ix

Illustrations

INTRODUCTION

IF I could take a journey back in time, Melbourne House in the late eighteenth century would be one of my first stopping-places. I should like to see the people who came to the mansion which Lady Melbourne built in Piccadilly— the Prince of Wales before he became fat and ludicrous, the young Georgiana Devonshire with giant plumes nodding above her charming and expectant face, Horace Walpole's god-daughter, the talented Mrs. Damer, Charles James Fox and handsome Charles Grey. These are among the first characters in the story of Albany. Then, after a few royal years as York House, Lady Melbourne's mansion is divided into apartments, new buildings are erected in her garden, and in 1803 the property has changed into Albany—the Albany that we know.

The story of Albany is largely the story of the people who have lived there. A list of names is not inspiring, and I could not write about them all, so I have chosen a few and I must admit that they are those who interest me most. I have tried to give a picture of their lives while they were there, but this would have made little sense without some account of what had gone before. One thing is shared in common by all about whom I have written—their stay in Albany was important to them, though in very different ways. To Byron and Lytton it marked a turning-point in their lives, a moment when each took an irrevocable decision—Byron to embark on his disastrous marriage, Lytton that he could never again live with his wife. To 'Monk' Lewis, though he did much work there, it was somewhere to live and entertain, and a setting for his collection of *bibelots*, constantly to be re-arranged and re-displayed. To Gladstone it was a place where he rested for a moment at the outset of his public career, convenient for the House of Commons, but quiet enough for him to be able to meditate without distraction on the relation of Church and State. To Macaulay it was a prize won by his own efforts, and the place where he could at last live the life he most aspired to—'a college life in London'. To John Lane it was an achievement—the base from which he helped to revolutionize the literary and artistic world of London.

The stillness in Albany, which you cannot fail to note, seems to hold within it echoes of events long past and voices that are silent. 'Monk' Lewis's Venetian gondolier-turned-manservant, with his enormous mustachios, Byron's hideous old maid, of whom he was so inexplicably fond, 'the great Wilson' who cosseted his 'gentlemen' of *The Saturday Review*, are as much a part of its past as are those they served.

In that timeless tranquillity it requires little effort of the imagination to see them there—the dandy, Bulwer Lytton, sitting down to pen his bitter warning to the future Mrs. Disraeli on the penalties of slander; the aged Wordsworth joining Gladstone and his servant in impromptu prayers, and carefully peeling off his silk stockings, to replace them with worsted before venturing out; Jane Austen's favourite brother, handsome and over six feet tall, setting up his business in the courtyard; Macaulay returning to his rooms to re-read *Persuasion* after a visit to the Great Exhibition in Hyde Park; the consumptive Beardsley arriving at *The Bodley Head* with the black satchel which gave him the look of 'the man from the Pru', but which really contained his haunting drawings for the *Yellow Book*; the cavalcade of riders clattering out of Albany Courtyard at the turn of the century to join the fashionable parade in Hyde Park.

Wherever possible I have quoted directly from contemporary letters or journals, as I believe that they paint the most vivid picture of people and events.

The main sources of information are given at the end

of this book, but it is difficult to make the list complete. In the quest for details about the everyday life of residents in Albany, only sometimes successful, I found crumbs of information in most unlikely places. I have enjoyed the search.

My grateful thanks are due to the Trustees of Albany, who so kindly allowed me to read the Minute Books of their meetings, which began in April 1803, the Minutes of the General Meetings of the Proprietors, the Albany Register and all the many documents in their possession. And here I must express my especial debt to Captain Charles Adams, Secretary of Albany since 1930, who has not only allowed me to study these documents in his rooms, but has been unfailingly helpful with advice and information from his unrivalled store of knowledge about Albany.

I must also record my thanks to Mr. William Stone for reminiscences of his sixty-five years as a resident of Albany; to Mr. R. Brook-Caws, Curator of Messrs. Coutts & Co.'s Archives, for helping me with the complicated financial negotiations which preceded the conversion of York House; to Mr. R. W. Lloyd for allowing me to make use of his collection of prints and documents; to Lord Home for permitting me to quote from the unpublished volumes of Lady Mary Coke's Journal; to Sir Harold Nicolson for advice about Byron's portrait; to Mr. Kennish Brown for allowing me to read his thesis on the architecture of Albany; to Mrs. O. Copland-Griffiths for information about the Copland family; and to Lady Gage, Lady Hermione Cobbold, Mr. John Wyndham, Lord Brocket, Lord Forteviot, Brigadier F. A. V. Copland-Griffiths, Mr. John Murray, Mr. C. A. Gladstone, and the Directors of Messrs. Coutts & Co. for permission to reproduce pictures in their possession.

Peace in Piccadilly

———

THE STORY OF ALBANY

CHAPTER I

MELBOURNE HOUSE

I

WE COME into London from the west, through the turnpike at Hyde Park Corner, and our twentieth-century eyes have difficulty in recognizing our surroundings. Where we are accustomed to see a pillared screen only the turnpike stands with its little lodge, and an apple-stall on ground given by George II to a man who had fought at Dettingen. We look in vain for Apsley House as we pass an inn called the 'Hercules Pillars' and make our way along Piccadilly.

If we had come this way a few years earlier, we should have seen an untidy huddle of stables and small houses on our left at the end of Park Lane, and innumerable taverns, the haunts of drovers from the cattle-market in Brook Fields. Now May Fair, held for so many years in the meadows behind Piccadilly, where you could see elephants and tigers, fire-eaters, ass-racing and bull-baiting, has been abolished. The theatre and the roundabouts have gone—only Shepherd Market remains. With their clientèle departed, the inns have given place to stone-faced mansions which look over Piccadilly to the Green Park. So quickly was this transformation achieved that Horace Walpole, driving this way a few years before us, 'stared today at Piccadilly like a country squire; there are twenty new stone houses: at first I concluded that all the grooms that used to live there had got estates and built palaces.'[1]

We pass some of these palaces as we walk on down

[1] H. W. to Montagu, 8 November 1759.

1

Piccadilly—Coventry House, whose hostess was the elder of the beautiful Gunning sisters; Egremont House, where five years ago the rebel Wilkes was interviewed by the Earls of Egremont and Halifax after his arrest;[1] and Bath House on the corner of Bolton Street. As we wander down Piccadilly we catch occasional glimpses of the Green Park through gaps in the brick wall fenced in by railings.[2] The grass slopes into the valley where the Tyburn Stream, spanned by a stone bridge, flows under the road into a large pool surrounded by trees.

Even in this busy thoroughfare we must be on our guard against pick-pockets and the possibility of more violent robbery. The Green Park, like Hyde Park, is a favourite haunt of footpads and some of the more daring have been known to send scouts out into Piccadilly. When one of these rascals has done his work he will dash across the road, where his accomplice will be ready to slam and lock the Park gate in the face of his pursuers.[3] So, keeping a wary eye on anyone who seems inclined to jostle us, we make our way past Lord Eglinton's new house on the corner of Stratton Street, past the wall bounding the courtyard of Devonshire House, which has been re-built since the old building was destroyed by fire some forty years since. We catch a glimpse of Arlington Street on the other side of Piccadilly, where Horace Walpole is still living, and where so many Cabinet Ministers have their town houses that he says, 'From my earliest memory Arlington Street has been the Ministerial Street.'[4]

The crush of carriages in this part of Piccadilly is so great that we make better progress on foot. We are fortunate not to have made this expedition ten or fifteen

[1] Sir N. W. Wraxall, *Historical and Posthumous Memoirs*, Vol. I, p. 340. This house is now the Naval and Military Club.

[2] James Ralph, *A Central Survey of the Public Buildings in and about London and Westminster*, 1731.

[3] *St. James's Chronicle*, 2 November 1769.

[4] H. W. to Geo. Montagu, 1 December 1768.

years earlier. Then we should have found a stinking ken-
nel running down the centre of the street, into which slops,
manure, rotten vegetables and even dead dogs and cats
were thrown. We should have been separated from passing
carriages only by posts placed at intervals along the side
of the road, while doorsteps jutting into the pathway
would have forced us out into the street every few yards.
Since the Westminster Paving Act, passed nine years ago,
things have changed for the better, and now we can walk
on a raised pavement with no obtruding doorsteps in our
way, while gutters have been constructed on either side
of the street.

Deafened by the roar of wheels on cobbles, we thread
our way through the carriages which are turning into
Bond Street, keep on past the high wall in front of Burlington House, and now we come to what I have brought
you so far to see—a new red-brick house rising from its
foundations to join the other noble mansions in Piccadilly,
with a courtyard in front and a long garden behind. Its
owners, like itself, are rather lately come to the fashionable
world, for it is only two years since Peniston Lamb,
second Baronet, married Sir Ralph Milbanke's beautiful
seventeen-year-old daughter, who is destined to be one
of the great hostesses and most influential women in this
era of remarkable women.

II

Elizabeth Lamb showed at the beginning of her married
life that judicious deference for convention which was to
colour her career by presenting her husband with a son and
heir. This duty done she turned to other things.

Sir Peniston Lamb was an indolent, dull and almost
illiterate young man. He had little to recommend him
except kindliness, good humour and nearly a million
pounds. These advantages his wife turned to good

account. He was proud of her beauty and popularity and he liked to boast that on his marriage he had given the whole of his wife's fortune back to her in diamonds. Soon after the birth of his son he was rewarded by the King for two years' silent but undeviating support in the House of Commons with an Irish peerage, an honour nicely calculated to encourage his loyalty to a monarch who checked every list of voters, yet not to destroy his future usefulness. As an Irish peer he could still sit in the House of Commons, where the Government votes were needed. He took his title from his Yorkshire estate and became (though he had never been to Ireland) Baron Melbourne of Kilmore in the County of Cavan.

Their son was born in May 1770. During that autumn Lady Melbourne was painted by Sir Joshua Reynolds, with her child in her arms. But she was by no means occupied exclusively with her maternal duties. She was eighteen years old, beautiful, wealthy, with unusual intelligence and a strong personality. She soon became friendly with other young married women of high rank and though some of the older generation might disapprove of them, their beauty and high spirits were welcomed at fashionable London gatherings. In those days they dined early and went on to the Opera-house or a play from which they returned for a late supper, with card playing afterwards, or political talk with the men who had come straight from the House of Commons. Sometimes there would be evening expeditions to Ranelagh. Sir Joshua saw Lady Melbourne at a Masquerade with the Duchess of Ancaster and Lady Fordyce, all dressed like men, 'the pretty fellows appearing in dominoes as masculine as many of the maccaroni things we see everywhere.'[1]

It was towards the end of this winter of festivities that Lord Melbourne became aware that it was his duty to

---

[1] The Maccaroni Club was composed of 'travelled young men'. Its members dressed foppishly, carried 'spying glasses' and wore their hair in long curls.

maintain an establishment more worthy of his new rank. Lady Melbourne was flying high. To the east of Burlington House stood a large, irregularly-shaped dwelling with a garden running back to Vigo Lane, which had originally formed three separate houses. The present owner, Lord Holland, no longer lived there, preferring his house at Kensington. His health was failing and the extravagance of his sons was threatening to dissipate the fortune which he had accumulated during his period as Paymaster-General. In a deed dated 1 April 1771, Lord Melbourne bought 'Holland House in Piccadilly' for £16,500—£500 more than Lord Holland had given for it eight years before.[1]

Lady Melbourne intended to build on this site a house which would compare with the mansions of the greatest families in England. It was to be a house where the fashionable world of London could be entertained in the utmost splendour. She would run no risk with its building and decoration; none but those already at the top of their profession would be employed. As architect she selected Mr. William Chambers, who had been 'architectural tutor' to George III when he was Prince of Wales and had since been appointed by Royal Letters Patent to be one of two 'Architects of the Works' at a salary of £300 a year. Robert Adam was his colleague.

Some years before Lord Holland had considered demolishing the old house and building a new mansion on the site. It is interesting to compare the plan prepared for him by Robert Adam, its oval, colonnaded forecourt and its house built round a central open courtyard, with the design executed for Lord Melbourne by Chambers.

This Melbourne House was to be set a hundred feet back from Piccadilly, protected from the street by a high wall surmounted by ornamental lamps. Two gates, with a tall, classical, pedimented arch between them, would lead into the Great Court. Coach-houses and stables for thirteen

[1] Deed in possession of Trustees of Albany.

horses were to be on the left side of the courtyard, on the
right the Porter's Lodge and the kitchen premises. Ten
steps at the front door would lead the visitor into a large
hall, and through three archways he would see ahead
the whole central space of the house to the roof filled by the
Great Stair and adorned by classical statues standing in
recesses. Magnificent reception rooms on the ground
floor and again above would overlook the garden at the
back of the house. On each floor the central room faced
down the garden with three tall, large-paned windows,
while the rooms on either side would end in rounded bays
twenty feet across.[1]

Such was the plan which was finally adopted. But with
all this settled to her satisfaction Lady Melbourne had
still to arrange for the decoration. The 'rage for painting',
which Robert Adam had regretted earlier in Italy, had
now spread thence to France and England. Lady Melbourne engaged the Florentine Cipriani, most fashionable of decorators,[2] to paint the ceiling of the fifty-two-
foot-long saloon. Biagio Rebecca was to beguile the eye
with *trompe-l'œil* decoration, of which he had shown
himself a master at Windsor and at Kew, and Wheatley
was to decorate the walls with landscapes.[3] The dining-
room, below the Saloon and of the same size, was panelled,
the panels being painted 'Green on a White Ground' and
the surrounds 'Pale Buff'. The ceiling was richly moulded.
At one end of the room a large bay window looked on to
the garden, at the other stood a colonnade of Ionic columns.[4]

It was perhaps fortunate that Lady Melbourne's mag-

---

[1] It is interesting to find that two water-closets were included in the
plans for Lord and Lady Melbourne's private apartments.

[2] Giovanni Cipriani painted allegorical pictures on the panels of the
State Coach first used in 1782 by George III and still in use today.

[3] Of all this wealth of decoration little remains today; only the
beautiful plaster-work of the ceiling in what was the State dressing-
room, and part of Cipriani's frieze in the Saloon, which has been concealed for some years past by a false ceiling.

[4] Plans in possession of Mr. R. W. Lloyd of I. 5 and 6 Albany.

nificence was in part restrained by a friend whose taste was less flamboyant than her own, Mrs. Damer, the only child of General Conway, Horace Walpole's friend. Artistic and gifted, a favourite of Walpole's since her earliest years, she had worked on his advice in several artists' studios and had studied anatomy with Cruickshank. At eighteen she had married—without love, it was said— Lord Milton's eldest son, the heir to a fortune of £30,000 a year. Now she and her husband were living an extravagant life in London—a modern, fashionable life, disapproved by the older generation, whereby they shared the same house but no common interests, and rarely met. He spent his nights with 'troops of women' and his days in the ease and idleness of the London clubs, she passed her time in all the pleasures of a life of fashion. But her knowledge and advice were valued by Lady Melbourne and were of great service to her in the decoration of the house. She was rich, beautiful and talented. Many must have envied her and no one can have anticipated the dreadful change that was so soon to come.

Lord Melbourne already played little part in his wife's life, save to pay the bills and accompany her to the play or to more formal gatherings. Within a year of their marriage he had contrived a meeting with a Mrs. Baddeley —an actress whom he had admired at Ranelagh. He persuaded her to leave the stage and to live under his protection in a house in St. James's Place, with a Mrs. Steele for her companion. In her hands he proved equally malleable. Presents of two, three and four hundred pounds were left (in notes) for her on the table. In one expedition she spent £700 'shopping'. Lord Melbourne, when told, does not seem to have protested, but apologized mildly for 'not having sufficient about him' to defray these expenses on the spot, and 'hoped, as he always did, that we had pleased ourselves'. He could not, he said, 'suffer a day to pass without seeing his dear love, tho he must return to his dear Betsy in the evening.'

Although he never came in his own carriage, but always in a hackney coach to avoid attention, news of his attachment must quickly have spread. His 'dear Betsy' must soon have heard of it, though there was nothing unusual in her position. Lady Melbourne was a woman of hard common sense. She had decided what she wanted from life and she would not make it difficult for her husband to occupy himself happily.

One day the story appeared in a newspaper, with thinly disguised names, that a diamond necklace chosen by Lord Melbourne for Mrs. Baddeley had by an error been delivered to his wife. The husband reported to Mrs. Baddeley that 'Lady Melbourne, reading the paragraph, only smiled at the tale, and said the paper might have been better employed'.[1] But Mrs. Baddeley gathered that she was not the only one to have expensive fancies. 'Lord Melbourne came again in the evening. Sat himself down saying he was tired to death, with prancing about all day with his Betsy a-shopping.'

It was fortunate that Lord Melbourne's father and uncle had been such industrious men. For the cost of Melbourne House was enormous. Even Lord Melbourne seems to have been surprised at its eventual price. Mrs. Steele wrote in her diary that when he came to see Mrs. Baddeley one day, 'she spread out some silks which she had bought for Lord Melbourne to see. His Lordship seeing them said they were beautiful, but not so handsome as they ought to be, considering who was to be the wearer, and being told the price, gave me one hundred pounds to pay them, saying, "Why did not she buy more silks, whilst she was about it? King has done well today, for my Betsy has been there and bought silks to a great amount, in order to hang her rooms; and when they are completed, they will be very elegant." And so indeed they ought, for His Lordship declared to me, upon his honour, that when the house in Piccadilly which he was

[1] *Memoirs of Mrs. S. Baddeley*, Vol. I, p. 136.

building, was finished, and the furniture in it complete, so as to sit down in it to dinner, from a just calculation, it would cost him one hundred thousand pounds. "An astonishing sum!" exclaimed I. "It is a much greater sum," continued His Lordship, "than I intended, when I first began"; for Mr. Chambers' the surveyor's estimate of the house and offices complete, did not exceed thirty thousand pounds; but after they had gone on some way, and had made by his orders, some few alterations, it came to twenty thousand more. So that the buildings of that house came to fifty thousand pounds besides the sixteen thousand pounds paid for the old house and ground.'[1]

Lady Melbourne did not worry about the cost. Her object was to produce a magnificent setting for the entertainments which she proposed to give, and in the meantime there were visits to the opera, to the play, parties at Ranelagh and private theatricals, of which she and Mrs. Damer were very fond. The ubiquitous Horace Walpole watched them dance in a quadrille at the French Ambassador's Ball.

'The quadrilles were very pretty: Mrs. Damer, Lady Sefton, Lady Melbourne and the Princess Czartoriski in blue satin, with blond and collets montés à la reine Elizabeth; Lord Robert Spencer, Mr. Fitzpatrick, Lord Carlisle, and I forget whom, in like dresses with red sashes, de rouge, black hats with diamond loops and a few feathers before, began; then the Henri Quatres and Quatresses . . . all in white, the men with black hats and white feathers flapping behind, danced another quadrille, and then both quadrilles joined.'[2]

The building and decoration of the mansion in Piccadilly took some time. In November 1774 Lord Melbourne wrote from Brocket to William Chambers: 'I was in Town for a few Hours yesterday and think the Ceiling extreamley Pretty. I am afraid they will be a considerable

---

[1] Baddeley, op. cit., Vol. II, pp. 202–4.
[2] H. W. to the Countess of Upper Ossory, 27 March 1773.

time about it yet. I wish you to make Mr. Evans determine to finish it in a Month, at all Events I must beg the
workmen may be all out by New Year's Day.' He hoped
that when he returned to London at the end of the week
he would find the scaffold taken down from the gateway
and 'the Yard and Coach Houses Cleared from the dirt
the Stone Masons Have made'.[1] At last the ceilings were
painted or decorated with plaster-work, the marble chimney-pieces were installed,[2] Lady Melbourne's silks were
stretched on the walls, and after four years' activity the
house was completed to her satisfaction.

Now the courtyard was filled with carriages, and the
ladies with powdered hair and nodding feathers climbed
the double staircase in the large central hall and whispered to each other of the latest scandal, while the men
talked their endless politics. This was the beginning of
Lady Melbourne's career as a great hostess. The Melbourne title was a very new one and Lord Melbourne
himself would be of no assistance to her ambition, save to
provide the money.

The indolent, good-natured man continued to pay the
bill and to admire 'his Betsy', but it was not to see or talk
to him that guests thronged to his house. His happiest
hours were those spent in shooting at Brocket or hunting
at Melbourne, his days in London were passed in lazy
dissipation. Yet at Melbourne House the younger fashionable set assembled, attracted by its beautiful hostess and
by the hospitality which might appear almost too lavish
for good taste, but in which it was undoubtedly pleasant
to share.

[1] Correspondence of Sir Wm. Chambers in library of the Royal
Institute of British Architects.

[2] Those in 'the great dining-room, the middle drawing-room and
Lady Melbourne's dressing-room' were designed by James Paine and
executed in statuary marble, that in the dining-room being 'inlaid with
verd-antique'. The designs may be found in Paine's *Plans, Elevations
and Sections of Noblemen's and Gentlemen's Houses* (1767–83), Vol. II.

Then, just as Melbourne House had been completed, a new figure appeared in London Society, whose intimates were to include all who were most outstanding politically and socially in her generation, who with her friends was to revolutionize manners and fashion—Georgiana Duchess of Devonshire.

Her mother, wife of the first Earl Spencer, was a woman remarkable for her piety and common sense, with strong views on the importance of education. Georgiana and her younger sister were brought up in the strictest and most simple way. Just after her seventeenth birthday Georgiana was married to the Duke of Devonshire, and in Piccadilly the dust sheets were put away and Devonshire House was re-opened to receive the bride. The Duke was a strange figure in a period of original and often violently eccentric men. 'Constitutional apathy formed his distinguishing characteristic . . . He seemed to be incapable of any strong emotion.'[1] Taciturn and formal in manner, he spent much time at his clubs, discussing politics and Shakespeare, from whose works he could quote at length, drinking and playing cards. In London he never waked before four.[2]

The Duchess had been filled with high ideals of wifely duty by her strong-principled mother whom she adored, but affectionate as she was and wanting to do right, she found it impossible to achieve any intimacy with this phlegmatic man of the world who spent so much of his time away from home. It was not that their ages were so different—the Duke was only twenty-four at the time of their marriage, but he was one of those who never experience the irresponsibility and careless gaiety of youth, while his Duchess, as Lady Mary Coke sourly observed, 'cannot walk into a room; She must come in with a hop and a jump. She seems to have unfortunate good spirits, and tho' I believe she is perfectly good

[1] Wraxall, Vol. III, p. 342.
[2] Iris Leveson-Gower; *The Face without a Frown*, p. 43.

humour'd and innocent, I don't believe she will ever be a day older.'[1]

It was not great beauty that made her the most fascinating woman of her day, but an overpowering charm. Describing her own appearance she wrote:

'I've oft puzzled to find, why hard 'tis to trace
The features and looks of my comical face,
Since a moderate drawing might surely comprize
A snub nose, a wide mouth and a pair of grey eyes,'

and in her portraits the face that 'seldom wore and never met a frown' does not seem more beautiful than those of many of her contemporaries. Nevertheless she quickly became pre-eminent among them. 'The Duchess of Devonshire effaces all without being a beauty'; wrote Horace Walpole, 'but her youth, figure, flowing good nature, sense and lively modesty, and modest familiarity, make her a phenomenon.'[2] This fresh, natural charm captivated everyone, and with her great position and wealth made her the most outstanding and popular personality to appear in London society for many years.

Lady Melbourne was a few years her senior and already what the Duchess longed to be—the mother of a little son. Sophisticated, clever and a knowledgeable guide to all the amusements of a young wife in London society, she was soon the Duchess's intimate friend, though in character they were entirely dissimilar. While Georgiana was all sensibility—affectionate, generous and impulsive, a believer in high ideals and conscience-stricken when she lapsed from them—Lady Melbourne was of tougher fibre. She was, as Lord David Cecil has said, a man's woman. Her creed was tolerance and common sense.

Lady Melbourne was the ideal confidante, discreet, clever and unsentimental, who could give shrewd advice and would never censure on moral grounds. She would

[1] *Journal of Lady Mary Coke*, 13 October 1775.
[2] H.W. to the Countess of Upper Ossory, 1 February 1775.

accept failings and deceptions with a tolerant smile, her disapproval was reserved for those foolish enough deliberately to flout convention or the opinion of the world. The role of confidante and guide was always a favourite one with her and she exerted herself to bind the Duchess to her by every bond of affection. Her friends were young married women, well-bred and gay, whose admirers were more in evidence than their husbands. To the Duchess's surprise she learned that it was vulgar to be seen with your husband. Well might she sigh, 'The most unsafe and critical situation for a woman is to be young, handsome and married to a man of fashion.'[1]

The new friends arranged to have their portraits painted together. 'Has Lady Greenwich told you,' wrote Lady Mary Coke, who in spite of her critical comments seems as fascinated as anyone by their doings, 'of the Duchess of Devonshire, Lady Melburn, and Mrs. Damer all being drawn in one picture in the Characters of the three Witches in Macbeth? They have chosen that Scene where they compose their Cauldron, but instead of "finger of Birth-strangled babe, etc." their Cauldron is composed of roses and carnations and I daresay,' she adds venomously, 'they think their Charmes more irresistible than all the magick of the Witches.'[2]

The seal was set now on Lady Melbourne's success by her friendship with the Duchess, and the society at Melbourne House at last attained its proper form with the addition of the stars who shone at Devonshire House. Their acknowledged hero was Charles James Fox, whose forceful, saturnine face, with its shaggy black eyebrows, was frequently to be seen at Melbourne House. With him came his friends, all young like himself, and drawn together by his magnetic leadership in opposition to the Court party—Fitzpatrick, Hare, Grenville, Fawkener, and another whose brilliance rivalled Fox's own, Richard

[1] Iris Leveson-Gower, op. cit., p. 32.
[2] 14 July 1775.

Brinsley Sheridan. His play, *The Rivals*, had created a
sensation in London and his wit and charm made him an
enchanting companion.

Fox had lately abandoned his youthful dandyism, when
he had worn feathered hats and the red high heels which
were the distinguishing mark of privilege at the French
Court. Now he wore always a blue coat and buff waistcoat,
the colours of Washington's army, to show where his
sympathies lay. It was observed that 'neither of these
garments seemed in general new, and sometimes appeared
to be threadbare'.[1] In Parliament he and his friends were
making every effort to force the Government to abandon
the war against the American Colonies.

Among these friends was one who we may guess was
foremost in Lady Melbourne's thoughts, whose name was
to be coupled with hers for several years—young Lord
Egremont, handsome, immensely rich, 'in his voice and
manner a fascination for women, and even for men, which
neither knew how to resist.'[2] Owner of a vast estate at
Petworth in Sussex and of Egremont House in Piccadilly,
in later years the patron of Constable and Turner, he was
reserved in company but a fascinating companion to his
intimates. At Petworth he bred race-horses, having sixty
or seventy brood-mares, and eventually he won both the
Derby and the Oaks five times. In London his postilions
had white jackets trimmed with muslin, and clean ones
every two days.[3] He was the most eligible bachelor in
London and all mothers' eyes were on him. To their
chagrin he appeared not to notice the young ladies brought
to his attention; his admiration seemed reserved for Lady
Melbourne.

She must at this time have been a very attractive
woman. She wore her bright brown hair unpowdered. Her
complexion was brilliant and her eyes large and blue.

[1] Wraxall, op. cit., Vol. II, p. 2.
[2] W. M. Torrens, *Memoirs of Viscount Melbourne.*
[3] H.W. to the Countess of Upper Ossory, 7 October 1773.

Tallish, graceful, sophisticated, lively, she was interested in men and men's conversation. But perhaps the most attractive thing about her was her splendid zest for life, not in its more spiritual or intellectual forms, but just for living. Her energy was unbounded, her good-humour almost unshakeable. She enjoyed her food and drink 'in a very unusual manner', though it was noted that 'it did not seem to have the least effect, her spirits were just as equal after dinner as before'.[1] She was at ease in men's society and enjoyed their conversation. 'A commanding figure, exceeding the middle height, full of grace and dignity, an animated countenance, intelligent features, captivating manners and conversation. All these and many other attractions, enlivened by coquetry, met in Lady Melbourne.'[2] Lord Egremont found her combination of feminine charm and masculine intelligence irresistible.

Many years later he wrote to Lord Holland: 'When I came into what is called the *world*, Voltaire and Rousseau were both alive, their wit and their doctrines engrossed the attention of everybody, and not a day passed without hearing their names talked of, either with admiration or censure; and added to this, everything in fashionable life, dress, food, amusement, morals and manners, all must be French. Grammont's *Mémoires*, the French novels, Crebillon, etc., came in aid of the two living Philosophers, as standards of ethics, and there was hardly a young married lady of fashion, who did not think it almost a stain upon her reputation if she was not known as having cuckolded her husband; and the only doubt was, who was to assist her in the operation.'[3]

They led a carefree life for the first two years after Melbourne House was completed. Lady Melbourne was painted for the third time by Sir Joshua, this time holding her little son by the hand. Georgiana had quickly accus-

[1] Lady M. Coke, op. cit., 23 November 1783.
[2] Wraxall, op. cit., Vol. V, p. 371.
[3] The Earl of Ilchester, *The Home of the Hollands*, p. 205.

tomed herself to the extremes of the current fashions and delighted in exaggerating their follies. With their pow-dered hair piled high into towering head-dresses decorated with flowers, ribbons and even fruit, crowned by huge feathers or with wide hats cunningly balanced on their heads, they were the cynosure of all eyes.

The *Morning Post* published in 1776 an analysis of the charms of the reigning toasts of London:

Scale of Bon Ton.

	Beauty	Figure	Elegance	Wit	Sense	Grace	Expression	Sensibility	Principles
Duchess of Devonshire	15	17	13	11	10	5	3	9	16
Duchess of Gordon	12	5	0	14	13	5	15	13	3
Countess of Derby	4	11	5	2	3	7	4	9	11
Countess of Jersey	11	6	1	2	0	11	12	5	0
Countess of Barrymore	19	18	18	19	18	19	17	19	18
Countess of Sefton	14	16	13	3	4	6	9	12	13
Lady Harriot Foley	9	17	14	13	7	12	11	13	16
Lady Anna Mar. Stanhope	7	17	13	15	12	11	2	18	17
Lady Melbourne	9	0	11	3	5	14	6	8	15
Mrs. Damer	7	16	15	13	14	12	14	5	2
Mrs. Crewe	15	7	4	6	8	0	15	14	12
Mrs. Bouverie	12	16	14	7	9	10	8	19	12

It seems likely that the anonymous judge was in love with the Countess of Barrymore, who must have been delighted with the marks awarded her. Lady Jersey, on the other hand, can scarcely have been pleased to see it stated in public that she had no sense and no principles.

The Duchess of Devonshire was already in debt—her new carriage alone had cost 500 guineas, without the upholstery[1]—but her extravagance and addiction to high play, combined with fear of her husband, had not yet shadowed her life as they were to do her later years. 'At Ranelagh the Duchess of Devonshire and her Company amused themselves with puffing out their cheeks, and letting their friends strike them on each side to bring them to their natural form . . . The *bon ton* are still in Town, Duchess of Devonshire, Ly Melburn, Mrs. Damer etc., they have dinners, suppers, etc., and live much together.'[2]

Even their troubles did not seem very serious. Lord Foley's sons had run into debt and borrowed money at such a high rate of interest that they were said to have 'contracted to pay eighteen thousand pounds a year'. Lady Harriot Foley's position does not seem to have produced a qualm in Georgiana when she visited her friend. 'Her Grace's Misfortune is a very unnatural one, that of being too happy, and delighted with everything She hears and sees, so the situation in which she found Lady Harriot was, in her Grace's opinion, Charming. Ly Harriot told her she had no Clothes; this was Charming above measure. She added that Bailiffs were then in the House. "Delightful," said her Grace, "Lord, I am afraid we shall never have Bailiffs in Devonshire House." '[3]

But a tragedy was to fall on one of their intimate circle which could not be laughed away. In August 1776 the three Damer brothers 'unexpectedly notified to their father that they owed about 70 thousand pounds'. The two

[1] Jacob Larwood, *Story of the London Parks*, p. 166.
[2] Lady M. Coke, op. cit., 6 July 1776.
[3] Ibid., 12 July 1776.

younger brothers were inveterate gamblers but John
Damer was said to be 'cool, reasonable and reserved, but
passed his life as he died, with troops of women'. Their
father, Lord Milton, sent them a message, refusing to see
them or to pay their debts. His two older sons, he said,
were to leave for France at once and to take Mrs. Damer
with them. She hurried to the country to bid farewell to
her family and was to return to London and prepare for
their departure on Friday.

'On Thursday,' wrote Walpole, 'Mr. Damer supped at
the Bedford Arms in Covent Garden with four common
women, a blind fiddler and no other man. At three in the
morning he dismissed his seraglio, bidding each receive
her guinea at the bar, and ordering Orpheus to come up
again in half an hour. When he returned, he found a dead
silence, and smelt gunpowder. He called, the master of the
house came up, and found Mr. Damer sitting in his chair,
dead, with a pistol by him, and another in his pocket!'[1] It
was clear that his action had been deliberately thought out;
the balls he had bought were too large for his pistols,
'upon which, as it was found afterwards, he had sat down
and pared them with a pen-knife till he had made them
fit.'[2]

Poor Mrs. Damer, on her return to London, stopped at
the door of Lady Harriot Foley's house, where she saw
Lady Harriot in her coach and her husband leaning upon
the coach door. Although they had heard the news of John
Damer's death, neither had the courage to tell her. After a
short conversation she drove on, when luckily the Foleys
'spied Charles Fox on horseback . . . He accepted the
commission with alacrity, and tho' he did not absolutely
tell her, said so much that she guess'd what had happen'd
but *would* go home, where Mr. George Damer mett her
and told her his Brother had kill'd himself: upon which she
was hardly in her senses and insisted upon seeing him, for

[1] H. Walpole to Sir H. Mann, 20 August 1776.
[2] Lady M. Coke, op. cit., 5 September 1776.

LADY MELBOURNE, AGED 18, WITH HER SON, PENISTON,
BY SIR JOSHUA REYNOLDS
Detail from the large portrait in the possession of Viscountess Gage

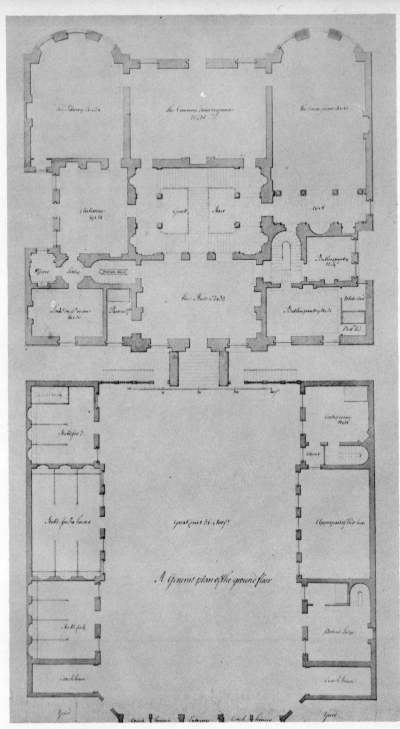

PLAN FOR THE GROUND FLOOR OF MELBOURNE HOUSE
BY SIR WILLIAM CHAMBERS
From the Soane Museum

they did not tell her where he had shot himself till some time after . . . The next day she saw Lady Milburn.'[1]

Mrs. Damer's troubles were not yet over. Her career as a leader of the *ton* was ended in an hour. Her father-in-law blamed her entirely for his son's death. He vented his fury on her by selling her jewels, which were magnificent, 'her furniture, carriages and *everything* . . . to pay the debts with, and he abused her for staying *in another man's house* (for she stay'd a few days there before she went to the country, and the house is another's being seiz'd). Upon hearing this she left it, and chose to go in a hackney coach, taking only her ink-stand, a few books, her dog and her maid with her out of that fine house . . . It was spirited and noble in her; she had but 3 guineas in her pocket, which was to last her till Michaelmas, for Lord Milton did not offer her any assistance.' The servants were owed fourteen months' wages. 'She paid . . . those servants who were in immediate want, the rest were too generous to take any, and absolutely refused to take more than would serve them for immediate use; they are all fond of her and cried bitterly at her leaving the home, in such a way too, but . . . she walk'd through the house amidst them all, into her hackney carriage with a firmness that is quite heroic, for though she may be accused of not loving her husband she cannot be accused of not loving her house and all her grandeur.'[2]

Lady Melbourne, with her other friends, was sympathetic and helpful, but Mrs. Damer decided to retire to the country and live with her father for a year, to save one year's income in order to pay the debts which remained after all her husband's possessions had been sold. There she settled down to work seriously at her sculpture. 'She is very ingenious and is now amusing herself with molding wax. She has taken Ly Ailesbury and made a striking re-

[1] Lady Mary Coke, op. cit., 21 September 1776.
[2] Life and Letters of Lady S. Lennox, ed. Countess of Ilchester and Lord Stavordale, Vol. I, pp. 251–2.

semblance. She is . . . copying an antique of Sir William Hamilton's.'[1] Mrs. Damer also modelled the heads of the two rivers, Thames and Isis, which one can still see on Henley Bridge.

So, for a time, one familiar face was lacking from the parties in Melbourne House. But the great bow-windowed Saloon still resounded to music and laughter until the candles guttered and the cold dawn light showed the coaches and sedan-chairs and the groups of weary footmen in the courtyard. Not content with their high play at faro, quinze and hazard, the *ton* led a new fashion for speculation on the stock market.

'I supped after the Opera at Mrs. Meynel's with a set of the most fashionable company,' wrote Horace Walpole to a friend, 'which I very seldom do now, as I certainly am not of the age to mix often with young people. Lady Melbourne was standing before the fire, and adjusting her feathers in the glass, says she, "Lord! they say the stocks will blow up: that will be very comical." '[2]

The long political discussions raged fiercely, led by Charles Fox, proclaiming the doctrine of liberty, while Sheridan, Selwyn and Hare added wit and gaiety. Present at all these entertainments, whether card-party or supper, or an expedition to Ranelagh or Vauxhall, Lord Egremont was never far from Lady Melbourne's side. He was her acknowledged admirer and when she was reported to be again with child the gossips' tongues were soon wagging.

In those days, when everything rested on the system of primogeniture, whereby the eldest son inherited all the fortune, houses and estates, while his younger brothers existed on a pittance in the Army or the Church, it was the unwritten code that a wife must not deceive her husband until she had first provided him with an heir. Lady Melbourne had already done her duty. No doubt, with her

[1] Lady M. Coke, op. cit., 26 September 1776.
[2] H. W. to Rev. W. Mason, 12 May 1778.

scrupulous observance of society's laws, she would not otherwise have carried her love affair to such lengths.

'Yesterday Mrs. Lloyd had many of the fine world, Ladys and Men in the uniform of the Oaks,' wrote Lady Mary Coke on 7 June 1777. 'Lord and Lady Derby went there yesterday and the *bon-ton* were to go there in the evening. The Duchess of Devonshire came in leaning upon Lady Melburn's arm; her Ladyship is with child which occasions great joy; to my surprise, thinking as they had spent the greater part of their fortune, it was happy they had but one Child, but it seems they are of different opinion.'

A month later she noted: 'The Melburns are still in Town and their House open to all of the *bon-ton* who remain in Town: I hear of parties and suppers frequently: her Ladyship lies inn in December.' And on 25 October: 'The news of the day was Ly Melburn being brought to bed of twins, but as she was considerably before her time, the son died soon after it was born, but the daughter was alive and they hoped might be brought up.' She then quotes Lady Greenwich's opinion that Lord Egremont was their father and adds, 'Lady Greenwich is you know a little scandalous, but . . . Lady Egremont said something to the same effect to His Majesty in the Drawing-Room, who answer'd he was sorry her Grandson was· dead.' Lady Mary refers frequently in her journal to 'the fine Ladies going on in their usual stile' and a year later writes, 'Some of the fine Ladies are come to Town, Lady Derby, Ly. Melburn etc. the latter is again with Child.'

Contemporary gossip subsequently averred that Peniston Lamb was the only one of Lady Melbourne's children to have Lord Melbourne as his father. Certainly the son born to her at Melbourne House in 1779, two years after the unfortunate twins (for the daughter died, too), bore little resemblance to his elder brother, who was then nine years old. Generally thought to be Lord Egremont's son, and destined to be Prime Minister of England, William

Lamb was christened at the parish church of St. James's, a hundred yards down Piccadilly.

The year after his birth there was the anti-Catholic outburst in London, when for five days, between the 3rd and 7th June 1780, the mob surged round the city, wantonly destroying and sacking the houses of prominent Catholic sympathizers. Many people left for the country, taking with them their jewels and more valuable possessions. The Fleet Prison was set on fire, Lord Mansfield's house in Leicester Square burnt down and Devonshire House was said to be menaced by a similar fate.[1] The Duchess took refuge in Lord Clermont's house in Berkeley Square, where she slept on a sofa for several nights. But troops were rushed to the city and soon things quieted down. Hyde Park and St. James's Park were transformed into military camps and cavalry rode round the larger streets and squares in the west of the town.

'Two troops of Mr. Fitzroy's are to patrole up and down Piccadilly,' wrote the Duchess, 'and as the Duke don't like having the soldiers here again (as there is no need) the depot of guards for this part of the town is to be at Lord Melbourne's.'

And now that other figure appears on the scene whose name and habits were to be the subject of gossip, censure, wit and sometimes praise for years to come—the Prince of Wales. The future Prince Regent, at eighteen years old, made his official début. The Duchess of Devonshire described him at this time as 'rather tall, his figure too fat and womanish, but his graceful movements and extremely handsome face counteracted these defects'. Another observer described his countenance as 'handsome and prepossessing and commonly gay, though at times it became suddenly overcast and sullen' and added that he had 'a vast quantity of light-brown hair, which then adorned his forehead and temples'.[2] Brought up in the narrow home-life

[1] Wraxall, op. cit., Vol. I, p. 236.
[2] Ibid., Vol. V, p. 356.

of George III and his Queen, he was determined to get away from the rules and restrictions with which his life had hitherto been bounded. He knew himself to be handsome and talented. He spoke French, Italian and German fluently, and having a retentive memory, he could quote readily from Homer and Virgil, an accomplishment at that time thought indispensable to any man of taste. 'For music he nourished a passion,' and he possessed an excellent voice. His tutor had judged him at the age of fifteen, saying that he would be 'either the most polished gentleman or the most accomplished black-guard in Europe—possibly both'.

Reacting violently from the narrow-mindedness and lack of culture in his home the Prince, finding himself admired and courted on all sides, threw himself with enthusiasm into the whirl of London life. The two houses which quickly claimed him as a constant guest were Devonshire House and Melbourne House. He was heard to say that he was 'glad the King's parties ended so soon as none of the agreeable entertainments began till after ten o'clock'. He found the Court gatherings formal and disagreeable and after a party at Windsor for the Princess Royal's birthday, he muttered that 'he would rather have been at the Cathedral'.[1]

No doubt he enjoyed some evenings more. 'The *beau-monde* goes on much as usual,' wrote Lady Sarah Lennox in August. 'The few that remain in town go down to Windsor to keep up the ball as well as they can. Lady Melbourne loves her son so much that she goes twice a week to see him at the Christopher at Eaton, where she and Lord Melbourne give a dinner which the Prince of Wales honours with his presence.'[2]

He began to frequent Brooks's Club, to protest his devotion to Charles Fox. He and Georgiana called each other 'Brother' and 'Sister'. History does not tell us in

[1] Lady M. Coke, op. cit., 4 October 1782.
[2] Lady S. Lennox, op. cit., Vol. II, p. 23.

what terms he and Lady Melbourne referred to each other
in their more intimate moments, but it is unlikely that
Lady Melbourne's more robust personality would have
encouraged such high-flown expressions of platonic love.
In any case his devotion to her was soon evident. 'The
Prince of Wales is *desperately* in love with Lady Melbourne,
and when she don't sit next to him at supper he is not
commonly civil to his neighbours: she *dances* with him,
something in the cow stile, but he is *en extase* with admiration at it.'[1]

Lady Melbourne had achieved her object. She was a
worldly woman and she wanted worldly success for herself
and for her family. When she married a man who could
have had no interest for her but his money, when she
persuaded him to build the mansion for her in Piccadilly
and to enrich it with everything that money could buy,
when she threw herself into the activities of society, when
she set herself to attract a man or to charm a woman, it
was always with her over-riding aim in mind. And now
she could admit success. Ladies who wanted the Prince of
Wales to attend their parties would approach him through
Lady Melbourne.[2] He presented her with a large portrait
of himself by Sir Joshua Reynolds which 'is placed in the
great room at Brocket Hall; . . . Mr. Fox pays her great
attentions in consideration of her high favour.' Finally,
when the Prince had moved into Carlton House, he
appointed Lord Melbourne Lord of the Bed Chamber
'which no doubt is procured him by his Lady'.[3] With the
Duchess her friend and the Prince her admirer, she was
secure in the place to which she had always meant to
climb.

True, there were some old-fashioned ladies who
thought the Melbourne House circle rather raffish and their
morals doubtful, but she could afford to ignore them. True,

[1] Lady S. Lennox, op. cit., Vol. II, p. 36.
[2] Lady M. Coke, op. cit., 2 November 1783.
[3] Ibid., 23 November, 13 June 1783.

her fourth son, George, born in 1784, was said by many to be the Prince's son. True, too, that the Prince did not remain her lover for long. He passed on, as was his way, but with her usual tact and good humour she contrived that they should remain the best of friends and he turned to her often for advice.

Mrs. Damer, too, had returned to London and bought the lease of a house in Sackville Street which backed on to the east side of the garden at Melbourne House. The deed is still extant of 'Lord Viscot Melbourn's Agreement to Lett The Honoble Mrs. Damer have a Door through the Garden Wall and a window looking into it'.[1] Here she sculpted a bust of Lady Melbourne and another of Lady Elizabeth Foster, Georgiana's new friend and protégée. Of these works it was written:

'Long with soft touch shall Damer's chisel charm,
With grace delight us and with beauty warm.
Foster's fine form shall hearts unborn engage
And Melbourne's smile enchant another age.'[2]

Horace Walpole was as devoted to Mrs. Damer as ever and she would take Lady Melbourne to dine with him at Strawberry Hill, the old man declaring himself 'vastly pleased with the party'.[3] When Walpole died he left his beloved Strawberry Hill to Mrs. Damer, with a legacy of two thousand pounds to maintain it. In the papers Lady Salisbury and Lady Melbourne were constantly named as 'the most elegant equestrians' in Hyde Park. Lady Melbourne was one of the leaders of the *ton* and Melbourne House rang to the clamour of the world of rank and fashion.

Old-fashioned guests would not always feel at ease in Melbourne House. Though the meals, when they came, were sumptuous, nobody was certain of their time. There was little formality, people did as they pleased, the conver-

[1] In the possession of the Trustees of Albany.
[2] Darwin's *Economy of Vegetation*, Vol. II, p. 113.
[3] H.W. to Hon. H. S. Conway, 27 August 1783.

sation was forceful and free. Politics were vehemently discussed. Arguments, robustly phrased and barbed with wit, raged over the changing topics of the day—the coalition between Fox and North, the thorny question of the Prince's allowance and his debts, the Westminster Election, in which Lady Melbourne and Mrs. Damer took a part which was as enthusiastic, though more discreet, than Georgiana's.

What secrets must have been confided to Lady Melbourne in that house! Her level judgment was acknowledged by her friends; she was so interested in their problems, so helpful and yet so discreet. 'No man is safe with another's secrets, no woman with her own,' she once said. There was Georgiana's impulsive sentimental friendship with Lady Elizabeth Foster, her passion for faro, her mounting debts and at last the birth of a child—after eight years of marriage—a daughter, and then another. There was the secret marriage of the Prince and Mrs. Fitzherbert, and Charles Fox's denial of it in the House of Commons. There were the first rumours of the King's madness and the resultant feuds in the Whig party, who sighted power ahead, with Charles Grey and Sheridan quarrelling violently; the hand-bill sent to Mrs. Fitzherbert warning her that tomorrow '500 libels will be published declaring the Prince had forfeited his right to the Crown by marrying her'; the Prince's alarm; Sheridan sent to stop it; and then suddenly the King pronounced by his physicians to be quite recovered; the Pitt-ites jubilant, the Whigs in despair.[1]

Lady Melbourne's reign at Melbourne House must have ended in an orgy of confidences, *tête-à-têtes* and secret interviews. In the midst of the political crises, in which the women played an important part, she had her own relationships to manage—platonic friendships and others not so platonic. Lady Melbourne, although plumper

[1] Duchess of Devonshire's Diary of Regency Crisis, quoted by W. Sichel, *Sheridan*, Vol. II, p. 422.

than she used to be, was still very alluring. Lord Egremont did not marry until very late in his long life, though he had a number of illegitimate children who were brought up beneath his roof at Petworth, but he was by no means her only admirer now that the Prince was only a valued friend. Francis, 5th Duke of Bedford, was believed by the world to be at her feet, and Georgiana's letters to her[1] when there were rumours of his becoming engaged to the Duchess of Gordon's daughter seem to confirm this. Contemporary records have not vouchsafed to us the name of the father of Emily, born in 1787, her only daughter to survive to maturity, who lived to be the wife of one great Prime Minister and sister to another, or of little Harriet Ann, born two years later.

While discreet management of her own relationships cannot have been simple, Lady Melbourne delighted in managing also her friends' and her children's affairs and would spare herself no trouble to bring them success. But more even than her common sense and tact were needed to save the Duchess of Devonshire. Overwhelmed by debts which she was too frightened of her husband to acknowledge to him, still longing to justify herself in his eyes by bearing him a son, she realized at last the true nature of his relationship with her protégée, Lady Elizabeth, the 'poor little soul' whom Georgiana had encouraged from compassion to make her home with them, when she left her husband after a short, unhappy married life.

In spite of this her sentimental friendship with Lady Elizabeth survived all the vicissitudes of their joint life with the Duke and continued to the very end of her life. The two children whom Lady Elizabeth had discreetly borne the Duke on the Continent were eventually brought into the nursery with Georgiana's own children. The daughter, known as Caroline St. Jules, and supposed to be the daughter of a French nobleman, afterwards married George Lamb, Lady Melbourne's fourth son.

[1] Mabell, Countess of Airlie, *In Whig Society*, pp. 29–36.

At twenty-nine Georgiana's private life was misery and frustration, but her house was still the brilliant *rendez-vous* for the Opposition, with the Prince of Wales and the fascinating Charles Fox always present at her parties. To the Devonshire House circle she welcomed a newcomer, seven years her junior. Charles Grey came fresh from scholastic triumphs and Fox, quickly recognizing his brilliance, determined to mould his opinions. He was a very handsome young man and he fell at once under Georgiana's spell. He became an *habitué* of Devonshire House. At what moment her friendly interest changed to deeper feeling we do not know, but five years later, after the birth of her long-awaited son in 1790, she gave way to the passionate love she felt for Grey, who was now twenty-seven years old, and soon she found that she was with child by him.

Somehow the Duke found out, or was told. He discovered, too, that her debts now totalled more than £60,000. Weeping, unhappy, repentant, the Duchess was sent off to the Continent, accompanied by her sister, Lady Bessborough, and Lady Elizabeth, leaving her friend and confidante, Lady Melbourne, to forward her letters under cover to Grey, to send his letters on to her and to give each news of the other. As always, Lady Melbourne was efficient and reliable. Even the Duchess's sister, who had never liked her, admitted that 'Lady Mel: wrote constantly'.[1]

Now a hush fell on the great house. One month after the Duchess's departure for the Continent Lord Melbourne signed a document giving up all rights to Melbourne House in Piccadilly. The Duke of York, when dining there one night, had told his hostess that he was tired of his house in Whitehall and that he longed for a house like hers 'which he particularly admired'. With her usual good humour Lady Melbourne remarked that 'she would like the opportunity of looking on the park every morning

[1] *Lady Bessborough and Her Family Circle*, ed.: Lord Bessborough, p. 67.

when she rose and that were it possible, she would willingly exchange the chimes at night of St. James's for those of the Abbey. H.R.H. vowed that anything was possible to her'.[1]

In this casual way the idea of an exchange originated, but soon even Lord Melbourne was persuaded to consider its feasibility. What his wife's motives were it is difficult to imagine. It seems a big sacrifice, even for Lady Melbourne, to make for a Royal whim. Now that the mansion had been completed, decorated and entertained in, was she bored with it? Did the idea of moving to a new house, and one just vacated by a Royal Duke, appeal to her? Did the view over St. James's Park really attract her, or with the King's return to sanity, did she think it a prudent move to oblige his favourite son? Or was it that, as Lady Mary Coke had hinted, even the Melbourne fortune was beginning to be affected by such profusion?

In 1775 when the building had not long been completed, Lord Melbourne had already mortgaged the house to Theodore Henry Broadhead of Soho Square for £8,000, and later for a further £2,000. These mortgages had never been paid off and he was continuing to pay interest on them. In March 1789 he executed a further mortgage of £3,000 on the house to his Architect, now Sir William Chambers, 'in consideration of . . . the sum of three thousand pounds due and owing.'

This was evidently only after Chambers had made repeated attempts to claim payment. In November 1784 Lord Melbourne wrote a conciliatory letter to his architect from Brocket Hall. 'I confess myself sorry that your interest should be Two Y^{rs} in Arrear, and It is not from a wish to be resolute as you term it in refusing your Capital or denying to Pay your Interest. A very unexpected Draft on account of the new Parliament so much called before its time, made with me money very scarce and I Hope S^r you

[1] Torrens, op. cit., p. 34.

will be Content with the Payment of a Year's Interest now, and the rest shall be kept back as little longer as Possible.' He is hoping to raise money by the sale of a house in Sackville Street or by 'another Person purchasing back a Rent Charge I Have on His Yorkshire Estate'.[1]

These documents incline one to think that the exchange of houses, attributed by most writers to Lady Melbourne's anxiety to oblige Royalty, may really have been a way for the Melbournes to escape from financial difficulties with no loss of prestige. Whatever their reasons, on 25 December 1791 'His Royal Highness Frederick Duke of York and Albany did . . . agree to Exchange . . . with . . . Peniston Lord Viscount Melbourne the . . . premises . . . at . . . Whitehall and the Furniture therein. Together with the old Lottery office and other the premises which His Royal Highness then held or had made application to the Treasury to hold . . . by lease from the Crown for the Term of Fifty Years and also to pay to Lord Viscount Melbourne the several sums of £16,000, £5,811 and £1,760 making together £23,571 and . . . Viscount Melbourne agreed . . . on payment of the said £23,571 . . . to grant and release to His Royal Highness Frederick Duke of York and Albany . . . the Premises . . . situate in Piccadilly.' In pursuance of the agreement 'His Royal Highness on or about the twenty-fifth day of December (1791) . . . entered into and took possession of the . . . premises in Piccadilly lately called Melbourne House and . . . Lord Melbourne entered into and took possession of the . . . premises at Whitehall lately called York House.'

It is not surprising that the legal agreement was not completed and signed until nearly a year after the exchange had been made. The lawyers had a difficult problem to untangle. The Duke of York, like his elder brother, was recklessly extravagant. He had borrowed money from his banker, Thomas Coutts, on the security of his lease of York House. This had now to be transferred to a mortgage

[1] *Correspondence of Sir Wm. Chambers* at R.I.B.A.

on his new house. Meanwhile two brothers, Oliver and James Farrer,[1] had paid off Broadhead's £10,000 mortgage on Melbourne House, at the Duke's request, and this sum was secured to them by a fresh mortgage, partly on the same house and partly on 'Oatlands and other His Royal Highness' . . . estates in the County of Surrey'. There is significant mention of 'several other principal sums heretofore advanced' by the Farrers to the Duke. The £3,000 mortgage to Sir William Chambers had been paid off by the Duke's trustees, an unusual note being struck by the statement that the said sum was 'the proper money of His Royal Highness Frederick Duke of York and Albany.'

By 7 November 1792 these tortuous financial arrangements had been set out in a long document by the lawyers and signed. During the three years that the Whitehall house had been in the Duke of York's possession it had been entirely re-decorated by Henry Holland, the Prince of Wales's architect at Carlton House, and its courtyard had been converted into a huge, circular domed hall entered from a portico in Whitehall.[2]

The Melbournes settled down in the new Melbourne House, free of mortgages and with ten thousand pounds in cash. Here they would continue their brilliant entertainments. Here the young Lambs were to grow up and here William was to bring Lady Caroline, his bride, to live on the first floor of the house.

But all this lies in the future. Melbourne House in Piccadilly has changed its name and its character, too. Though it has passed to a Royal Duke it will never know such brilliant days again.

[1] Partners in the firm of solicitors, Messrs O. and J. Farrer, now Messrs. Farrer & Co., of 66 Lincoln's Inn Fields. Sir Leslie Farrer, K.C.V.O., the present head of the firm, is the great-great-grandson of James Farrer.

[2] This house is now the Scottish Office and with the exception of Brooks's Club is the finest surviving example of Holland's interior decoration.

CHAPTER II

YORK HOUSE

REDERICK WAS the King's favourite son. He was
born, a year after the Prince of Wales, in 1763. As an
infant of seven months his father had made him
Bishop of Osnaburg, 'one of those secular dignities, with
an ecclesiastical designation, which are peculiar to Germany.' The revenue of the bishopric was about £20,000
per annum and George III, as Duke of Luneberg and
Elector of Hanover, had the right to nominate him.

Frederick was very strictly brought up, in close companionship with the Prince of Wales, but at seventeen
years of age he was separated from his brother and sent
to study military arts in Germany. He had always shown
great interest in military affairs and stayed in Germany,
studying the Prussian system of training, accompanying
Frederick the Great to reviews and exercises and learning
from his uncle, the Duke of Brunswick, who was thought
a great soldier. At twenty-one he was created Duke of
York and Albany and Earl of Ulster. He had already been
gazetted Colonel of the regiment which is now the Life
Guards and later Major-General.

On his return to England two years later he was rap-
turously received by his family after his six years' absence.
His parents and sisters were waiting for him at Windsor
and the Prince of Wales travelled post-haste from Brighton
as soon as news came of his brother's arrival. While
Henry Holland was completing the 'repairs and additions'
to the house bought for the Duke in Whitehall, conveni-

ently near to Horse Guards Headquarters, he moved into Carlton House with the Prince of Wales and, to his parents' distress, became his brother's boon companion in every activity.

The two young princes were very different in character, the elder being more cultivated, appreciating music and showing discrimination and taste in his collection of pictures and furniture. There is no doubt that the Prince of Wales was exceptionally gifted and, in his youth, possessed extraordinary charm of manner. But his great gifts were corrupted by a selfishness which grew greater with the years. His brother, though less cultured, had a warmer heart and a bluff, loyal, straightforward character which in spite of his many indiscretions endeared him to those who knew him. 'He is the only one of the Princes who has the feelings of an English Gentleman,' wrote Charles Greville.[1] The brothers shared a reckless love of pleasure and lack of restraint. They enjoyed race-meetings and late parties, they gambled and drank heavily, but we must remember that these tastes were shared by the majority of their contemporaries. There were few like their father and his Queen who lived quietly, and disapproved of the frivolity and laxity of London life.

When he had been home for a year the Duke accompanied his parents to Cheltenham, where the King, who had not been well, had been advised to rest from official duties and to take the medicinal waters. Soon after the King's return to Windsor he showed the first undoubted signs of insanity and the Duke hastened to him, to find his brother already there. Then began over the mad King that struggle for power between the Queen, supported by Pitt, and the Prince of Wales, advised by Fox. All through this crisis, in which the Duchess of Devonshire and Lady Melbourne were kept well informed by their friends, the Duke of York was firmly on his brother's side, consulting

[1] *Greville Memoirs*, edited Lytton Strachey and Roger Fulford, p. 59.

with Sheridan and Fox, whose party openly proclaimed themselves 'the Prince's Friends'. He spoke more than once in the House of Lords during the debate on the Regency Bill, and then all argument was suddenly ended by the King's recovery.

The Queen did not conceal her resentment that during the King's illness the Duke had sided with his brother. He continued to live at Carlton House and it was from here that he set out to fight a duel on Wimbledon Common with Charles Lenox, the Duke of Richmond's nephew and an officer of his own regiment of Coldstream Guards.[1] This young man was well liked by the Queen and 'had been amusing himself all winter with abusing . . . the Prince of Wales and the Duke of York in the most scurrilous way'. At Daubigny's Club, where he was 'talking offensive language about them and their friends' in the Duke's presence, Colonel St. Leger interrupted him, saying it was 'very odd that he always chose to say these things to persons who could not resent them', and suggested that he might say them 'to some of us who can answer you'.[2] Lenox did not take up this challenge, but he afterwards apparently believed that the Duke of York had been telling the story and resented the imputation that 'he had put up with language unfit for any gentleman to hear'. He therefore called the Duke out.

During this affair of honour, which had been thrust on him, the Duke behaved with great courage. 'The ground was measured at 12 paces and both parties were to fire at a signal agreed on . . . Lieutenant-Colonel Lenox fired, and the ball grazed his royal highness's curl. The Duke of York did not fire.' He explained, when pressed by his opponent, that he had come out at Lenox's

---

[1] Colonel Lenox (always spelled so in contemporary accounts) was a Company Commander. This position carried the rank of Colonel in the Guards. He later succeeded his uncle as Duke of Richmond and was the host at the Ball in Brussels in 1815, on the eve of Waterloo.

[2] *Life and Letters of Sir G. Eliot*, Vol. I, p. 313.

desire, to give him satisfaction, and had no animosity against him, but that if Lenox 'was not satisfied he might fire again'.[1] This Lenox refused to do and honour was satisfied. The affair 'made a great noise all over the Kingdom' and the Duke's courage was much admired, though his father showed acute distress when told of the danger to which his son had been exposed.

The alterations to York House in Whitehall were soon complete and the Duke gave a splendid party to celebrate his move. But he was already deeply in debt and his thoughts turned to marriage, the best way in those days for spendthrift princes to recoup their losses. During his residence in Germany he had become acquainted with the Princess Royal of Prussia, niece of Frederick the Great. In September 1791 negotiations for their marriage were completed and he returned to Berlin for the ceremony. Parliament voted him £18,000 a year from the Consolidated Fund on his marriage, which made his income £37,000 a year. Nevertheless his devotion to gambling and his extravagant habits left him constantly in debt throughout his life.

It was a few weeks after the happy couple's arrival in London and the second marriage ceremony at Buckingham Palace that the Duke signed the agreement with Lord Melbourne to exchange their houses, though he had only been living in his own for two years. The novelty of a Royal marriage in England had an exhilarating effect on the country. 'The nobility and gentry in town' all left their cards, but it was soon evident that the Duchess preferred life in the country at Oatlands with her dogs to the delights of London society. The Duke, though self-indulgent, took his military career very seriously. He had been promoted Lieutenant-General soon after his first return to England and when the French Convention, having murdered their King, declared war on England, it was as Commander of

[1] This account is from the report drawn up by the two seconds for publication, quoted J. Watkins, *Frederick, Duke of York* p. 137.

the British expeditionary force that he left England fifteen months after his marriage. England's long struggle against the Revolutionary forces had begun.

On the 25th of February 1793, at half-past six in the morning, the three battalions of the Guards which composed the expeditionary force paraded before the Horse Guards. 'At seven the King, attended by the Prince of Wales and the Duke, came down the Mall from Buckingham Palace. After His Majesty had been about half an hour on the parade, the battalions marched by him in companies, moving to slow time, the officers saluting as they passed. They then went off by Storey's Gate, and took the Kent road.' When they had all passed, the King, Queen and the three elder princesses rode down to Greenwich to watch the embarkation. 'The Duchess of York was so much depressed in her spirits that she could not bear to witness the departure of her consort in the career of peril and glory.'[1]

So the great house in Piccadilly was deserted. The traffic rolled past the entrance and filled the air with the roar of wheels on stone, but rarely did a carriage turn into the courtyard. The Duke returned, after a year's absence, for a brief four weeks' visit. A few months later the servants were flustered by the news that the Duchess had narrowly escaped death in a fire at Oatlands which had destroyed the greater part of the house. But she continued to prefer it to London, and the accident gave the opportunity to rebuild in the new Gothic fashion.

After two years abroad the Duke was home again. The English troops had been forced to retreat from Holland into Germany, and the Stadtholder and the Princess of Orange had fled to England. The Duke was now made a Field-Marshal and Commander-in-Chief of the British forces, in succession to Lord Amherst who was nearly eighty. As an administrator he gained a higher reputation than as a general in the field. He was only thirty-one years old

[1] Watkins, op. cit., p. 211.

when he took up his office. Tall, stout, loud-voiced and jolly, his good nature made him popular with his subordinates.

During the week he would leave his house in Piccadilly, now known as York House, early every morning, and would be at his desk in the room over the archway at the Horse Guards soon after nine o'clock. As he had usually not repaired to bed until the early hours of the morning, this punctual appearance showed his enthusiasm for his work, which was no less than an attempt, long over-due, to re-organize the British Army. He would stay at the Horse Guards sometimes until nearly seven in the evening. His Duchess passed only a small part of the year in London and the Duke would drive to Oatlands on Saturday, where large parties would assemble for the week-end. As soon as dinner was over the Duke would sit down to whist 'and never stirs from the table as long as anybody will play with him . . . He is equally well amused whether the play is high or low, but the stake he prefers is fives and ponies.'[1] On Monday morning, he would set off punctually at nine o'clock for London, leaving the Duchess with her dogs, which now numbered nearly forty, and a rapidly growing menagerie which included monkeys, parrots, kangaroos and ostriches.

It is for his work at the Horse Guards that the Duke of York and Albany should be remembered. Many were the abuses in the Army which he ended and reforms which he instigated. His first important regulation made it impossible for anyone to be promoted captain without first having served two years, or field officer without six years in the Army. 'Prior to his being appointed Commander-in-Chief an officer . . . could purchase up to the rank of lieutenant-colonel in three weeks or a month.'[2] He founded the Royal Military College for the instruction of

[1] Greville, op. cit., Vol. I, p. 58.
[2] Colonel Willoughby Gordon's testimony at the investigation, 1809.

cadets who, after a four-year course, were granted commissions, and a school to train officers on the staff which later became the Staff College. He nearly doubled the private soldiers' pay and reformed their uniform and living conditions. Their barracks and rations were improved, great-coats were provided, powdered hair and pig-tails were abolished. Minute regulations for military hospitals were issued and he urged all ranks to be vaccinated against smallpox. His experience with an army in the field had evidently left a deep impression on his mind, and even his enemies had to admit his practical concern for the welfare of his troops.

After four years at the Horse Guards he once again left England as Commander of an invasion force—this time composed of British, Dutch and Russian troops—which was intended to expel the French army of occupation from Holland. But the expedition was a complete failure. The Duke and all his army were evacuated in less than two months. For this fiasco he had to face much criticism, but it is doubtful if he was truly to blame. The whole expedition was badly conceived and the campaign had already begun under General Abercrombie before the Duke arrived. His command was more political than military, it being thought helpful for the supreme commander to be the King's son, so that he could deal more easily with his allies—the Prince of Orange and the difficult Russian general. The conduct of the expedition was violently attacked in Parliament and it was probably at this moment that the rhyme was first heard in the London streets:

> 'The grand old Duke of York
> He had ten thousand men.
> He marched them up to the top of a hill
> And he marched them down again.'

But he was supported by his father and by Pitt and the Cabinet, and he returned to the Horse Guards to continue his peaceful campaign to improve the conditions and efficiency of the Army. His private life remained extravagant and irresponsible. He continued to gamble wildly at cards and on the turf, he drank and ate heavily and kept doubtful company. The years of good living left their mark. He was stouter and redder of face, his tongue wagged too easily after a good dinner, but his frank, kindly manner still made him popular. Extravagance led to constant financial embarrassment and little more than two years after his return from the disastrous Walcheren expedition he had arranged for the sale of York House in Piccadilly.

Whether he decided to sell it only to pay off pressing creditors, or whether other reasons weighed more heavily we cannot tell. The Duchess spent little 'time in London and they had no children. With another man one might have supposed the sale to have been made with motives of economy. But not with the Duke. Even at the age of sixty-two, when he was heavily in debt and unable to pay his tradesmen's bills, he was to pull down his house in Stable Yard, St. James's, and embark light-heartedly on the building of another enormous mansion.[1]

It was about this time that the Duke first met that lively Mrs. Clarke who was to prove so disastrous to his reputation. Certainly it was not long afterwards that he had installed her in a furnished house in Park Lane and only two years later that she was living under his protection at No. 18 Portman Square[2] with more than twenty servants and two coaches and ten horses for her personal use.[3] Her allowance was fixed by the Duke at £1,000 a month. But the lady, who later described her royal lover in public as 'a great big baby', was not blinded by affection to the possibilities of her position. She used the two years to improve her finances.

[1] Now Lancaster House
[2] W. Clarke, *Life of Mrs. Mary Anne Clarke*, p. 19.
[3] Miss Elizabeth Taylor, *Authentic Memoirs of Mrs. Mary Anne Clarke.*

The Duke, as can be seen from his ingenuous love-letters, was infatuated with her, and it must have been easy for a clever woman to encourage him to talk indiscreetly about military affairs. Large sums of money were paid to her by men who were seeking promotion in the Army and she professed to be able to satisfy them by interceding with the Duke. From the evidence it seems unlikely that he was guilty of more than indiscretion, but the affair was taken up by the Opposition as a stick with which to beat the Government, and after public investigation before a committee of the whole House of Commons, the Duke resigned his post.

Three weeks had been occupied by taking evidence. The attractive Mrs. Clarke, whose quick tongue was never at a loss for a witty or a pert reply, was recalled again and again. She became a public figure. Crowds ran behind her carriage, and even the Members of Parliament were not insensible of her attractions. 'The idlers at White's, and the frequenters of the opera—whom at other times it had been found difficult to drag from the claret bottle or the ballet—were now unfailing in their Parliamentary attendance.'[1]

Public feeling ran high against the Duke and he was burnt in effigy. The House of Commons cleared him by a majority of eighty-two votes, but the Opposition were known to be planning a motion calling for his resignation. Before they could do so, he had resigned. The curious sequel to the whole affair was the speed with which public opinion was reversed. Scarcely a year after his resignation, while the Duke was living quietly—though perhaps not in great amity—with his Duchess at Oatlands, a lawsuit was brought against the Member of Parliament who had been the instigator of the charges against him and it was revealed, in the course of evidence, that this man had promised Mrs. Clarke to furnish her new house for her and had given her five or six hundred pounds to persuade

[1] Lieut.-Colonel A. Burne, *The Noble Duke of York*, p. 295.

her to give the necessary evidence against the Duke. This was borne out by the book written by Mrs. Clarke herself, in which she frankly stated, 'If I had not been well satisfied of receiving the remuneration agreed upon, not all the Jacobinial parties in Europe should have introduced my letters and person to the notice of Parliament.'[1]

Public opinion swung violently back again and the Duke, who had always been popular with the Army, was regarded as 'the victim of a foul conspiracy'. Two years after his military career had apparently ended in public shame, he was back at the Horse Guards. In this post he was to remain until the long war with France was at last ended at Waterloo. His father had now relapsed into insanity, from which he would never recover. During his brother's Regency and when the Regent at last became King, he remained Commander-in-Chief. As the years passed he became increasingly stout and increasingly popular, and Mrs. Clarke was forgotten. But that is not our story.

When the Melbournes left their house in Piccadilly its character to a visitor would have seemed unchanged. It remained a great house, like so many others which stood along Piccadilly between Sackville Street and Hyde Park Corner—a house for splendid entertainments, with stately rooms where candles by the hundred lit the elegant crowds who gathered there to dance or talk. But now a change is coming. We must look for the last time, as the Duke must have looked, at the long garden running behind the house back to Vigo Lane, and with that stout figure we will leave by the stone steps at the front door and drive out of the courtyard and away down Piccadilly.

When we come here again the house will look the same, but all will be transformed within. All change is to be crammed now into a few fateful years and then, for it, time will stand still and it will be preserved by loving

[1] Mrs. Clarke, *The Rival Princes*, Vol. I, p. 74.

hands and protected from the changing world outside. It is no longer to be a family house, a private mansion, but a curious new community which will grow and develop and yet remain unique, not in London only, but in the world.

CHAPTER III

ALBANY, EARLY DAYS

I

THE GREAT banking firm of Thomas Coutts & Company was deeply involved in plans for the future of York House. The mortgage to the bank was now £22,000. It was only natural that, knowing the Duke's reckless extravagance, Coutts should have thought the conversion of York House or the development of its site the best hope of obtaining repayment of the loan.

In 1801 a young builder in St. Martin's Lane named Alexander Copland proposed the first scheme to Coutts. This was to demolish the mansion, leaving a site 600 feet deep from Piccadilly and a hundred feet wide. A row of houses would be built with their backs to those in Sackville Street, facing west over a new road which would run from Piccadilly to Vigo Lane by the side of the garden wall of Burlington House. This plan was worked out in detail, carefully considered and then discarded.[1]

The next plan was a proposal to preserve the mansion and convert it into 'a magnificent and convenient Hotel in single and double apartments, for the Complete Accommodation of Families for any Length of Time, and of the Subscribers in particular. Also to contain a Coffee Room, Dining Room, extensive Kitchen, wine cellars, etc., to be called The Royal York Hotel. To be formed on a Plan that

---

[1] Messrs. Coutts have in their archives a questionnaire with sixteen queries of the most searching character written out in Thomas Coutts's hand and answered, in pencil, sometimes rather testily, by Copland.

will be profitable to the Subscribers and advantageous to the Public.'

Prospectuses were printed setting out these particulars. It was hoped to find one hundred subscribers of six hundred pounds each and various proposals were made as to what should then be done. From these it can be seen that The Royal York Hotel was the seed from which sprang the idea of Albany, the independent community controlled by elected representatives. These proposals for the Hotel laid down that as soon as forty persons had subscribed, a Meeting should be called at which the subscribers should choose first three Trustees and secondly a committee of seven, to whom should be entrusted the furnishing of the Hotel and the erection of additional buildings. Seven subscribers should have the power at any time to call a General Meeting and the majority at General Meetings and Committees was to bind the rest.

This plan, too, came to nothing, but in 1802 a new printed prospectus was produced. It was the birth of Albany. '*Proposals for Dividing and Disposing of the Mansion House and Premises lately occupied by His Royal Highness The Duke of York in Piccadilly.*—It is proposed to make extensive additions to York House and Offices, and to distribute the whole into elegant and convenient Sets of independent Freehold Apartments, appropriating a Part of the Premises for a large Dining-Room, Kitchen, extensive Cellars, Hot and Cold Baths etc. for the exclusive Convenience of the Inhabitants of the Apartments, and also for a Residence for a Maître d'Hôtel.

'The Dining-Room will be supplied by the Maître d'Hôtel, and great Convenience will be derived to the resident Proprietors from the Facility of obtaining from him every Requisite in their own Apartments.'

II

The financial arrangements, as always with the Duke of York's affairs, were complicated and protracted. On 22 January 1802 the Duke agreed 'to sell to Mr. Copland[1] . . . for the price of £37,000 All that . . . Mansion house called York House . . . with all the Offices Coach-houses Stables and other erections and Buildings and all the Court Yards Gardens and other Grounds . . . and also all . . . the Household Goods Furniture Fixtures and Effects . . . now in upon or about the . . . Mansion House . . . which are mentioned or specified in a certain Inventory . . . lately made out thereof and signed by the said Parties.[2] And the said parties mutually agreed that Mr. Copland should be let into possession . . . on the 25th March 1802,' when the first instalment of the purchase price was paid, but that no conveyance of the property should be made to him until he had paid the whole.

Copland reserved the right to rescind the agreement, if he was not within three months 'able to procure Subscribers to the . . . House and premises as a Subscription House or Hotel to the amount of £50,000 or upwards'. The purchase price was to be paid in seven instalments over the period ending 25 March 1804. But on 7 March 1802 Mr. Copland signed a Memorandum to the original agreement, waiving his power to determine the agreement and becoming absolute purchaser of the house 'on terms above mentioned except as far as the same is altered by this Agreement with an Intention of making extensive

[1] In this and other Deeds the name is sometimes spelled Copland and sometimes Copeland.

[2] There is no trace of this inventory among Copland's papers which are now in the hands of the Trustees of Albany, and the Duke's copy must have been destroyed by his executor, who burned many papers after his death.

additions thereto and of building on part of the said premises and converting the Buildings into and selling the same in separate Lots of Apartments'. The instalments of payment were altered and not to be completed until September 1805, 'with the privity of Thomas Coutts and Oliver and James Farrer Esquires who are Mortgagees of the said Premises.'

The Duke of York also agreed with the mortgagees that after the first two instalments, amounting to eight thousand pounds, had been paid, they would join in 'proper Conveyances of each set of Apartments as soon as the same is finished and sold and in granting Building Leases of such part of the said Premises as shall be let on such Leases upon receiving such sum of Money as with the Instalments then paid shall be equal to half of the Value thereof or upon a Fee Farm or Ground Rent (of equal value with such Money) being reserved to him . . . until the whole £37,000 and Interest have been paid and then such fee farm or Ground Rents and the residue of the said premises are to be conveyed to Alexander Copland'.[1]

In September 1803 a document was drawn up, stating that of the £37,000 which Copland had agreed to pay for York House and its contents, £9,500 had already been paid to Coutts's bank and £9,300 to the Duke of York, leaving £12,500 still due to the bank and £5,700 to the Duke. On the security of the property Coutts Trotter and Edward Marjoribanks, both partners in Thomas Coutts & Co., agreed to advance £12,500 and £5,700 respectively, so that these sums could be paid. The Farrer brothers released the premises from their mortgage of £38,000 'they having other security for the Same'.

It may well be that this was a critical moment for Cop-

---

[1] The arrangement whereby the freehold of part of a building could be granted was then a novel one, though less uncommon now. The unusual feature at Albany is that a freehold 'set of apartments' may consist of rooms on three different floors—living-rooms on one floor, with servants' rooms in the attics and a cellar below.

land. The building was completed but some sets of chambers remained vacant. No doubt the cost of the work already done had to be met and he may have felt uncertain whether he would be able to make his future payments on the dates already agreed. His fears proved groundless. The records do not show if the loans from Trotter and Marjoribanks were ever made. The money may have been merely held at Copland's disposal in case of need. In any case the bank was paid by June 1804 and the final payment to the Duke of York was made in February 1805, nearly eight months before the appointed date.

III

On Friday 22 April 1803 a meeting was held at the Thatched House Tavern in St. James's Street of 'the Proprietors of Apartments at Albany . . . for the purpose of choosing Trustees conformably to the proposals for dividing and disposing of the Mansion House and premises lately occupied by His Royal Highness the Duke of York in Piccadilly'. The Minutes of this meeting were carefully inscribed in a book bound in green calf, with engraved brass clasps and a red label, lettered in gold *Minutes of the General Meetings of the Proprietors of Albany.* The original proposals, which had been agreed to by each proprietor before his purchase, were read to the meeting.

'It is proposed to make extensive additions to York House and Offices, and to distribute the great part into elegant and convenient Sets of independent Apartments or Chambers, the Inheritance to be vested in the Trustees not exceeding seven with a view to general regulation and so as to give each purchaser a Freehold Estate in Equity, a part of the premises to be appropriated for a large Dining room, Kitchen, extensive Cellar, hot and cold baths etc. and also for the Residence of a Maître d'Hôtel . . .

'Each Proprietor shall be subject to such Rules and

Regulations, to be framed by the Trustees, respecting the occupation Letting, or otherwise disposing of the apartments by each proprietor, and respecting the general management and Regulations of the whole concern, as will in the Trustees' judgment be most conducive to the benefit of the Proprietors in general.

'As soon as contracts for the sale of 20 sets of Apartments are entered into the Trustees are to be chosen at a meeting of the then Proprietors . . .'

A list of the names of proprietors 'who have contracted for sets of Apartments, amounting to more than 20' was produced by Mr. Copland and read to the meeting, and seven Trustees were elected.

Six days later, on 28 April 1803, the Trustees of Albany met for the first time 'at Albany House'. Since that date they have been meeting regularly to administer the affairs of the community for whom they are Trustees. Amenities of main water, gas, electricity and telephones have been added, not always without protest, but the appearance and structure of the house remain today as they were at that first meeting in 1803.

These Trustees came quickly to business. At their first meeting, as recorded in a smaller book, bound in green calf, and labelled *Albany Trustees Minute Book*, they appointed a Secretary, who was to act as Steward to the Proprietors, and 'Ordered that he do attend from the Hours of Eleven to Four'. Mr. Copland was requested 'to specify the Apartments appropriated for the Maître d'Hôtel' and Mr. Richard White 'to prepare a Draft of the Rules and Regulations'.

Articles of Agreement were drawn up on 28 February 1804, between the Trustees and the Proprietors of Albany, and the Rules and Regulations were attached. This document relates the whole story of the purchase by Copland of the house, the conversion of it into apartments, and their sale to various gentlemen, who had all previously agreed that the entire premises should be conveyed to

Trustees and that they, and every future owner of their apartments, would be subject to any rules made by the Trustees. It was also agreed that the Dining Room and offices of the Maître d'Hôtel should be conveyed to the Trustees, who could let them 'to a desirable tenant', and devote the money thus obtained, after paying the Fee Farm Rent of £22, which was the first charge on the property, to 'expenses of lighting, paving, cleansing, watching and the general outgoings . . . and to divide the surplus among the Proprietors'.

Alas, the last clause was never to be invoked, as the Dining Room and Hotel were to be a consistent failure. However, the Agreement added 'that in case the rents and profits . . . shall not be sufficient to answer the purposes aforesaid then . . . it shall . . . be lawful for the . . . trustees to make a rate not exceeding one shilling in the pound upon the yearly value of each set of Apartments'. This is the way in which the expenses of maintaining this little town within a town have been met, since the agreement was signed. It was also agreed that if a Trustee died or resigned or 'became incapable of acting . . . by . . . ceasing to be proprietor of one set of apartments' then another should be nominated by 'the majority of all the . . . Proprietors of Apartments or Chambers present at a Meeting'.

This long and comprehensive document ends by Trustees and Proprietors binding themselves and their executors to observe the Rules and Regulations which are attached. These are strictly observed to this day. The first rule is 'That the premises mentioned in the aforegoing articles shall be called Albany'. No changes in walls, windows or 'any alterations whatever varying the present Figure of the Buildings shall be made without the consent in writing of the majority of the trustees first obtained. No profession Trade or Business is to be carried on in any of the Apartments or Chambers without the approbation of the majority of the trustees in writing . . . All Conveyances and Leases of the Apartments are to be registered with the Secretary . . .' These are the most important of the fifteen Rules, and it can be seen from them how great is the authority of the Trustees. No change of any kind can be made without their approval.

In the *Albany Register Book* you will find the names, in alphabetical order, of those who have owned apartments in Albany since *The List of Original Proprietors* was copied into it in beautiful copperplate in 1804.

IV

Henry Holland planned the conversion of York House to Albany. He had been previously employed by the Prince of Wales as architect at Carlton House and the Pavilion, and by the Duke of York for his houses in Whitehall and at Oatlands. His major commissions had all come from the great Whig families. He was the architect of Brooks's Club and as much associated with the Whig aristocracy in the capacity of architect as Coutts was as banker.

The twenty-eight-year-old Copland had previously been apprenticed, at the age of fourteen, to Holland's cousin. Also associated with them in the new enterprise was another young builder, Holland's nephew, Henry Rowles. Copland had already achieved some success in his profession. Six years before, at the age of twenty-two, he had obtained the first of innumerable contracts for the building of Army barracks and hospitals all over the country, and even in the Isle of Wight and the Channel Islands. He must quickly have become prosperous, for before negotiations for Albany began he had bought a country estate at Gunnersbury for £10,000[1] which had belonged before her death to Princess Amelia, the King's aunt. Central London already had one building of his construction—the Guard House in Hyde Park (now called the Powder Magazine)

[1] Mrs. Papendiek, *Time of Queen Charlotte*, Vol. I. p. 267.

THE ENTRANCE TO MELBOURNE HOUSE FROM PICCADILLY.   ON THE LEFT IS THE
WALL OF BURLINGTON HOUSE
From the Soane Museum

A SECTION OF THE GREAT
HALL AND STAIRCASE AT
MELBOURNE HOUSE
*From the Print Room, Victoria and
Albert Museum*

THE CEILING OF
THE STATE
DRESSING-ROOM AT
MELBOURNE HOUSE,
NEXT TO THE
DRAWING-ROOM.
THIS CEILING IS
STILL IN
EXISTENCE
*From the Print Room,
Victoria and Albert
Museum*

and he was by then at work on the Duke of York's School in Chelsea. A few years later he was to build the Royal Military College at Sandhurst, the new Covent Garden Theatre, which like its predecessor was destroyed by fire, and St. Katherine's Docks.

These four then were responsible for the venture— Coutts, the banker, Holland, the successful architect, not averse from speculation in real estate, his nephew and heir, who, after his uncle's death, was responsible for dispersing his papers and drawings, and Alexander Copland, the enterprising young builder.

The two gateways, the porter's lodge and the Piccadilly wall were soon demolished, and by September 1803 four houses had been built in their place and let on ninety-nine-year leases. The shop-fronts designed by Holland for these houses reflected the French influence everywhere the fashion. Six eagles, finely modelled in Coade stone, stood on the piers which framed the shop windows, and appeared to support the balconies above them on their heads and outstretched wings.[1]

The buildings round the courtyard were re-modelled to make sets of chambers, and the house itself was divided into twelve apartments. Lady Melbourne's magnificent rooms were cleverly converted, sometimes by cutting off part of a room and dividing the space horizontally as well, making a little top floor with a tiny staircase, and a lower room, perhaps a kitchen, in the space below. In other, larger apartments one room would remain untouched as a lofty, well-proportioned living-room and the smaller rooms adjoining would be used as bedrooms.

There is mention, in a document dated September 1803, of 'those Ranges of Buildings lately erected and built on the East and West sides of the garden'. These were two

---

[1] These shops have all been demolished, the last in 1937, but two of the eagles have just returned to Albany, after an exile of several years, and now stand in the small paved gardens on each side of the door leading from the mansion to the Rope Walk.

long blocks of buildings which Holland designed to run the full length of the garden, with a paved and covered walk between them. They were of cream-painted stucco, three storeys high, with large-paned Regency windows. Balconies on the first floor bore simple wrought-iron balustrades of the same design as those over the shops in Piccadilly. Each entrance was marked with a letter (B to F on the west side, G to L, coming back to the mansion, on the east), and the chambers by a number—One and Two being on each side of the entrance, on the ground floor, with their kitchens in the basement, while the first and second floor chambers had their kitchens in the attics. These sets of chambers each consisted of a hall or ante-room with a fireplace, a living-room which opened by fine double-doors into the bedroom (both looking on to the covered way), and a dressing-room behind with a water-closet and a hip-bath. Each set of rooms included a cellar in the basement and a 'garrett' on the top floor.[1]

A long underground corridor ran underneath each of these buildings, from the back of the mansion to the end of the property, with good cellars leading off them.[2] At the far end of the garden Holland finished the two rows of stucco buildings with two larger buildings in brick, whose lofty rooms were the same height as those in the brick-built mansion at the other end. These buildings, F and G, contained larger apartments than those off the covered way. There were two small shops and a porter's lodge between them guarding the northern entrance to Albany. Holland's design for the entrance from Vigo Street was as

---

[1] Many of these chambers have now been altered so that the original bedroom, which looked into the Rope Walk, is used as a dining-room, and the dressing-room behind is divided to make a bedroom and small bathroom. Holland's plans for the conversion and for the new buildings can be seen in the Crace Collection at the British Museum.

[2] The corridors still exist and are used by tradesmen to deliver their goods.

happy as for the shops in Piccadilly, and it remains very little altered to this day.

In April 1804, at the Trustees' twenty-first Meeting, Mr. Copland 'applied to obtain from the trustees leave for certain persons to Pass and Repass from Savile Row to Piccadilly under the covered way and through the House'. So the 'Rope Walk'[1] was already completed by that date.

Block F was fully let by 1804, but Mr. Copland was not so fortunate with all the other buildings. Some remained for several years with one or more sets of chambers empty. In December 1804 the trustees 'ordered that two Lamps be placed on each of the Staircases in the New Buildings where there are Inhabitants', and that 'each of the Entrances to the staircases in the New Buildings be Lettered'. Porters were engaged, one for the front gate at 'a salary of £50 per annum with a livery and allowance of Coals and Candles for one Room', and another for the back gate at a salary of £45 per annum with a livery.

At the fortieth Trustees' Meeting, on 17 January 1805, the Secretary reported that he had 'caused Lamps to be placed on the Staircases in the New Buildings and had caused the entrance to each of the Staircases to be lettered'.[2] He was ordered at this meeting to provide livery for the two porters, 'a Plain round Hat' costing eight shillings, 'a Coat with scarlet cuffs and collar with white buttons' for two pounds and twelve shillings, 'a scarlet Waistcoat' for nineteen shillings, 'a pair of Velveteen breeches with leather lining' costing one pound five shillings and sixpence, and 'a Livery Great Coat with 2 rows of Buttons, Pockets behind and scarlet collar' for three pounds and six shillings.

The Secretary, having provided the two porters with these liveries, is ordered at the following meeting 'to provide another round Hat for each of the Porters with a

---

[1] It is not known who first gave this name to the covered way, or at what date.

[2] These lamps are still in place but are now fitted for electricity.

gold edging and gold lace band'. Both porters were
shortly afterwards found guilty of grave negligence when
a robbery had taken place and were 'immediately dis-
patched'. The Trustees ordered 'that the porters admit
no Person thro' Albany on any pretext whatever except
such as reside there or have business with the Inhabitants'. A night porter was engaged in June 1805 'to
Watch at the back Gate from eight at Night till five in
the Morning and to Pump the Water into the several
Cisterns,[1] and to sweep the Passages, Staircases and
Covered Way at one guinea per week'.

Seven estimates were received in answer to an advertisement for proposals to contract for lighting the lamps in
the courtyard, mansion house, covered way and staircases.
I am delighted to find that a Mr. Patrick's estimate to do
the work for a year for £90 was accepted. His letter
begins, 'Gentlemen, I much wish to become your Lamp
Contractor not for emolument only, but equally for the
honour of working for so respectable a foundation . . .'

V

Apartments in the mansion were known as A.1, A.2 etc.
and were fully occupied in 1804, with only one exception.
Houses in the courtyard, too, soon found tenants. At Number Two, Henry Angelo, the famous swordsman, had his
Fencing Academy from 1804 to 1809. He must have found
the position a good one for his clientèle, though the Trustees
were not sympathetic to his request to be allowed to put
up a board outside his house, saying that it would not be
consistent with the Rules of the Institution.[2] It is probable
that 'Gentleman' Jackson, the pugilist, had an arrangement to make use of the same premises. Farington said,

---

[1] From wells at the back of the new buildings. Water for each
building had to be pumped up by hand.
[2] Seventeenth Meeting, 2 February 1804.

'He has a room in Albany building, Piccadilly, where He gives lessons in Pugilism, and is supposed to make four or five hundred a year.'

There is no trace in the records of his having taken a lease in his own name, but we know that Byron boasted of having 'knocked down Mr. Purling, and put his kneepan out (with the gloves on), in Angelo and Jackson's rooms in 1806'.[1]

In 1810 George Wyatt took over the lease from Angelo when it still had ninety-one years to run, at a rent of £40 per annum. Two years later he transferred it to Lewis Wyatt. These Wyatts were members of the well-known family, of whom no fewer than thirteen followed the profession of architect in the hundred years after 1770. The most famous of them was James Wyatt, who succeeded Sir William Chambers and rivalled Robert Adam as the most fashionable architect of his day. Lewis Wyatt was his nephew and after being apprenticed to another architect-uncle, Samuel, he worked for a year in his Uncle James's office before beginning to practise independently, when he was twenty-five years old. Even then he continued to help James in his official work as Surveyor-General to the Office of Works and Architect to the Board of Ordnance.

James Wyatt was the architect of many buildings in Gothic style, of which Fonthill and Ashridge were among the largest. At Oxford he had designed the Radcliffe Observatory, Canterbury Gate and Quadrangle in Christ Church, and the library at Oriel. He built the new Palace at Kew for George III which cost £500,000 and was never furnished or lived in, and made alterations or additions to many famous houses including Belvoir Castle, Wilton House, Windsor Castle and Badminton.

Lewis Wyatt, as his assistant, must early have had much work and responsibility, for his uncle was an erratic and unreliable man, extraordinarily casual in business matters, although brilliant and charming. He liked to dash

[1] Moore, *Life of Byron*, p. 118.

off a design for a building and leave the details to be
worked out by his assistants. James Wyatt is often abused
for the destruction of ancient monuments in the cathedrals
which he restored, and his romantic buildings in eighteenth-
century Gothic style have long been out of fashion. But at
the end of his life when his nephew, Lewis Wyatt, and his
brother Samuel were working with him, they developed
together a fastidious style of classical architecture and
interior decoration which rivalled that of the Adam
brothers.

When Lewis Wyatt took over Number Two, Albany
Courtyard, he was thirty-five years old and was just completing the re-modelling for Lord Bolton of his house,
Hackwood, near Basingstoke, which took him eight years,
from 1805 to 1813. His Uncle James died the year after he
had moved in, but Lewis Wyatt continued to practise
from these chambers until 1827.

VI

In March 1804 Number One, The Courtyard, 'on the
south-west corner . . . next Mr. Angelo's', was let 'for
97 years to Messrs. Henry Thos. Austen & Henry
Maunde'.

This Henry Austen was Jane Austen's favourite brother,
four years older than she, the handsomest, most charming
and least reliable of an intelligent and lively family. Their
father, the Rev. George Austen, was a classical scholar, a
Fellow of St. John's, who had been known at Oxford as
'the handsome proctor'. He augmented the income from
his two Hampshire livings by taking in a few carefully
chosen pupils to educate with his own children. His wife
was niece to the Master of Balliol and their large family
was a devoted one.

Henry Austen, after his father's tuition, graduated at
St. John's, but Jane spent only two years of her life at

school, from seven to nine, and those mainly because she would not be separated from the sister two years older than herself. This sister, Cassandra, Jane adored; she was a second self. But Henry was her best-loved brother, tall, handsome, witty and gay. 'He cannot help being amusing,' Jane said.

He must have been an attractive personality. His niece remembered him as 'brilliant in conversation' and said that he seemed to create a perpetual sunshine. But he was the most erratic of the family—always with some new plan or fresh enthusiasm which within a short time would be altered or abandoned altogether.

The two younger brothers joined the Navy, one rising to Admiral and the other to be a Knight and Admiral of the Fleet. The eldest brother took Holy Orders and Henry, too, was destined by his father for the Church. But in the excitement of the war with France he joined the Oxford Militia as a lieutenant, becoming captain and adjutant four years later, and even contemplated transferring into a regular regiment. This was prevented by his marriage to his first cousin, the daughter of his father's sister, who was ten years older than himself.

His parents, although very fond of their niece, did not approve of the marriage. She had been born in India. She was attractive and frivolous and had always been spoilt. Warren Hastings, her god-father, had settled ten thousand pounds on her and later her widowed mother took her to live in Paris, whence she sent letters to her Austen cousins describing the Court at Versailles and the *toilettes* of Marie-Antoinette. At nineteen she married a wealthy French nobleman, the Comte de Feuillide, of whom she reported: 'It is too little to say he loves me, since he literally adores me.' He was guillotined thirteen years later in the Revolution.

After three years as a widow she married her cousin, Henry Austen. But she would never have tolerated a husband in a regular regiment, liable to be sent at any moment to the Cape of Good Hope (for such had been Henry's choice). He soon left the Militia and with a brother officer named Maunde, set up a new firm of bankers and army agents. After an ineffectual attempt to reclaim the Comte de Feuillide's property, which nearly ended in a French prison, he moved his office to Albany Courtyard. His wife, in a house in Upper Berkeley Street, was happy to keep up her acquaintance with the many French *émigrés*. She loved entertaining and Henry shone in society.

Jane probably visited them just before he moved his office to Albany, bringing with her the original version of *Northanger Abbey*, and trusting to Henry's experience of the business world to get it published.[1] She was too shy to brave publishers herself and had already been rebuffed by one who had refused even to read the first version of *Sense and Sensibility*. Henry's man of business sold the novel to Crosby & Co. of Ludgate Street, who paid ten pounds for it. But the anticipatory excitement soon turned to disappointment. Mr. Crosby did not like this novel by 'A Lady' well enough to take the risk of publishing it and nothing more occurred.

Eventually, after six years' silence, Jane wrote a rather pathetic letter, under an assumed name, reminding him that his firm had paid ten pounds for a manuscript novel in two volumes. 'Six years have since passed, and this work of which I am myself the Authoress, has never . . . appeared in print, tho' an early publication was stipulated for at the time of sale. I can only account for such an extraordinary circumstance by supposing the MS. by some carelessness to have been lost.' She offered them another copy and asked for a reply, adding, 'should no notice be taken of this address, I shall feel myself at liberty to secure the publication of my work, by applying elsewhere.' She signed herself 'Mrs. Ashton Denis'.[2]

[1] Austen-Leigh, *Life and Letters*, p. 75.
[2] *Jane Austen's Letters*, ed. R. W. Chapman, 2nd edition, pp. 263-4.

Mr. Richard Crosby replied at once, acknowledging that his firm had paid ten pounds for the manuscript, but denying that there was any time stipulated for its publication. He stated brutally that they were not bound to publish it, but that if anyone else did they would take action to prevent its sale. He ended by offering the manuscript back to the author at the price paid for it.

Jane, with her mother and Cassandra, had been left in straitened circumstances when the income from her father's livings ended with his death early in 1805. Mrs. Austen's sons had immediately offered all they could from their earnings and mother and daughters lived almost entirely on this money. Jane was in no position to produce ten pounds, in those days a large sum, and had no alternative but to leave her manuscript with the unpercipient Mr. Crosby. It was not until shortly before her death that she succeeded in recovering it. By this time four of her books had been published, all successfully, and Henry, acting for his sister, repaid Mr. Crosby his ten pounds and thus regained the copyright. He then took great pleasure in telling the publisher that the book which he had willingly surrendered was written by the author of *Pride and Prejudice*.

A year after moving his business to Albany, Henry took a small house in the village of Brompton, among the market gardens, from which he rode every morning to his office. It was a favourite district with the French *émigrés* and his wife must have had many friends there. But his business venture cannot have been very successful, as in 1807 he and Maunde had to leave their office in Albany, which was then let to another firm, 'the original Lease granted to Austen and Maunde having been forfeit.'[1]

Another officer from the Oxfordshire Militia, the Colonel's younger brother, now joined them as partner. His name was James Tilson and his family was probably rich, as the father lived at Watlington Park in Oxford-

[1] Note in book of leases in Albany records.

shire. The firm of bankers and army agents now became
known as Austen, Maunde & Tilson and opened a
new office in Henrietta Street, off Covent Garden. Here
the business appeared to prosper. Henry became even
more elegantly dressed, and two years later he and his
wife bought one of the newly-built houses on the west side
of Sloane Street. There was no building as yet on the east
side and they had an uninterrupted view across the Five
Fields[1] to the backs of the distant houses in Grosvenor
Place and to Hyde Park Corner. Jane talked about 'walking
into London' to do her shopping.

It is probable that Jane visited Henry and his wife while
he still worked in Albany, but we cannot be sure of it. We
know that during this time he and his wife spent their
holidays with his parents and his two sisters, Jane and
Cassandra. Jane was more intimate with him than with
any of her other brothers and she had always been very
fond of his wife. Unfortunately all her letters to Henry
have been destroyed and Cassandra burned many of Jane's
letters to her which she thought too intimate for other
eyes. Of the four years when Henry worked in Albany,
only six of her letters have survived, and her letters are
almost the only record of her movements.

There is a hint that she may have been in London with
Henry in the summer of 1805, their father having died in
Bath the previous January. In August she was staying with
a married brother, Edward, at Godmersham, and complained of delay in the delivery of a letter. 'On its way from
Albany to Godmersham (it) has been to Dover and
Steventon,' she wrote. The Austens often stayed in London for a few days on their way to Edward's home and it
sounds as though Jane had done so on this occasion.

If she did visit London then, or at other times while
Henry's office was in Albany Courtyard, she would certainly have inspected it, watching with interest, perhaps,
as she did at Henrietta Street on one of her many visits,

[1] Now Belgrave Square.

the opening of a new account. She rejoiced in Henry's success, which she felt he had achieved by his own efforts. 'The progress of the bank is a constant source of satisfaction.'

We know from the accounts of other visits, in letters which have been preserved, how she would have spent her time: shopping—for dress muslin and silk stockings, material for a new *pélisse* or trimming for a bonnet—visits to the theatre, small parties with the Henry Austens' friends, pleasant walks in Kensington Gardens, a visit to a museum, perhaps, and several to picture galleries of which Henry was very fond, though Jane said her preference for Men and Women always inclined her to attend more to the company than the sight. She describes her brother collecting her from a friend's house: 'Henry, who had been confined the whole day to the Bank, took me in his way home; and after putting Life and Wit into the party for a quarter of an hour, put himself and his Sister into a Hackney coach.'[1]

Remembering her intimacy with Henry, the one brother associated with her writing, her affection for his wife and the amount of time which they spent together in the months and years which are recorded for us, it seems very likely that she would have stayed with them in London between 1804 and 1807, perhaps even more than once. But it is sad that one does not know for certain if the immortal Jane ever visited Albany.

By 1811 a publisher had been found for *Sense and Sensibility* and Jane came to London to correct the proofs. Published anonymously in three volumes for fifteen shillings, it eventually made £150 for its author. *Pride and Prejudice* followed, with excellent reviews. Henry, who had always admired his sister's work, was made happy by her success, but his wife was already very ill and two months afterwards she died. Family affection is precious at such a moment and as soon as he could he drove down

[1] Letter, 18 April 1811.

to Hampshire to his mother and sisters. No doubt they felt deeply for his distress and when he returned to London Jane drove with him in his curricle.

As they were in mourning they went to no theatres, but visited several exhibitions of pictures where Jane, whose mind was full of *Pride and Prejudice*, delighted in finding portraits of the characters in her book. She detected 'a small portrait of Mrs. Bingley, excessively like her. I went in hopes of seeing one of her Sister, but there was no Mrs. Darcy—perhaps however, I may find her in the Great Exhibition which we shall go to, if we have time;—I have no chance of her in the collection of Sir Joshua Reynolds's Paintings which is now shewing in Pall Mall, and which we are also to visit.—Mrs. Bingley's is exactly herself, size, shaped face, features and sweetness; there never was a greater likeness. She is dressed in a white gown, with green ornaments, which convinces me of what I had always supposed, that green was a favourite colour with her. I dare say Mrs. D. will be in Yellow . . .' The characters which she had created were alive for her—as they are for us. 'We have been both to the Exhibition and Sir J. Reynolds',—and I am disappointed, for there was nothing like Mrs. D. at either. I can only imagine that Mr. D. prizes any Picture of her too much to like it should be exposed to the public eye.—I can imagine he would have that sort of feeling—that mixture of Love, Pride and Delicacy.'[1]

Henry could not restrain himself when he heard two ladies discussing *Pride and Prejudice* with admiration, and confided in them that it was his sister who had written it. He gave a copy, too, to Warren Hastings, after a visit to Daylesford, and Jane was pleased to hear that Mr. Hastings expressed a high opinion of it and particularly admired Elizabeth Bennet. The carefully guarded secret of Jane's authorship was soon a secret no longer. She was distressed, but determined to harden herself.

[1] Letter to Cassandra Austen, 24 May 1813.

Jane was much with her brother after his wife's death, helping him to move from his house in Sloane Street to rooms over the Bank and staying with him frequently. She saw that he would not long be inconsolable. 'His Mind is not a Mind for affliction,' she said. 'He is too Busy, too active, too sanguine.'[1] She was convinced that he would marry again and a year after his first wife's death he had bought another house, 23 Hans Place, and was already introducing his sister to possible candidates. *Mansfield Park* was published that year. Jane read it aloud to Henry as they travelled together from Hampshire to London in a post-chaise.

The following year in October, while she was staying at Hans Place to correct the proofs of *Emma*, Henry became dangerously ill and for more than four weeks she had to nurse him. Even when he was pronounced by the doctors to be out of danger his troubles were not ended. It was the year of Waterloo and in the economic confusion which followed the end of the war Henry's bank was about to fail. She wondered that he could get better 'with such Business to worry him', but slowly he gained strength.

One of the Prince Regent's doctors had attended Henry during his illness and he told Jane that the Prince greatly admired her novels, 'read them often, and kept a set in every one of his residences.'[2] As a result of his informing the Prince that their author was in London, His Royal Highness's librarian was instructed to wait on her and show her any civility in his power. This had two results— the first that, when Henry was convalescent, Jane was shown over Carlton House, and the second the intimation that if Jane wished to dedicate her next book to the Prince Regent permission would be granted.

Emma was already in the printers' hands—John Murray was to publish it—but she was distressed by the slowness with which the proofs were coming to her for correction. A

[1] Letter to Francis Austen, 3 July 1813.
[2] Austen-Leigh, op. cit., p. 311.

letter on her behalf from Henry on his sick-bed had no effect. In an effort to expedite publication she wrote to Mr. Murray, mentioning the Prince's suggestion about the dedication. 'Whether it has done any . . . good I do not know, but Henry thought it worth trying,' she wrote at the end of November. Perhaps it did help, because *Emma*, with a dedication 'To His Royal Highness The Prince Regent', was published two weeks later. She wrote humorously to John Murray: 'You will be pleased to hear that I have received the Prince's thanks for the *handsome* copy I sent him of "Emma". Whatever he may think of *my* share of the work, yours seems to have been quite right.'[1]

There was no such satisfactory end to Henry's troubles. In March he was declared bankrupt. But his resilient nature triumphed over this, as over other set-backs. He immediately left London and business for good, and determined on a return to his original vocation, which his career, first as a soldier and then a banker, had temporarily superseded. After a brief, intensive study of the New Testament in the original Greek, he presented himself to the Bishop of Winchester for ordination in August 1816, five months after his bankruptcy had been declared. He was disappointed when the Bishop, no doubt thinking that he was easing an awkward moment, indicated a Greek Testament which lay near him, saying: 'As for *this* book, Mr. Austen, I dare say it is some years since either you or I looked into it.' He became curate of the village of Bentley, near Alton, and Jane said that he wrote 'very superior sermons'.

A year later Jane was dead, and it was Henry who prepared *Northanger Abbey* and *Persuasion* for publication, adding a short memoir of his sister written in a florid style very unlike her own. Handsome, changeable, witty and gay—soldier, man of business and finally a curate— Jane's affectionate words describe him best: 'Oh, what a Henry!'

[1] 1 April 1816.

VII

Reading the accounts of the Trustees' meetings it sur-
prises one with how little fuss the novel idea of Albany
was made to work. The one part of the concern which gave
continual trouble, until at length it had to be abandoned,
was the Tavern or Hotel. At first Copland ran it himself
with a paid maître d'hotel, but gave it up after only a few
months when he found that he was losing money, abandoned the idea of converting the two large basement
rooms into baths, and the Trustees then let the Hotel to a
Mr. John Mollard for £22 per annum.

He promised to keep the dining-rooms 'well-supplied
with good wines and provisions, to provide Laundresses
to be employed and paid by the Inhabitants, and to take
care of such of the Chambers as are committed to his care
by any of the Proprietors . . . also to keep the staircase
and passages in the House clean and in good order'. The
Trustees explained that they had made this agreement at
such a low rent because 'from the present infancy of the
Undertaking, and while many of the Apartments remain
uninhabited, it was not possible to find an eligible Tenant
who would risk giving such a rent as the Trustees think
may be expected when the Apartments shall be fully in-
habited'. It was evidently their idea that owners of
chambers in Albany should have the advantages of what
we should now call 'service flats'. But Mr. Mollard had
decided in less than a year 'on adjusting his accounts very
minutely' that his enterprise was 'attended with great
loss'.

The Hotel was then let to a Mr. Cross for £100 per
annum. Mr. Cross applied to the Trustees for leave to
insert the following advertisement in the Public Papers:

'Albany Tavern and Coffee Room (late York H^{e}) Piccadilly.
H. Cross most respectfully Invites the Nobility and Gentry to

the Inspection of the above Tavern and Coffee Room fitted up in a most superior Stile of Elegance for their accommodation, hopes for their Patronage and support by reasonable charges and Wines of superior Vintage, Dinners, Turtles drest & sent out on the shortest Notice.

Soups made, Dishes Wines and Spirits.'[1]

But a year later Mr. Cross became bankrupt and the next tenant, Macdonagh, followed suit at the end of a year's tenancy. After this, not surprisingly, no tenant was forthcoming and the Trustees requested Mr. Copland again to undertake the management. 'For the purpose of throwing the Coffee Room open to the Public' he spent nearly £400 in making a direct entrance from the court-yard to the Tavern, under the supervision of Robert Smirke, officially appointed architect to the Trustees. But in less than a year Copland again despaired. One further attempt was made, but the tenant finding that he had lost 'more than £500 by the undertaking', in spite of paying no rent, the proprietors agreed that it was no use con-tinuing a Hotel and authorized the Trustees 'to let it as best they can'.

Up to this date Lady Melbourne's dining-saloon had probably remained untouched, as it is referred to as 'the Great Room', but now all the premises hitherto used by the Hotel were converted into two apartments. That in the Mansion was numbered A.14 and was let from 1811 for twenty-one years to Robert Smirke, at a rent of £126 a year. Sir Robert Smirke was one of the most successful architects of his day, with a reputation for reliability and knowledge of the technical side of building. The Trustees could have found no better guide and he remained their official architect, advising them, without remuneration, on all structural alterations to the buildings for some years.

'The Kitchen and Cooks' apartments originally be-

[1] Fifty-ninth Meeting of Trustees, 24 October 1805.

GEORGE WYNDHAM, 3RD EARL OF EGREMONT, SAID TO BE
THE FATHER OF LADY MELBOURNE'S SHORT-LIVED TWINS,
WHO WERE BORN IN 1777, AND OF WILLIAM LAMB, BORN IN
1779, LATER 2ND LORD MELBOURNE AND PRIME MINISTER

This portrait by Thomas Phillips was painted some 20 years later, in 1798, when he was 47 years old. It is in the possession of John Wyndham, Esq., at Petworth house

THE PRINCE OF WALES, AGED 21, BY SIR JOSHUA REYNOLDS.
THIS IS THE PORTRAIT GIVEN BY HIM TO LADY MELBOURNE
IN 1783 WHEN HE WAS "DESPERATELY IN LOVE" WITH HER.
SHE PLACED IT IN THE SALOON AT BROCKET HALL, WHERE
IT STILL HANGS. IT IS NOW IN THE POSSESSION OF LORD
BROCKET. GEORGE LAMB, BORN IN 1784, WAS GENERALLY
THOUGHT TO BE THE PRINCE OF WALES'S SON

THE DUKE OF YORK, AGED 31
Detail from the painting by Hoppner now in the Ashmolean Museum

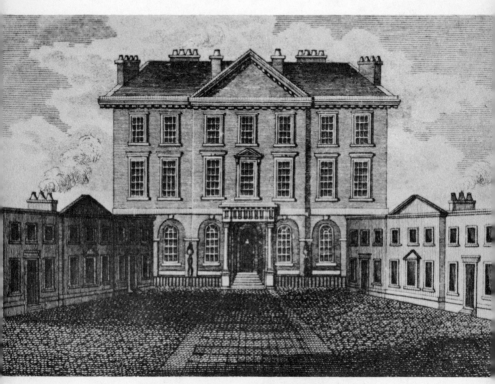

VIEW OF YORK HOUSE IN PICCADILLY
From the Carlton House Magazine

longing to Melbourne House'[1] were let in the same year to Thomas Hill Mortimer, who wrote offering to convert them into a set of chambers at an estimated cost of £600 and to pay £63 per annum rent. 'Being by Profession a Solicitor and having understood an objection might arise to admitting me within the Precincts of the Establishment I think it necessary to add that my connexions are but few and of the first Situation in Life, who generally expect me to wait upon them, rather than attend me—and my communication with Lincoln's Inn and the Law Offices being naturally through Piccadilly the apprehension that such a Tenant might disturb the privacy of the Society . . . will be less reasonably entertained.'[2]

Thus the curious community of Albany was shaped, fulfilling a need—'for the casual residence of the nobility and gentry, who had no settled town residence.'

For more than one hundred and fifty years Albany has provided comfortable, compact quarters in the centre of London for their fortunate owners, and the hush and calm of an earlier day still seem to cling about them. As one stands on the steps leading down from the Mansion to the covered way between the long stuccoed buildings one is reminded of cloisters, of that calm which reigns in college gardens, where the noisy movement of the world can be sensed far off and yet one stands in stillness.

There is a strange timelessness about the long paved vista of the Rope Walk which would make it scarcely surprising if a figure from another age should saunter out of one of those lettered entrances—K.1 perhaps, on our right as we stand with our backs to the Mansion and the whole five hundred feet of the covered way stretch ahead of us. He is a tiny, foppish figure. He turns our way and we catch a glimpse of his face—with round black eyes and skin dark above his high, starched cravat. It is not the sort

[1] Thus described in letter to Trustees from Mortimer on expiration of lease. Minutes of Trustees' Meeting, 8 August 1842.
[2] 6 June 1811.

of face one would expect to see in this place or in the elegant clothes which he is wearing. He has checked, turns and retraces his steps. Let us follow him and see what kind of a man he was who lived here, in K.1, so long ago.

CHAPTER IV

IN THE DAYS OF LEWIS AND BYRON

I

MATTHEW GREGORY LEWIS was known to his friends as Mat, but from the publication of his first book he became to the world 'Monk' Lewis. He must have been one of the most notorious of the early inhabitants of Albany.[1]

His parents had separated while he was still a child, owing to an 'indiscretion' on the part of his pretty mother, and he wrote sadly that he was made 'almost an umpire' between them. He was deeply attached to his mother who, though her husband made her an allowance, often found herself short of money. As an undergraduate at Christ Church her son would send her money which he had saved from his own allowance and, when he heard she was in need, appealed to his father for twenty pounds, though 'being obliged to apply so frequently to my father is very painful to me'. For once his father was unsympathetic and refused to advance him any money. 'The question is not whether you shall deny yourself pleasures to give satisfaction to others; but whether you shall continue to supply wants which perhaps are not necessary to a person to whom I have already been very liberal. If you continue to

---

[1] The records in Albany give June 1809 as the date on which M. G. Lewis bought the lease of the Chambers K.1 from Wm. Thorogood. But he is known to have moved to Albany about a year after his estrangement from his father towards the end of 1802, so it is probable that he took the apartments for a short time and later decided to buy the lease.

be found an easy exchequer, there will be no income I can allow you will be sufficient to satisfy their avidity who are imposing on your mother.'

This rebuke from his father, who had always treated him with the greatest kindness, did not stop Mat from wishing to help his mother, and it was then that he first had the idea that he would make money for her by writing and that no one could object if he chose to give her money which he had earned by his own work. 'I have begun something which I hope, and am indeed certain, will, hereafter, produce you a little money . . . It is a romance, in the style of *The Castle of Otranto.*'

Although he was still an undergraduate his father had arranged for him to spend the summer months at Weimar learning German, and this visit was to have a lasting influence on his tastes and thought. Among the first people whom he met in Weimar was 'Monsieur de Goethe, the celebrated author of *Werter,*' he wrote to his mother, 'so you must not be surprised if I should shoot myself one of these fine mornings. As to my own nonsense, I write and write . . . I have got hold of an infernal dying man, who plagues my very heart out. He has talked for half a volume already, and seems likely to talk for half a volume more; and I cannot manage to kill him out of the way for the life of me.'[1]

He was not yet eighteen but he had already written one comedy, one farce (besides translating another from the French), two volumes of a novel, two of a romance and numerous poems. Even recognizing his extreme facility for composition, which led people to say later that he could 'throw off a couple of stanzas while the applicant for them has been describing of what nature they were to be', this is a remarkable achievement for a seventeen-year-old boy. After his stay in Germany, where he became fascinated by the thrills of gloom and horror which animated the contemporary German school of literature, he

[1] *Life and Correspondence of Matthew Gregory Lewis,* Vol. I, p. 72.

returned for the winter to Oxford and then left the following summer for The Hague to take up a position as attaché at the British Embassy. His mother had been acting as his literary agent at home, but she could send him only news of disappointments—books, plays and poems refused. Nevertheless startling success was soon to greet him.

'They say that practice makes perfect; if so, I shall one day be a perfect author, for I practise most furiously. What do you think of my having written, in the space of ten weeks, a romance of between three and four hundred pages octavo? I have even written out half of it fair. It is called "The Monk", and I am myself so much pleased with it that, if the booksellers will not buy it, I shall publish it myself.'[1] He had barely finished the fair copy when his father, alarmed at the course of the war in the Low Countries, recalled him to England.

The previous year Mrs. Radcliffe had made a sensation with her book *The Mystery of Udolpho*, for which she had received what was then the enormous sum of £500. This was the book which had so stimulated Mat's imagination that he had returned in haste to his unfinished romance.

There was no shadow of doubt which book made the greatest sensation in 1795. *The Monk* was scarcely published (anonymously) before it was assailed by critics for immorality—always an advertisement for a book by an unknown author—and it was more discussed and more widely read than any other published during that summer. But it was not, like so many others, quickly forgotten. A year after its publication the Attorney-General was instructed by a society for the suppression of vice to move for an injunction to restrain its sale. The prosecution was subsequently dropped, but the book retained its popularity. The improbable story of mystery and despair, its cult of the monstrous and supernatural, satisfied the public appetite for the macabre which had been awakened by

[1] Lewis, op. cit., 23 September 1794, Vol. I, pp. 133–4.

Mrs. Radcliffe. 'Is it *horrid?*' the female reader would inquire at the circulating library. *The Monk* was undoubtedly horrid and its success was phenomenal.

For a short time Mat was able to hear his book discussed, guesses hazarded as to the writer's identity, and on occasions to overhear strangers claiming to be close friends with the author. From the moment that the shield of his anonymity was pierced, he became 'Monk' Lewis, and for the rest of his life it was only to his family and intimates that he would be 'Mat'. As 'Monk' Lewis his name was on every tongue. Hostesses competed for the presence of this new literary celebrity. He was returned to Parliament as member for Hindon in Wiltshire, a seat until then held by William Beckford of Fonthill.[1]

In this broadening world his character developed and hardened into lines which changed little in after-life. Above all he loved social gatherings and conversation. He was incredibly loquacious and at the same time subject to sudden moods of depression and extreme sensitivity, when tears would well in his large, dark eyes and sometimes roll down his sallow cheeks at a sad story or a touching sentiment. This failing, frequently indulged in public, was embarrassing to his friends, but he appeared to feel no *gêne*. In person exceptionally small, with large, dark, shining eyes, he was always talking. 'Nothing was more tiresome than Lewis when he began to harp upon any extravagant proposition,' wrote Walter Scott. 'He would tinker at it for hours without mercy, and repeat the same thing in four hundred different ways. If you assented in despair, he resumed his reasoning in triumph . . . If you disputed, daylight and candlelight could not bring the discussion to an end.'[2]

A second edition was printed of *The Monk* and Lewis, bowing to the critics, struck out various phrases which he thought were responsible for 'the outcry raised against

[1] He never spoke in Parliament and resigned after a few years.
[2] Intro. to *The Monk*, p. xxiii.

the book'. He always protested that the most he could be accused of as the author was imprudence, and 'twenty is not the age at which prudence is most to be expected. Inexperience prevented my distinguishing what would give offence . . . the objections rested entirely on expressions too strong, and words carelessly chosen.'[1]

Soon afterwards he began a collection of 'marvellous ballads . . . ancient as well as modern.' Erskine, the brilliant lawyer, showed him some poems of this kind written by Walter Scott who, though four years older than Lewis, was still unknown. Lewis was so impressed by these poems that he wrote to Scott, suggesting that he should contribute to his collection, which was to be called *Tales of Wonder*. A few months later, in the house of Lady Charlotte Campbell,[2] a lady with whom he was on terms of innocent sentiment and who entertained a literary *salon* in Edinburgh, Lewis met Scott for the first time. Years afterwards Walter Scott confessed to a friend that he had never felt such elation as when the 'Monk' invited him to dine for the first time at his hotel. Lewis's good nature led him to arrange with his own publisher to bring out some of Scott's work. The person who first set him on trying his talent at poetry, Scott said, was Mat Lewis.

When *Tales of Wonder* were published shortly afterwards (in 1801) he and Scott became the targets for a satirical attack from Byron:

> 'Oh, wonder-working Lewis, Monk and Bard,
> Who fain would make Parnassus a church-yard,
> Lo! wreaths of yew, not laurel, bind thy brow,
> Thy muse a sprite, Apollo's sexton thou!
> Whether on ancient tombs thou take thy stand,
> By gibbering spectres hailed, thy kindred band;
> Or tracest chaste descriptions on thy page

[1] Letter to his father, 23 February 1798.

[2] Daughter of the Duke of Argyll, her mother was one of the beautiful Gunning sisters. As a widow became Lady-in-Waiting to the unfortunate Princess of Wales, wife of the Prince Regent. Afterwards Lady Charlotte Bury.

To please the females of our modest age;
All hail, M.P., from whose infernal brain
Thin-sheeted phantoms glide, a grisly train;
At whose command "grim women" throng in crowds,
And kings of fire, of water and of clouds,
With "small grey men"—"wild yagers", and what not,
To crown with honour thee and Walter Scott;
Again all hail! if tales like thine may please,
St. Luke alone can vanquish the disease;
Even Satan's self with thee might dread to dwell,
And in thy skull discern a deeper hell.'

But this collection of ballads was by no means Lewis's only activity. To his father's regret, he showed little bent for politics, while his interest in the theatre remained very lively. Already he had had one play successfully produced at Drury Lane—*The Castle Spectre*, with Mrs. Jordan as the heroine. Sheridan had no very high opinion of the play, and as manager advised Lewis to omit the appearance of the spectre from the final scene. In spite of similar recommendations from friends who had read the play and actors who were to perform in it, he insisted on retaining the ghost and was proved right in the event as the ghost continued to appear nightly, 'with increased applause'. Both Byron and Lady Holland have left reports of an exchange between Lewis and Sheridan over this play. They had got into a dispute. 'I will bet you, Mr. Sheridan,' said Lewis, 'a very large sum; I will bet you what you owe me, as manager, for my *Castle Spectre*.' 'I never make large bets,' Sheridan replied, 'but I will lay you a very small one; I will bet you what it is worth.'

Lewis then thought he would try his hand as a writer of comedies. A farce, taken from a French play, *The Twins; or, Is it he, or his brother?* was given as a benefit for Bannister at Drury Lane but never repeated. Then *The East Indian*, a comedy written when he was sixteen, accepted by Mrs. Jordan but never yet performed, was given for her benefit and subsequently played for some little time at

Drury Lane. Lewis blamed Sheridan for the comedy not being a greater success and for its being taken off before he thought necessary—'Mr. Sheridan having blocked up my road, mounted on his great tragic war-horse *Pizarro*,[1] and trampled my humble pad-nag of a comedy under foot, without the least compunction.'[2]

Relations between Lewis and Sheridan were clearly strained, but an opera by Lewis was performed at Drury Lane, with Mrs. Jordan and Charles Kemble in the leading parts, before an open break came over the production of another tragedy, *Alfonso, King of Castile*. Lewis immediately transferred his play to Mr. Harris, manager of Covent Garden, who received him with flattering attentions and accepted the play 'with great joy, and praises it extremely'. This tragedy must surely have been in Sheridan's mind when he wrote that devastating farce, *The Critic*, as Lewis slaughtered his characters wholesale, by poison, dagger and sword. The rift between them was never mended—jealousy must have played a large part in their quarrel. Years later, Lewis, usually so good-natured and kind, wrote this epigram upon Sheridan:

'For worst abuse of finest parts
  Was Misophil begotten;
  There might indeed be *blacker* hearts,
  But none could be more *rotten*.'

Lewis's most horrific effect in the theatre was yet to come. His monodrama, *The Captive*, threw Covent Garden Theatre into confusion. It was a picture of madness. Mrs. Litchfield, an actress of great reputation at the time, took the part of the Captive, a poor lunatic woman chained in a dungeon. So horrifying was the effect of the short scene that women cried, fainted and shrieked with terror. 'Two people went into hysterics during the performance, and two more after the curtain dropped. . . I immediately

[1] A tragedy by Sheridan based on *Rolla* by Kotzebue.
[2] Lewis, op. cit., Vol. I, p. 222.

withdrew the piece,' said Lewis. 'I did not expect that it would succeed. . . The only chance was, whethèr pity would make the audience weep; but, instead of that, terror threw them into fits.'

While working for the theatre, Lewis's facility for composition enabled him to write ballads and verses, for many of which he also composed melodies. Some were written to order for operas or plays, when the manager wished to introduce a song, others were published as poems and when set to music became immensely popular. A large proportion of the songs then most widely sung in drawing-rooms and whistled in the streets were written by him.

Inspired, perhaps, by her son's success, Mrs. Lewis told him that she was thinking of publishing a tragedy which she had written. His mother's 'former errors' had been almost forgotten by this time and she lived a life of comfort, though not with her family, receiving an allowance from her husband and frequent presents from her son. The latter's reaction to her suggestion was violent: 'It would be useless to say that it should be published without your name . . . The book-seller . . . would not fail to insert in the newspapers that it is whispered, that such a novel is written by Mrs. Lewis, and then would follow paragraph after paragraph, with all our family affairs ripped up, till everyone of us would go mad with vexation. I cannot express to you in language sufficiently strong how disagreeable and painful my sensations would be, were you to publish any work of any kind, and thus hold yourself out as an object of newspaper animadversion and impertinence. I am sure every such paragraph would be like the stab of a dagger to my father's heart . . . As for myself, I really think I should go to the continent immediately upon your taking such a step.'

Poor Mrs. Lewis quickly gave up her idea of becoming an authoress and was rewarded by a letter of thanks from her son, further explaining his views: 'I hold that a woman has no business to be a public character, and that in proportion as she acquires notoriety, she loses delicacy. I always consider a female author as a sort of half-man.'

Among his many friends he had intimate connections with the two families who had previously lived in the house now known as Albany. William Lamb, Lady Melbourne's favourite son, had collaborated with him in a poem, and he was a frequent visitor to Oatlands, where—great mark of favour—the Duchess of York gave him a dog, a spaniel named Folly. But even in Royal circles the 'Monk's' too ready emotions were liable to overflow. 'Lewis at Oatlands was observed one morning to have his eyes red, and his air sentimental: being asked why? he replied, that when people said anything *kind* to him, it affected him deeply; and just now the Duchess had said something *so* kind, that—here tears began to flow again. "Never mind, Lewis," said Colonel Armstrong to him, "never mind, don't cry. *She did not mean it.*" '[1]

He entertained the Duchess of York at a *fête champêtre* in his country cottage at Barnes, but in the bustle of preparation, a friend found him in a sudden mood of gloomy abstraction. 'A gust of wind swept a blossom to his feet. He regarded it for a moment. . . "See," said he, "it is still in the pride of its bloom. . . Still it is broken!" His large black eyes filled with tears, and his voice had that sort of choking sound that I *so hate*.' Later the same observer described the scene when Lewis's favourite tortoiseshell cat, Minnette, settled herself comfortably on the Duchess's shawl, which was lying on the seat beside her. She would not allow the cat to be moved, saying, 'Poor little ting! I do tink she love me,' and talked happily with Lewis about cats, dogs ('I av many dog, as you know') the slave trade and Mr. Wilberforce.[2]

If Lewis had not quarrelled with his father he would

[1] Byron's story from *Detached Thoughts*.
[2] Lewis, op. cit., Vol. I, pp. 336–46.

probably never have become an inhabitant of Albany. But the two were estranged when the father became infatuated with a woman who, it was reported, had said that he was only waiting for his wife's death 'to give her the greatest proof of his regard'. After hearing this Mat infuriated his father by treating her very coldly when she came, as she frequently did, to the family house in Devonshire Place, and steadfastly refused either to call on her, as his father wished, at her house in Baker Street, or to greet her 'with *warmth* and *pleasure*' when she came to his own home.

Mat was as devoted as ever to his mother. '*Ought* a son,' he asked, 'to be on friendly terms with a person who he *knows* is waiting with impatience for the death of his mother, and who has had the imprudence to avow that she is doing so?' It is much to his credit that he should have taken such a firm stand, for he was by everyone expected to inherit a large fortune from his father, as the eldest and only surviving son. After this difference his father's manner became extremely cold towards him and shortly afterwards he received a letter telling him that his father had 'ceased to consider me as part of his domestic establishment—that after what had passed it was disagreeable to him that I should remain an inmate of his house—and desiring me to leave.'[1] But this was not all. In his resentment he considerably reduced Mat's allowance, and knowing that he enjoyed riding, refused to keep his saddle-horses in his stables and dismissed the groom, telling his son that if he chose to have horses now he must pay for them himself.

This reduction in his income distressed Mat particularly because he had for several years been giving his mother nearly half the thousand pounds a year allowed him by his father. His friends said at the time that his father had written to him, 'As I find you can live upon £500 a year—the half of what I have hitherto allowed you—I do not see why I should furnish you with more.' A man whose

[1] Lewis, op. cit., Vol. I, p. 288.

feelings were so sensitive that he could cry at a sad thought or an affectionate word, must have suffered greatly from this harsh treatment by his father. But love for his mother and the strong feeling that his father was requiring of him conduct which he had no right to demand, supported his spirits.

After leaving his father's house in Devonshire Place he drove north with the Duke of Argyll in his landau, for a visit to Inverary Castle. Here he cannot have had much time to ponder on his estrangement from his father, 'dining at eight, supping at two, and going to bed at four in the morning.' Yet he protested to his mother that he was regular in his mode of life compared to the other inhabitants of the castle. 'Many of them do not go to bed till between six and seven; and between four and five in the morning is the time generally selected as being most convenient for playing at billiards.' Happening to wake at six o'clock and 'hearing the billiard balls in motion, I put on my dressing-gown, and . . . looking down into the great hall, I descried Tom Sheridan and Mr. Chester (who had not been in bed all night) playing with great eagerness. Fortunately, Tom was in the act of making a stroke on which the fate of the whole game depended; when I shouted to him over the balustrade, "Shame! shame! a married man!" on which he started back in a fright, missed his stroke, and lost the game'.[1]

William Lamb was a fellow guest at the Castle. The 'Monk' wrote to Lady Melbourne in October 1802: 'Your *Darling* arrived here on Wednesday last dripping wet, but otherwise in good care and in good spirits. He is at present busily employed upon the composition of a Domestic Newspaper which has been lately established at Inverary and of which he has been appointed Editor for the present week. Three have already been published with great applause, but (in spite of all care) not without *some* heart-burning: the Fourth *of course* will possess all the merits of

[1] Lewis, op. cit., Vol. II, p. 5.

the three former, unaccompanied by any of their defects; for *you know* it would be impossible for William not to do everything better than anyone else. To tell you the truth . . . I have some difficulty not to be of the above opinion myself. Inverary is as full as it can hold—and *fuller* too as the Irishman said. Bedrooms are in great request and William and Kinnaird being the last comers, are moved about from chamber to chamber, never knowing one night where they are to sleep the next. Whoever passes a few hours out of the Castle is certain of finding one of the two new-comers established in his room when he returns; and a formal complaint was lodged yesterday by a great Russian Count, that he only stept out for half an hour, and the first things which He saw lying on his bed when He came back, were a dozen pairs of Kinnaird's leather breeches.' All the guests took part in amateur theatricals and performed three different plays, in one of which William Lamb 'obstinately refused to be dressed as a shepherd with a wreath of roses and a bunch of cherry coloured ribbands ornamenting his hat'.[1]

On Mat's return from Scotland a half-reconciliation was patched up with his father, who shortly afterwards restored his allowance, but he was not invited to return to his father's house and in the circumstances would not have wished to, so he had to find somewhere to live in London. He chose the Chambers named K.1 in Albany and retained them until his death.

If his father's house was no longer open to him there were many others where he was a welcome guest. Inverary was not the only ducal establishment to which he was invited. There were more parties at Oatlands, there was a dinner at Bushey Park with the Duke of Clarence, who came up to him on Egham racecourse, called him ' "Lewis", *tout court*' and invited him 'as a man of romance and sentiment' to dinner to meet some Spanish Deputies. Then there were four pleasant days passed at Woburn Abbey

[1] Mabell, Countess of Airlie, op. cit., pp. 64–65.

with the Duke of Bedford, where the guests had 'turtle, venison, burgundy, and champagne, in profusion every day; and . . . at breakfast every person had a silver tea-pot appropriated to his own use.'

Many people criticized Lewis for being a snob. Even Walter Scott, who to the end of his life acknowledged his debt to him, said: 'Lewis was fonder of great people than he ought to have been, either as a man of talent or as a man of fashion. He had always dukes and duchesses in his mouth, and was pathetically fond of anyone who had a title. You would have sworn he had been a *parvenu* of yesterday, yet he had lived all his life in good society.'[1]

These criticisms were resented and denied by Lewis himself. 'I care nothing about rank in life,' he wrote, 'nothing about what other people may think or may say; and have always . . . shown (what Mr. Pitt was pleased to call) a pleasure in spitting in the face of public opinion. I live as much with actors, and musicians and painters, as with princes and politicians, and am as well satisfied, and better indeed, with the society of the first, as with that of the latter. But I absolutely require that people should possess some quality or other to amuse me or interest me, or I had rather be by myself.'[2]

Mat Lewis divided his time between his country cottage and his chambers in Albany. These chambers must have been quite unlike any others. He had 'almost a passion for mirrors' and his rooms were full of them, with flowers and books and pictures and here and there 'little elegant de-vices and poetic fancies'. He was constantly adding to his collection of *bijouterie* and 'all sorts of pretty knick-nackery', particularly of seals for which he was 'continually invent-ing new mottoes and devices'. His friends were sure of pleasing him if they gave him another seal. In one letter to his mother he mentioned that Lord Henry Petty had sent him 'a very pretty seal . . . Macdonald too has sent

[1] Introduction to *The Monk*, p. xxvi.
[2] Lewis, op. cit., Vol. I, p. 362.

one quite beautiful; and I hear that Lady Cowper and William Lamb have two more in hand for me.'

We get many glimpses of 'Monk' Lewis which bring him before our eyes so vividly that we can see him in his rooms at Albany, his little body hunched in a chair in a gloomy mood, or talking endlessly to a visitor, or dashing off a poem, designing a seal for his collection or examining a new German work or an old book of Scottish ballads to add to his library, or elegantly dressed, passing with neat little steps to the shelter of the covered way and through the Mansion on his way to dine at Holland House.

One never-to-be-forgotten evening he came home direct from Drury Lane Theatre where the curtain had been dropped before the end of his drama *Venoni; or, the Novice of St. Mark's*. The audience had shown their dislike of the third act in no uncertain fashion, an act where Lewis had attempted a modern scene by dividing the stage in two. On the left side of this stage wall the hero was confined in one cell, on the right Mrs. Siddons, the heroine, languished in another. The climax came when the gallant hero broke down the wall to rescue Mrs. Siddons. By this time the uproar was such that the curtain was dropped on a disconcerted cast. 'Call a rehearsal tomorrow morning,' said Lewis, 'and I'll see what can be done.' He hurried home. With pen, ink and strong coffee, and 'Pray go to bed and on no account disturb me till I ring', he settled down to write an entirely new third act to the play. By morning it was finished, and new parts were given out that day. Manager and actors were astonished and a week later the new version of the play began a successful career.[1]

'Mat had queerish eyes,' said Scott, 'they projected like those of some insects, and were flattish on the orbit. His person was extremely small and boyish—he was indeed the least man I ever saw, to be strictly well and neatly made. I remember a picture of him by Saunders being

[1] Lewis, op. cit., Vol. II, pp. 57–58.

SIR WILLIAM CHAMBERS,
ARCHITECT OF
MELBOURNE HOUSE, BY
SIR JOSHUA REYNOLDS
IN 1780 (THE
BUILDING ON THE LEFT
IS THE STRAND FRONT
OF SOMERSET HOUSE,
DESIGNED BY
CHAMBERS, SHOWING
THE ROOMS THEN
OCCUPIED BY THE
ROYAL ACADEMY)
*From the Council Chamber of
the Royal Academy*

MAKERS OF ALBANY

HENRY HOLLAND,
ARCHITECT TO THE
GREAT WHIG FAMILIES,
WHO PLANNED THE
CONVERSION OF YORK
HOUSE TO ALBANY,
THE CHAMBERS BUILT IN
THE GARDEN AND THE
SHOPS IN PICCADILLY
ON THE SITE OF THE
OLD WALL AND
ENTRANCE GATES
*The portrait by Opie is in the
possession of Lord Forteviot*

THOMAS COUTTS, THE
WHIG BANKER. HIS
BANK HAD A
MORTGAGE OF £22,000
FROM THE DUKE OF
YORK ON YORK HOUSE
AND HELPED TO
FINANCE ITS
CONVERSION TO
ALBANY

*The portrait by Sir William
Beechey is in the possession of
Messrs. Coutts and Co.*

MAKERS OF ALBANY

ALEXANDER COPLAND,
THE BUILDER WHO
CONVERTED THE HOUSE,
ERECTED THE NEW
BUILDINGS AND WAS
ACTIVE IN THE
AFFAIRS OF ALBANY
FROM THE BEGINNING
UNTIL HIS DEATH IN
1834

*The portrait by Sir Robert Smirke
is in the possession of Copland's
great-grandson, Brigadier F. A. V.
Copland-Griffiths, D.S.O., M.C.,
a Trustee of Albany*

handed round at Dalkeith House. The artist had ingeniously hung a dark folding mantle round the form, under which was half-hid a dagger, a dark lantern, or some such cut-throat appurtenance; with all this the features were preserved and ennobled. It passed from hand to hand into that of Henry, Duke of Buccleuch, who, hearing the general voice affirm that it was very like, said aloud, "Like Mat Lewis! Why, that picture's like a man!" He looked, and lo! Mat Lewis's head was at his elbow. This boyishness went through life with him. He was a child, and a spoiled child, but a child of high imagination; and so he wasted himself on ghost-stories and German romances. He had the finest ear for rhythm I ever met with—finer than Byron's.'[1]

In spite of the tears which rose so easily to his dark eyes, 'Monk' Lewis was not, as his readers pictured him, always a melancholy, or sinister figure. His gayer side, which had led him to delight in amateur theatricals and to throw himself with enthusiasm into the facetious newspaper produced by guests in the house-party at Inverary Castle, made him exert himself on other social occasions. One such function was a raffle for charity which the eccentric Lady Cork planned for a large evening party to be given at her house in London. He arranged with the hostess that every guest who took a ticket for the raffle should receive a prize, and diverted himself by choosing objects which would cause the maximum of embarrassment to each recipient.

The joke was most successful. 'The assembled guests were parading the brilliantly-lighted drawing-rooms burdened with the most out-of-the-way articles . . . while the inventor of this novel kind of *plaisanterie* was silently enjoying the joke [of] their distress. Gentlemen were seen in every direction, running about with teapots in their hands, or trays under their arms, endeavouring to find some sly corner, in which to deposit their prizes; while

[1] Quoted, Introduction to *The Monk*, p. xxvii.

young ladies were sinking beneath the weight, or the shame, of carrying a coal-scuttle or a flat-iron. Guinea-pigs, birds in cages, punch-bowls, watchmen's rattles, and Dutch-ovens, were perplexing their fortunate . . . proprietors.'[1]

His relationship with his father remained an uneasy one. The lady who had been the subject of their quarrel, being well aware of Matthew's feelings towards her, lost no opportunity of making trouble between father and son, and when Mr. Lewis fell ill in the spring of 1812, they were still estranged. An affectionate letter from Matthew was brought by his sister to their father's bedside, but he asked her to keep it for a little—'Don't give it me just now.'

Matthew, waiting for news in his rooms at Albany, heard from her eight days later that his father had never mentioned it again or asked to see it. He wrote to his mother, 'His illness makes me melancholy; his sufferings give me pain; I am sincerely anxious to hear of his being better. But as it is now above nine years since I have had any intercourse with him that carried with it any kindness, his loss will alter none of the habits of my life; . . . I shall not miss his place at table, nor the morning welcome, nor the affectionate good night. . . Nine years of constant harshness or indifference, on his part, have now made us strangers to each other; but still I dread so much the thought of witnessing his sufferings, that I scarcely know whether, for my own happiness, I ought to wish for a reconciliation *now* . . . In a mercenary view a reconciliation may be desirable for me, but in what other? Good God! to have his affection restored to me, merely that I may lose it again for ever—it seems shocking to me; and the kinder his treatment might be of me *now*, the more bitter will be my regrets at losing him.'[2]

But two days later he was sent for, and father and son

[1] Lewis, op. cit., Vol I., p. 365.
[2] Ibid., Vol. II, pp. 77–78.

were reconciled. 'He only said to me "God bless you",
two or three times. I was ordered not to speak: I made it
up in *crying*, as you may well believe.'

Soon afterwards his father died and was found in his will
to have left everything to 'his beloved son', save for a be-
quest of £500 to the lady they had quarrelled over, and a
release for her relations of sums lent by him, apparently
amounting to several thousand pounds.

Lewis's position was now entirely changed. He found
himself a very rich man and the owner of valuable plantations in Jamaica. He was able to give his mother a thousand pounds a year and bought for her a charming little
house in one of the loveliest parts of Surrey. He remained
himself perfectly content with his apartment in Albany
and his country cottage at Barnes. He continued his interest
in the theatre. His spectacular drama, *Timour the Tartar*,
had a tremendous success, being the first play in which real
horses trod the stage of Covent Garden. This was followed
by two of his plays which he had converted into operas.

He entertained small supper-parties of men in his
rooms. 'At a dinner at Monk Lewis's chambers in the
Albany, Lord Byron expressed . . . his determination not
to go there again, adding, "I never will dine with a
middle-aged man who fills up his table with young
ensigns, and has looking-glass pannels to his book-
cases." '[1]

Perhaps it was Lewis who first introduced Byron to
Albany. Certainly, in spite of what Byron had said, they
became friendly. Lewis called on Byron several times at his
lodgings in Bennet Street off St. James's. Byron would
dine with Lewis in his chambers and they went to the
theatre together. Byron commented in his journal. Once
Lewis seemed 'out of humour with everything'.[2] Another
time, 'Lewis called. It is a good and good-humoured man,
but pestilently prolix and paradoxical and *personal*. If he

[1] *Rejected Addresses*, (first published October 1812), p. 18 n.
[2] 14 November 1813.

would but talk half, and reduce his visits to an hour, he would add to his popularity. As an author he is very good, and his vanity is *ouverte* . . . and yet not offending.'[1]

This friendship with Lewis led Byron to re-read *The Monk* in the original, unexpurgated edition. 'I looked yesterday at the worst parts of *The Monk*. These descriptions ought to have been written by Tiberius at Caprea—they are forced—the *philtered* ideas of a jaded voluptuary,' he wrote in his journal. 'It is to me inconceivable how they could have been composed by a man of only twenty—his age when he wrote them . . . I should have suspected Buffon of writing them on the death-bed of his detestable dotage. I had never redde this edition, and merely looked at them from curiosity and recollection of the noise they made, and the name they left to Lewis.'

On another occasion Lewis was full of a visit to Oatlands, 'where he has been squabbling with Mad. de Staël about himself, *Clarissa Harlowe*, Mackintosh, and me,' wrote Byron. '. . . She bored Lewis with praises of himself till he sickened . . . She told Lewis wisely, he being my friend, that I was affected, in the first place and that, in the next place, I committed the heinous offence of sitting at dinner with my *eyes* shut, or half shut. I wonder if I really have this trick. I must cure myself of it, if true . . . I should like, of all things, to have heard the Amabaean eclogue between her and Lewis—both obstinate, clever, odd, garrulous, and shrill. In fact, one could have heard nothing else.'[2]

Two months after this meeting Byron had moved into Albany himself. His address he gave as 2, Albany. His rooms were in the mansion. From the front door, he would walk straight into the house and the door to his apartments would be on his left hand at the far side of the mansion. His living-room contained the great bow-window which in Lady Melbourne's day had lit the library. It no longer

[1] *Journal*, 30 November, 1813.
[2] Ibid., 16 January 1814.

looked into a garden, but down a wide space between the two new buildings, with the paved and covered walk in the centre. Thanks to the Rules and Regulations drawn up by the Trustees of Albany the rooms were absolutely quiet, and their new occupant could ask no better place in which to write undisturbed. Like all other apartments in Albany, a cellar in the basement and maids' rooms in the attics were included.

'This night,' he wrote in his journal, 'got into my new apartments, rented of Lord Althorpe, on a lease of seven years. Spacious, and room for my books and sabres. In the house, too, another advantage . . . Redde a little of many things—shall get in all my books tomorrow. Luckily this room will hold them.'[1]

Moore recalled that Byron had such a passion for arms of every description that 'there generally lay a small sword by the side of his bed, with which he used to amuse himself, as he lay awake in the morning, by thrusting it through his bed-hangings.'[2]

To his friend, Moore, he wrote a week later: 'Viscount Althorpe is about to be married, and I have gotten his spacious bachelor apartments in Albany . . . I have been boxing, for exercise, with Jackson for this last month daily. I have also been drinking, and, on one occasion, with three other friends at the Cocoa Tree, from six till four, yea, unto five in the matin. We clareted and champagned till two—then supped, and finished with a kind of regency punch composed of madeira, brandy, and *green* tea, no *real* water being admitted therein. There was a night for you! Without once quitting the table, except to ambulate home, which I did alone, and in utter contempt of a hackney-coach . . . I have also, more or less, been breaking a few of the favourite commandments; but I mean to pull up and marry, if any one will have me.'[3]

[1] *Albany*, 28 March 1814.
[2] Thomas Moore, *Letters and Journals of Lord Byron*, Vol. I, p. 74.
[3] 9 April 1814.

In contrast to the evenings when he sat up all night drinking with his friends, Byron would retire to his apartments on a strict regimen of near-starvation and violent exercise. He had a horror of becoming fat, saying that 'fat is an oily dropsy'. He would sometimes chew tobacco in place of a meal, thinking that it absorbed the gastric juice of the stomach and prevented hunger. 'Pass your hand down my side,' he said to an acquaintance, 'can you count my ribs?' 'Every one of them.' 'I am delighted to hear you say so. I called last week on Lady ——; "Ah, Lord Byron!" said she, "how fat you grow!" But you know Lady —— is fond of saying spiteful things!' 'It is to avoid your congratulations on *fatness* (which I abhor and you always inflict upon me after a return from the country) that I don't pay my respects to you today,' he wrote to Lady Melbourne. 'Besides which, I dislike to see L^d M^e standing by the chimney-piece, all horror and astonishment at my appearance while C.[1] is within reach of the twopenny postman. Today I have been very sulky; but an hour's exercise with Mr. Jackson, of pugilistic memory, has given me spirits, and fatigued me into that state of languid laziness, which I prefer to all other.'[2]

At this time Byron 'wore a very narrow cravat of white Sarsnet, with the shirt-collar falling over it; a black coat and waistcoat, and very broad white trousers, to hide his lame foot—these were of Russian duck in the morning, and jean in the evening. His watch-chain had a number of small gold seals appended to it, and was looped up to a button of his waistcoat. His face was void of colour, he wore no whiskers. His eyes were grey fringed with long black lashes; and his air was imposing, but rather supercilious.'[3] How much more we know of Byron's appearance and behaviour than of almost any other figure so

---

[1] The Melbournes' daughter-in-law, Caroline Lamb.
[2] 8 April 1814.
[3] *Rejected Addresses*, p. 19.

long dead. While he was alive nobody could take their eyes off him and we are still as fascinated by him today.

He wrote in his journal that he could not be long in any society 'without a yearning for the company of ym lamp and my utterly confused and tumbled-over library. Even in the day, I send away my carriage oftener than I use or abuse it . . . I have not stirred out of these rooms for these four days past: but I have sparred for exercise (windows open) with Jackson an hour daily . . . The more violent the fatigue, the better my spirits for the rest of the day; and then my evenings have that calm languor, which I most delight in. Today I have boxed an hour— written an Ode to Napoleon Buonaparte—copied it— eaten six biscuits—drunk four bottles of soda-water— redde away the rest of my time.'[1]

He arranged with Henry Angelo, the fencing master, to call on him at twelve o'clock, on as many days as possible, so that he could have what he called *'une bonne sueur* at the broadsword'. He preferred the broadsword to fencing, said Angelo, 'as the defect in his foot did not prevent it being an amusement to him, and at the same time it would be the means of reducing his size, for he was fearful of growing too lusty . . . His preparation for his exercise was rather singular, first stripping himself, then putting on a thick flannel jacket, and over it a pélisse lined with fur, tied round with a Turkish shawl.' When he had got hot enough, he would either lie down under a pile of blankets, or have his valet rub him down. Angelo was paid a gold half-guinea for each lesson and was careful, with this *'daily* scholar, far more lucrative than any of the others', to keep 'always on the defensive, retreating on his attacks'.

The only occasion when this tactful treatment almost failed was when Cam Hobhouse walked unexpectedly into the room where his friend was exercising. Byron, fired by an audience, did not give up but pressed his attack, seem-

[1] 10 April 1814.

ing 'determined to show his friend how well he could beat his broadsword master. Though I had always before been very politic,' said Angelo, 'yet here my pride was a little at stake, as we were no longer alone. Finding his attacks were getting desperate, I avoided his blows, and kept him at bay, till he was too fatigued to continue.' When Byron had recovered his breath and was anxious to go on, Angelo warned him with great politeness that he was but a man. Byron only cried, 'Bravo! . . Now take care of your numskull.' They went at it again, but Angelo, not liking to translate his warning into action, soon pleaded an engagement for another lesson elsewhere and left.

This was the only untoward incident. On all other occasions Byron was most friendly and would often persuade Angelo to stay talking with him for an hour or more. 'When I first attended him at Albany,' Angelo remembered, 'it was on the approach of spring; and often have I sat on the sofa next to a beautiful miniature of a lady, whose figure, I have heard him say, would serve as a model for Canova. At times this portrait seemed much to attract his attention.'[1]

To amuse him in his new rooms Byron had bought a macaw. A long table stood before the fireplace. It was always covered with books. In his living-room, too, were the silver urns which he had brought home with him from Greece. Now he added a screen made by Angelo which he had first seen at the Fencing Academy. It was decorated by prints of pugilists on one side and of actors on the other.

In addition to his books, his sabres, and his faithful valet, Fletcher, Byron had brought with him to Albany a maid known as Mrs. Mule. He had found this old crone in his last lodgings at Bennet Street, where her appearance had intimidated his visitors. Moore said that when Byron took chambers in Albany 'one of the great advantages which his friends looked to in the change was, that they should get

[1] *Reminiscences of Henry Angelo*, Vol. II, pp. 98–100.

rid of this phantom. But, no—there she was again—he had actually brought her with him.' He cited this as 'one of the numerous instances of Lord Byron's proneness to attach himself to anything, however homely, that had once enlisted his good nature in its behalf, and become associated with his thoughts . . . When asked how he came to carry this old woman about with him from place to place, Lord Byron's only answer was, 'The poor old devil was so kind to me!'[1]

Byron wrote of her in his journal: 'There is something to me very softening in the presence of a woman—some strange influence, even if one is not in love with them— which I cannot at all account for, having no very high opinion of the sex. But yet,—I always feel in better humour with myself and everything else, if there is a woman within ken. Even Mrs. Mule, my firelighter,— the most ancient and withered of her kind—and (except to myself) not the best-tempered—always makes me laugh,—no difficult task when I am "i'the vein".'

So Byron, scarcely three months after his twenty-sixth birthday ('Is there anything in the future that can possibly console us for not being always *twenty-five*?')[2] was established in this fine set of rooms. He was devoted to Lady Melbourne, who was now over sixty and rather stout, but still remarkably young in mind and appearance. He wrote to her when he had moved into his chambers: 'I am in *my* and *your* Albany rooms. I think you should have been included in the lease.'[3] He said she was 'the best friend I ever had in my life, and the cleverest of women'.[4] She was very fond of him, too, and quickly adopted with him her favourite rôle of confidante and adviser.

From the time, two years before, when Byron had come to London, unknown, proud and shy, and 'woke one

[1] Thomas Moore, op. cit., Vol. I, pp. 359–60.
[2] *Journal*, 1 December 1813.
[3] Letter 30 March 1814.
[4] *Journal*, 17 November 1813.

morning and found himself famous', he and Lady Melbourne had written to each other regularly, sometimes three or four times a week. They continued this correspondence until Byron left England in 1816.

'To Lady Melbourne I write with most pleasure,' he said, 'and her answers, so sensible, so *tactique*—I never met with half her talent. If she had been a few years younger, what a fool she would have made of me had she thought it worth her while.'[1]

Byron was restless and unsatisfied, his nature perpetually at war within itself. This inner conflict showed clearly in his habits. At one moment he would make himself ill by eating and drinking enormously, but then for days he would almost starve on biscuits and soda-water. He would dine out night after night and then for days on end stay gloomily alone in his rooms, the victim of intense *ennui*. He seemed to have two entirely different personalities—one the gay, clever companion, the other a moody, defiant sinner, haunted by mysterious guilt.

Lady Melbourne knew how to lighten his gloom. 'Your conversation is really champagne [to my spirits],' he said. With one part of his mind he longed to be married, but in darker moods he would throw out alarming innuendoes about sins and passions which set him apart. A wife would be his salvation, Lady Melbourne told him, and he agreed. In frequent letters they discussed the possible candidates. The two most favoured were Lady Adelaide Forbes, whose features reminded him of the Apollo Belvedere, and Lady Charlotte Leveson-Gower, who was said to have 'an air of *soul*' and 'the shyness of the antelope'. With Lady Melbourne's approval he was also corresponding with her niece in Durham, prim, academic Annabella Milbanke, her brother's only child—'Princess of Parallelograms' he called her in his letters to Lady Melbourne. He told Annabella that Lady Melbourne was in talent a *supreme* woman and with the kindest heart. He could never

[1] *Journal*, 24 November 1814.

perceive her defects as her society made him forget
them and everything else for the time. 'I do love that
woman (*filially or fraternally*) better than any being on
earth.'[1]

Years later he described her to Lady Blessington as 'a
charming person—a sort of modern Aspasia, uniting the
energy of a man's mind with the delicacy and tenderness
of a woman's.'[2] He particularly admired her forbearance
towards other women whose conduct was condemned by
society. 'She had always some kind interpretation for
every action that would admit of one, and pity or silence
when aught else was impracticable.'

Caroline Lamb's dramatic actions and disregard of public opinion during her disastrous and all too public love
affair with Byron had exasperated her mother-in-law. Now
that Byron had withdrawn, Lady Melbourne's only desire
was to suppress the scandal, keep Caroline from further
foolish extravagances in public, and for Byron's own good
and the peace of them all, to get him married. '(To please
you) I am trying to fall in love,' he wrote to her.

It was a summer of balls and masquerades. Byron, as an
admirer of Napoleon, did not share in the rejoicing which
greeted the newly-restored King, Louis XVIII, on his
triumphal entry into London in April. But the visit of the
Tsar and the King of Prussia made the summer a succession of brilliant entertainments and Byron was carried
along on the fast-running tide. Eight years later he would
write to Moore from Italy, reminding him of 'the year of
revelry 1814, the pleasantest parties and balls all over
London'.

Coming home to his rooms in the early morning too
excited to sleep, he would call to Fletcher for a glass of
brandy and would sit down to write poetry. 'It is a relief to
the fever of my mind to *write*,' he told Lady Melbourne,
and Moore, '*Lara* is finished, and I am copying him for my

[1] Letter, 12 February 1814.
[2] Lady Blessington, *Conversations with Lord Byron*, p. 225.

third vol., now collecting.'[1] As always, he was divided. In one mood he wanted to play the elegant patrician, moving easily and by right in the highest society. Then, abruptly, his mood would change, and the only object of his life would seem to be to excel as a poet.

After some months of quiet behaviour, Caroline Lamb now began to badger him again. A 'wrathful epistle' came from her, 'demanding letters, pictures, and all kinds of gifts which I never requested, and am ready to resign as soon as they can be gathered together; at the same signal,' he added bitterly, 'it might be as well for her to restore *my* letters as everybody has read them by this time.'

Two months after moving into Albany he complained to Lady Melbourne of 'an *inroad* which occurred when I was fortunately out',[2] and a month later, 'You talked to me about keeping her out. It is impossible; she comes at all times, at any time, and the moment the door is open in she walks. I can't throw her out of the window . . but *I* will not receive her.'[3] Two days later he is assuring her that he 'did not see nor hear of C. on Saturday, and that all bolts, bars, and silence can do to keep her away are done daily and hourly.'[4] Bolts and bars were evidently not enough. Coming home one day he found that she had been in his rooms and, on the title page of a book which lay open on the table, had written: 'Remember me!' Byron, enraged, sat down and wrote the bitter lines which are said to have hastened the collapse of her reason when, after his death, she read them for the first time:

> 'Remember thee! remember thee!
> Till Lethe quench life's burning stream
> Remorse and shame shall cling to thee,
> And haunt thee like a feverish dream!

[1] Letter, 14 June 1814.
[2] Letter, 28 May 1814.
[3] Letter, 26 June 1814.
[4] Ibid.

Remember thee! Aye, doubt it not,
Thy husband too shall think of thee:
By neither shalt thou be forgot,
Thou *false* to him, thou *fiend* to me!'

Her incursions into Albany must have caused considerable scandal amongst the inhabitants, as only gentlemen
could have apartments there and a lady's reputation would
be lost if she were seen entering Albany. Perhaps she
adopted her favourite disguise, dressing herself as a page,
a ruse which she had previously used to gain admittance to
Byron's lodgings.

Ten years later Caroline Lamb told the story of her
final visit to Albany, but by that time Byron had died in
Greece and Lady Melbourne, too, was dead and there was
no one to say whether her tale was true. According to her,
she visited his rooms in Albany 'disguised as a carman',
and Byron met her kindly. As he embraced her and pressed
his lips on hers, ' "Poor Caro," he murmured, "if everyone hates me, you, I see, will never change—no, not with
ill usage," and I said, "yes, I *am* changed, & shall come
near you no more"—For then he showed me letters, & told
me things I cannot repeat, & all my attachment went. This
was our last parting scene—well I remember it. It had an
effect on me not to be conceived—3 years I had *worshipped*
him.'

If her story was true, it is possible that Byron made these
rash confidences in the hope that he might at last be rid of
her. His friends were always deploring his regrettable
habit of confiding in any convenient listener. With his
detached interest in other people's emotions, did he want
to see how she would react to his revelations? Or, after
Byron's disgrace, and the rumours which everyone then
heard about his relationship with his half-sister, did she
invent the whole story? We do not know. But certainly
Byron made no reference to it in his letters to Lady
Melbourne, though he had few secrets from her, and it is
the kind of scene which he loved to describe.

Meanwhile Byron was still corresponding with Anna-bella Milbanke and, as with other entanglements, dis-cussing each move with Lady Melbourne, sending her niece's letters and his own replies for her to read. In July he went to the sea for a fortnight, returning to Albany in mid-August, where he wrote the final letter in what he described to Lady Melbourne as 'an extraordinary business'. Within a month he was engaged to be married to this highly-educated, serious girl whom he had not met for ten months.

He wrote at once to Lady Melbourne: 'I lose no time in telling you how things are at present . . . I shall be in town by Thursday, and beg one line to Albany, to say you will see me at your own day, hour and place . . . Seriously, I will endeavour to make your niece happy . . . Of my deportment you may reasonably doubt; of her merits you can have none. I need not say that this must be a *secret*. Do let me find a few words from you in Albany.'[1] On the same day he wrote Annabella an agitated reply to her letter accepting his proposal of marriage.

His stay in Albany was drawing to an end. When married he would have to live elsewhere, for Albany was sacred to bachelors and widowers. But his remaining weeks were not all happy. Looking into his financial affairs, getting his property 'into matrimonial array', he found them 'in so utterly embarrassed a condition as to fill him with some alarm'.[2] But Miss Milbanke was said to be 'a considerable *parti* . . . She is an only child, and Sir R.'s estates, though dipped by electioneering, are con-siderable.'[3]

A few weeks remained for him to enjoy his bachelor life—musical parties at the house of Douglas Kinnaird, his banker, when tears would rise in his eyes as he listened to Moore's *Irish Melodies*. Sometimes his favourite actor,

---

[1] 18 September 1814.
[2] Moore, Vol. I, p. 428.
[3] To Moore, 14 October 1814.

Kean, would be one of the party. Other evenings he spent with Gentleman Jackson or the champion, Tom Cribb, now retired and keeping a public house in Duke Street. When he was talking with the pugilists his boyish tastes seemed to revive. 'It was not a little amusing,' said his friend Moore, 'to observe how perfectly familiar with the annals of "the Ring", and with all the most recondite phraseology of "the Fancy", was the sublime poet of *Childe Harold.*'[1]

His departure for Seaham and matrimony was several times postponed and Lady Melbourne evidently became anxious. On 12 October Byron reassured her. 'Well, but I *am* going, am I not? What would mine aunt have?' But five days later he reports—still from Albany—that he is now quite alone with his books and his macaw, and 'horribly low-spirited'. At last he must leave London. 'Never was lover less in haste,' said one of his friends.

He was married in the first week of 1815 and with his bride remained in the North for the next two months. His publisher, Mr. Murray, was requested to make 'an occasional inquiry at Albany, at my chambers, whether my books, &c. are kept in tolerable order, and how far my old woman[2] continues in health and industry as keeper of my old den.'

The young couple returned to London, to 13 Piccadilly Terrace, which they had taken from Lady Elizabeth Foster, now the widowed Duchess of Devonshire. After Georgiana's death the Duke had married her, an action which scandalized his family far more than anything in his previous association with her. He had died only two years afterwards. Byron's books and swords were packed up and sent round from Albany. But news that he had married an heiress quickly reached his creditors, and financial worries, which had been dogging him for months, soon drove

[1] Moore, Vol. I, p. 427.
[2] Mrs. Mule.

them both nearly frantic. At the end of the year Lady
Byron was expecting a child. Before then bailiffs had been
several times in the house.

In November Byron wrote to Moore, 'Lewis is going to
Jamaica to suck his sugar canes. He sails in two days . . .
I saw him last night at D(rury) L(ane) T(heatre) for the
last time previous to his voyage. Poor fellow! he is really a
good man—an excellent man—he left me his walking-
stick and a pot of preserved ginger. I shall never eat the
last without tears in my eyes, it is so *hot*.'[1]

Since inheriting a fortune from his father, Lewis had
been able to satisfy the natural kindness of his character—
so different from what it was thought to be by his readers
—sometimes in eccentric fashion. He was well known to
all the beggars in streets through which he passed and
found himself embarrassed by long stories of hardship and
equally protracted protestations of gratitude. He was in
the habit of carrying loose sixpences in his pocket, and
when beset by a beggar would thrust one into his hand
muttering, 'No more words!' and hurry on. But when his
heart was touched, he on several occasions gave as much as
£50 to those whom he thought deserving, though they
were unknown to him. Now, towards the end of 1815, he
decided that he must go to Jamaica, to see for himself the
condition of his plantations and of those who worked in
them.

He had been gone only a month when a daughter was
born to Lady Byron and soon she left for the North to
visit her parents, leaving Byron with bailiffs in the house.
Though they had parted with friendly words, she never
returned to him and a letter from her father proposed a
separation. Public opinion turned violently against Byron.
He, who had been admired and courted by all the world,
found himself rejected and despised. Hostile paragraphs in
the newspapers, caricatures and pamphlets all presented
him as an odious figure, an unprincipled, licentious rake

[1] 4 November 1815.

whose wife, unable to countenance his excesses, had been forced to flee to her parents.

He, who had taken such pains to present himself to the public eye as a dramatic figure of unbridled passions and dark secrets, was horrified to find suddenly that the same public had accepted a picture of him far blacker and more discreditable than any he had striven to present. Broken in fortune, his books and furniture sold by public auction, only his privileges as a peer preserving him from a debtor's prison, deserted by his wife, condemned by all but a few faithful friends, he left his country, humiliated and resentful. But he was not crushed. He determined to show his critics that their verdict was not final, to hide from them the wounds that his pride had suffered and to force them to unwilling admiration.

In this mood he made his way 'through Flanders and by the Rhine' to Geneva, where after a few weeks at a hotel, he leased the Villa Diodati, on the shores of the lake. Here he was joined for a few days by Mat Lewis, just returned from his journey to Jamaica and on his way to Italy.

His three months in the West Indies had been full of interest for Mat. It was a strange moment in the history of the islands. The slave trade had been abolished; no new slaves were being imported, but those already in the island were still in slavery. 'The higher classes are all in the utmost alarm,' wrote Lewis, 'at rumours of Wilberforce's intentions to set the negroes entirely at freedom; the next step to which would be, in all probability, a general massacre of the whites . . . while, on the other hand, the negroes are impatient at the delay.'[1]

Mat drew up a new code of laws for the slaves at his plantation of Cornwall. No negro was to be struck or punished in any way without the trustee's express orders, a new hospital was to be built for them, a register of offences and punishments must be kept, no negro was to

[1] *Journal of a West Indian Proprietor*, p. 173.

be punished until twenty-four hours after his offence, 'in order that nothing should be done in the heat of passion.' Any white person having an improper connection with the wife of one of the negroes was to be discharged immediately. Allowances of clothing and food were detailed, in addition to the presents and money which Lewis had distributed personally during his stay.

Extra holidays were also arranged. Jamaican law allowed slaves all Sundays, every other Saturday and three days at Christmas. Lewis granted his slaves every Saturday as a right, and the second Friday in October and July, as well as Good Friday, making a full three-day holiday four times a year. The new October holiday he named 'the royal play-day', in honour of 'that excellent Princess, the Duchess of York.' On this day the head-driver was to announce 'The health of our good lady H.R.H. the Duchess of York.' With these words her health was to be drunk and three cheers given. Lewis solemnly announced to the negroes that he 'should not fail to let Her Royal Highness know, that the negroes of Cornwall drank her health every year'.[1] After all his kindness to them it was not surprising that his slaves' favourite song, repeated in chorus, often for hours together, and accompanied by dancing, ran:

'Since massa come, we very well off.'

This quite superseded the hitherto popular ballad, with the Duke of Wellington for hero:

'Ay! hey-day! Waterloo!
Waterloo! ho! ho! ho!'

But he was not so popular with the whites in the island. They complained that their slaves were being made discontented by his attentions to his own, and the Cornwall slaves soon spread the rumour that he intended to set

[1] *Journal of a West Indian Proprietor*, p, 243.

them free, or as an alternative that Wilberforce and the Regent had sent him to Jamaica to free all slaves, but that the other white folk were preventing him.

After three months in the island Lewis left Jamaica, and taking over two months on the voyage, landed at Gravesend early in June 1816. He stayed only a short time in England and then set out, as so many other English people did that year, with the long war over and Napoleon safely caged in St. Helena, for a tour of Europe. He reached Switzerland in mid-August and became Byron's guest at the Villa Diodati on the shore of Lake Leman, with a wonderful view across the peaceful water to the splendid mountains beyond.

Shelley with Mary Godwin, not yet his wife, were living in a cottage next to the villa, separated from it only by a vineyard, and with them was Claire Claremont, Mary's step-sister. Lewis may not have met the sisters. Mary was at this time writing her novel, *Frankenstein*, which was the result of an evening telling tales round the fire at the villa, when it was decided that everyone present must write a ghost story. Her step-sister was with child by Byron and although this was not yet known, scandalous reports had reached England that the two poets and the sisters were living together in general promiscuity.

During his short visit Lewis spent a day on the lake with Shelley and Byron, in a sailing boat of which they were joint owners. It seems strange now to think that at that time he would probably have been thought only slightly less gifted than Byron and considerably superior in genius to Shelley. His knowledge of German had not rusted and he read Goethe's *Faust* aloud to Byron, translating as he went.[1] It is probable that the idea for *Manfred*, the Nordic Faustian, came to Byron that evening; it was written shortly afterwards. Lewis told tales of the supernatural while they sat round the fire, and Shelley, who had been thrilled in his boyhood by *The Monk*, was so impressed

[1] Letter from Byron to Rogers, 4 April 1817.

that he wrote summaries of four of them in his journal. Byron and Lewis 'had some words' about Sheridan, who was one of the few people Lewis could not like, and Lewis was taken to visit Madame de Staël at Coppet, when as usual they quarrelled—this time about the slave trade.

But Lewis had not forgotten his responsibilities in Jamaica. While still at the Villa Diodati he drew up a long codicil to his will, dividing his two plantations between his sisters and laying down principles of conduct for his heirs. 'Having convinced myself that the negroes cannot with certainty be protected in their rights and comforts if they are . . . never visited by their proprietor; I wish to prevent this ever happening again, *to the very utmost of that power which the law allows me.* I therefore order that whoever shall after my death be in possession of my estate of Cornwall shall (if a man) pass three whole calendar months in Jamaica every third year, either in person or by deputing one of his sons or brothers.' A woman should be able to depute a husband, son or brother, but if three years should elapse without the heir fulfilling this condition, he should forfeit the estate, which should pass to the next heir subject to the same conditions. He also directed that no negro belonging to either of his estates at the time of his death should be sold, 'but I allow them to be set free'.

This codicil was witnessed by Byron, Shelley and Dr. Polidori, the temperamental young physician engaged by Byron to accompany him on his travels. After a few days Lewis moved on to Italy. He visited Florence, Milan and Rome, and then spent more than two months in Naples. By the first day of July he had been travelling round Europe for eleven months and had reached Venice, where he met Byron again.

The poet had now taken a villa, La Mira, on the banks of the Brenta, but hearing that Lewis had arrived in Venice, he joined him there to show him round the city. Byron's vanity must have been piqued when Lewis asked him, 'Why do you talk *Venetian* to the Venetians and not the usual Italian?' Byron replied that it was partly from habit, and partly to be understood, if possible. 'It may be so,' said Lewis, 'but it sounds to me like talking with a *brogue* to an *Irishman.*'

He stayed with Byron at his villa outside Venice. 'Monk Lewis . . . is a very good fellow,' said Byron. They went riding together in the summer twilight. 'Being short-sighted . . . he made me go *before* to pilot him,' wrote Byron later. 'I am absent at times, especially towards evening; and the consequence of this pilotage was some narrow escapes to the Monk on horseback. Once I led him *into* a ditch, over which I had passed as usual forgetting to warn my convoy. Once I led him nearly into the river . . . and twice did we both run against the diligence, which, being heavy and slow, did communicate less damage than it received in its leaders, who were *terrassé'd* by the charge. Thrice did I lose him in the gray of the Gloaming, and was obliged to bring to, to his distant signals of distress. All the time he went on talking without intermission, for he was a man of many words.'[1] Surviving these adventures, Lewis left for England after six weeks in Venice.

But again his sojourn in Albany was brief. He had deter-mined to re-visit Jamaica, to see that all the arrangements which he had made for the slaves at his Cornwall estate had prospered and perhaps to pay a visit to his other estate of Hoadley. It was a brave decision, as it was no easy voyage and there was always a real danger of being attacked by pirates. His over-sensitive nature showed itself again in his manner of leaving England. He quietly embarked on the same ship which had carried him on his last voyage to Jamaica and on his return. He did not say good-bye to his mother, but wrote to her as he was leaving: 'You know that I *never* will go through a leave-taking . . . If you have anything pleasant ever to tell me, send it to the Albany . . .

[1] Byron, *Detached Thoughts.*

But tell me nothing that can *possibly* agitate me, or you will be the death or the blindness of me.'

To his lawyer, as he was on the point of departure, he scrawled an agitated note: 'I leave my mother in such good health, that I have little apprehension that this note should be of use—still I may as well say, that *should* anything happen to her, I request you on *no* account to inform me of it. It would affect me too heavily and might kill me in such a climate.'[1]

This singular provision made for his peace of mind, he embarked, taking with him 'an excellent collection of modern books', including novels by Walter Scott, and a piano on which he used to play for hours at a time. When the vessel reached the Downs they found all other ships with their flags at half-mast and learned that Princess Charlotte had died, after giving birth to a still-born son, since they had left London. The voyage took nearly three months—from 5 November 1817 to the twenty-fourth of January.

His reception in Jamaica was most flattering, all his negroes beating drums, singing and dancing, to show their joy at his return, so whole-heartedly that those who should have been watching the cattle also joined in and the animals escaped into one of the best cane-pieces, which was ruined. Investigating events since his departure, Lewis found that the four bulls which he and Lord Holland had sent out from England, to improve the island stock, had all sickened and died within a few weeks of their arrival. He had also thought to lighten the slaves' labour by introducing ploughs to be drawn by oxen. But the negroes told to work with them 'broke plough after plough, and ruined beast after beast, till the attempt was abandoned in despair'. He also found that the season had been unhealthy and that he had lost several negroes, 'some of them young, strong, and valuable labourers.' With over three hundred and thirty negroes 'and with a greater

Lewis, op. cit., Vol. II, p. 191.

number of females than men, in spite of all indulgences and inducements, not more than twelve or thirteen children have been added annually to the list of births'. In consequence his 'sum total' had diminished since his last visit.

The infant mortality rate could not have been lessened, one would think, by the order he had given, before leaving, that all negro infants should be plunged, 'immediately upon their being born', into a tub of cold water. This, he had been 'positively assured. . . . infallibly preserved them from the danger of tetanus'.[1] On the other hand his slaves seemed contented and without complaints.

For three weeks he lived in the plantation, 'the doors of my house open all day long, and full liberty allowed to every person to come and speak to me without witnesses or restraint.' Not a single grievance was heard, but many of the negroes thanked him for treatment they had received in the hospital in illness and he was assured that during his absence his regulations had been obeyed implicitly. At the end of the three weeks Lewis opened a second hospital which he had had built for mothers, and there presented every male negro with a blue jacket lined with flannel and every woman with 'a flaming red stuff petticoat, and to every child a dress of white cotton'. The dancing and singing and drinking of rum lasted all night after the ceremony.

As all was going well at Cornwall he thought he would pay a short visit to his other estate at the extreme eastern end of the island. Here he 'expected to find a perfect paradise, and . . . found a perfect hell'. He had been told that 'Hoadley was the best managed estate in the island, and as far as the soil was concerned, report appeared to have said true'. But the slaves had been tyrannized and cruelly treated, not by the trustee, who was an excellent planter and confined his attention entirely to the cultivation of the soil, but by the four white book-keepers and the four black governors under him.

[1] *Journal of a West Indian Proprietor*, p. 320.

Lewis was exasperated to find conditions so different from what he had been led to expect. He had left himself only a week to spend there, which he had thought would be enough to grant two days' holiday for dancing, distribute a little money and establish the rules already adopted at his other plantation, all of which he imagined would be received with acclamation by the happy negroes who worked in such a paradise. Instead he was stunned by complaints from every quarter and the negroes declared that if he left them to work under the old tyranny they would follow his carriage all the way back to Cornwall. Lewis did his best, in the short time he could spend there, to remove the causes of discontent. He dismissed one book-keeper and another ran away; he got rid of the chief black governor and read aloud the regulations about holidays, rations and measures taken for the slaves' protection. Then, after distributing presents, he left in a violent thunder-storm.

His journeys to and from Hoadley were most arduous. He had to travel over primitive mountain roads and his adventures included being nearly swept away in his carriage when fording a flooded river, toppling in a curricle on a narrow shelf of rock at the edge of the sea, with one horse fallen into the water, and lodging in a hotel at Spanish Town where there was a fellow-traveller dying of yellow fever.

When he had first set out from Cornwall there had been 'such a quantity of horses, mules, servants and carriages collected for the journey' that Tita, the Italian servant whom Lewis had brought back with him from his travels in Europe, had clapped his hands in exultation and exclaimed, 'They will certainly take us for the King of England!' Tita's real name was Giovanni Battista Falcieri; he was a Venetian, with long black mustachios, who always carried two daggers about his person. Lewis was very fond of him and liked to tell the story of their meeting, when Tita had helped him to escape from bandits during his travels in Italy. By the time they were approaching Cornwall on their return journey the retinue had shrunk to 'one pair of chaise horses and a couple of miserable mules'. One horse after another had been left behind. 'I believe we shall return home on foot after all,' sighed Tita.

On 4 May Lewis, accompanied by his Italian servant, set sail from Jamaica. But he was never to reach London nor to set foot in Albany again. Early in the voyage the daughter of a white family returning to England became ill with the dreaded yellow fever. Lewis used frequently to rap at the door of their cabin and 'ask after her health in the gentlest tone, never forgetting to accompany such inquiries with some little gift . . . such as a shaddock or a bottle of soda-water—articles of which he had brought on board a plentiful supply'. Several of the crew were suffering from the same illness and after a few days Lewis, too, was stricken. After a gale when they first set out, they were now becalmed. The heat was intolerable. He could not lie quietly in his bunk but would rush up on deck and pace up and down for hours 'continually . . . spouting forth Italian and German poetry, in a wild impassioned tone, accompanied with violent gestures'.[1] As he grew worse he could no longer leave his berth. Tita nursed him faithfully, and sat always in the next-door cabin to be within call. Barely a week after leaving Jamaica Lewis was dead.

It seemed as though his preoccupation with the macabre and with scenes of horror must colour even the circumstances of his own death. The captain had no choice but to order his burial at sea. His small body was enclosed in a hastily-made wooden coffin, which was wrapped in a plain sailor's hammock and weighted with four eighteen-pound cannon balls. The Captain read the burial service and the coffin was lowered into the sea. The water closed over it, but in a second, to the horror of the spectators, it re-appeared.

[1] Lewis, op. cit., Vol. II, p. 369.

One end of the canvas hammock in which it was wrapped had come unfastened and the weights had escaped. The wind lifted the folds of the canvas like a sail and the coffin moved slowly away like a boat, rising and falling with the swell. Horrified passengers in the forward cabin saw it from the window passing on a level with their eyes. Then it was caught in the current and went dipping away over the sea, until the shocked spectators could see it only as a speck in the distance on the empty ocean, and finally it was lost to sight. It was a fitting end to the legendary 'Monk' Lewis, author in his life-time of so many terrifying Gothic horrors.

And what happened to Tita? He must have taken Lewis's belongings back to his chambers in Albany, those rooms so full of all the *bibelots* and conceits which Lewis had de-lighted to gather together. In his will he left 'my cham-bers in the Albany (for which I paid 600 guineas), with all the furniture' to the Honourable Thomas Stapleton,[1] and all his books to William Lamb. His fortune was carefully divided amongst his family, with bequests of money to friends and servants, and the dispersal of his collection of seals arranged to various intimates.

Tita Falcieri, by birth a Venetian, returned to his native city, and there entered the service of Lord Byron, who came to trust him and respect his courage. A year after Lewis's death Thomas Moore, staying for a few days with Byron at La Mira, writes of 'his portly gondolier Tita, in a rich livery and most redundant mustachios', and Shelley, to whom Tita acted as valet in Ravenna, de-scribed him as 'a fine fellow with a prodigious black beard who has stabbed two or three people, and is the most good-

---

[1] Hon. Thomas Stapleton, 1792–1829, of Mereworth Castle, Kent and Grey's Court, Henley-on-Thames. Only son of 6th baronet who, in 1788, inherited through his great-grandmother the ancient barony of Le Despencer, created in 1264. His only daughter succeeded her grandfather in the barony in 1831 and married the 6th Viscount Falmouth.

natured looking fellow I ever saw'.[1] He accompanied his master to Greece and was with him when he died. Byron left him two thousand dollars.

After serving Henry Bulwer (Edward Bulwer's elder brother who was sent out, fresh from Cambridge, after Byron's death, to carry £80,000 for the Greek Committee in London to Greece), and fighting with an Albanian regiment for the cause of Greek Liberation, Tita fell on evil days. James Clay, who was travelling in a small yacht with young Benjamin Disraeli through the Mediterranean, engaged Tita as his servant in Malta. At the end of their wanderings through the Greek Islands, Albania, Turkey, Syria and Egypt, Clay had no further need of Tita's services. In London Tita applied to Disraeli, bringing as a present a lock of Byron's hair which he had cut off the corpse at Missolonghi. Disraeli arranged for him to join his parents' household at Bradenham in Buckinghamshire. Here he quickly settled down and once again proved himself a faithful servant, his character belying his foreign appearance, outlandish dress and habits which at first excited alarm among the local population.

Sixteen years later old Isaac D'Israeli died in the devoted Tita's arms. Tita then married Mrs. D'Israeli's maid, who had stayed on, after her mistress's death, as housekeeper, and Benjamin Disraeli and his sister were much perplexed as to what should be done with them. Fortunately Disraeli happened to meet Byron's old friend, Cam Hobhouse, who arranged for Tita to be made a Government Messenger, first at the Board of Control and later, when that Office was abolished, at the India Office. He eventually retired with a pension and died in 1874 in England, at the age of seventy-six.

Byron must soon have heard of Lewis's death. 'Lewis was a good man, a clever man, but a bore, a damned bore, one may say. My only revenge or consolation used to be, setting him by the ears with some vivacious person who

[1] Moore, op. cit., Vol. VII, p. 237.

hated Bores, especially M<u>e</u> de Staël . . . But I liked
Lewis: he was a Jewel of a Man had he been better set. I
don't mean *personally*, but less *tiresome*; for he was tedious,
as well as contradictory, to every thing and everybody . . .
Poor fellow, he died, a martyr to his new riches, of a
second visit to Jamaica—

> 'I'll give the lands of Deloraine
> Dark Musgrave were alive again!
>
> *that is*
>
> I would give many a Sugar Cane
> Monk Lewis were alive again!'[1]

II

During the Napoleonic Wars the St. James's Volunteers,
of whom Leigh Hunt was one, mustered a thousand strong
next door to Albany, in the courtyard of Burlington
House. After Napoleon's defeat in 1814 it was arranged
that the European Congress should meet in September in
Vienna, but the London crowds had a prior opportunity
to cheer the King of Prussia and the Tsar—the heroes of
the hour—when they visited the capital, at the Prince
Regent's invitation, during the summer. Crowds of sight-
seers jostled outside the Pulteney Hotel in Piccadilly,
where the Tsar and his sister were lodged, and Clarence
House in St. James's where the King of Prussia and
Blücher were staying.

Hospitality was lavished on them and brilliant functions
were arranged for their enjoyment—a banquet at Carlton
House, to which the Tsar was driven in the Prince
Regent's state chariot with an escort of Household Cavalry,
and another at the Guildhall, visits to the Opera and the
House of Commons. They waltzed at balls given by Lady
Castlereagh and Lady Cholmondeley, for the Tsar was

[1] Byron, *Detached Thoughts*.

very fond of waltzing. It was observed at Lady Castlereagh's party that Blücher, who had previously dined at Carlton House, had some difficulty in getting up the stairs. They were rowed down the river to Woolwich in a procession of sixty barges, and they visited Ascot and Oxford, where there was a banquet in the Radcliffe—the Prince Regent wearing a silk cap and gown at the Encaenia—and dinner in Christ Church Hall. They were the centre of a glittering summer of pageantry.

On the 20th of June 1814 there can have been little sleep for the inhabitants of Albany. For the whole enormous garden of Burlington House was enclosed by tents, and in them two thousand people sat down to a brilliant banquet given by the members of White's Club in honour of the allied sovereigns. The evening's entertainment was said to have cost over nine thousand pounds. The Prince Regent honoured them with his presence, but so unfortunately did a number of less prosperous citizens who during the evening relieved their fellow-guests of many of their valuables.[1]

It was the unexpected news that her brother Henry had been at this magnificent entertainment that drew from Jane Austen the exclamation: 'Henry at White's! Oh, what a Henry!'[2]

III

In September 1814 Mr. Thomas Hill Mortimer, the solicitor who now lived in the converted kitchen apartments in the courtyard, wrote to the Trustees of Albany suggesting that they should erect gates between the two shops at the entrance 'to shut out disorderly persons'. He admitted

[1] H. B. Wheatley, *Round About Piccadilly*.

[2] To Cassandra Austen, 23 June 1814. Strangely enough, editors of Jane Austen's letters have failed to notice the significance of the date on which this letter was written and have left the reader to imagine that a visit by Henry to White's Club itself was sufficient to cause such excitement in his family circle.

that the narrowness of the entrance would make the gates inconvenient and that an extra Porter would be needed. 'It has occurred to me however that a Watchman might be established . . . to protect the Inhabitants passing to and from Albany from the lower Orders of Passengers through Piccadilly who constantly intrude for the most indecent purposes. It seldom happens that I return to my Chambers in the Evening, that I am not obliged to pass the Entrance to get rid of unfortunate Females, rather than allow them to follow me to my Door, even after I have submitted to the contributions which the lower Orders invariably levy—and a close pursuit has compelled me sometimes to knock at the front Door of the Great House rather than my own in order to deceive them as to my residence.

'I cannot but consider this a Nuisance which calls for remedy . . .'

As he contributed to the Trust Rates, without having the benefits of those who lived within the body of Albany and were protected by the Porter, he suggested that an extra Porter should be employed. The Trustees engaged a watchman at a guinea a week to supervise the courtyard from 10 p.m. to 6 a.m. and they urged the Board of Vestry of the Parish of St. James's to appoint a Parish Watchman 'to remain stationary in this Court Yard to guard this part of the Parish'. They remarked rather pointedly that 'this Establishment pays nearly £740 a year towards the Parish Watch and Poor Rates'. The Board of Vestry referred the complaint to the Watch Committee, who 'did not feel disposed to recommend the additional expense of another Watchman', but agreed to move the Watch Box from the bottom of Sackville Street to 'a situation as near as possible to the entrance of the Court Yard of Albany', on the 'East end of Burlington House Wall'.[1]

[1] Minutes of Trustees' Meetings, 29 November, 6 December and 13 April 1814.

IV

In 1815, the 6th Duke of Devonshire, Georgiana's son, sold Burlington House for £57,000 to his uncle, Lord George Cavendish. Lord George was a grandson of the famous patron of the arts, the 3rd Earl of Burlington, who had re-modelled the house a hundred years before and who at one time had both Handel and William Kent living under his roof. Sir William Chambers considered the circular colonnade which this amateur architect had built round his courtyard 'one of the finest pieces of architecture in Europe'. Lord George, contrary to some prophecies, left this colonnade and the high wall on Piccadilly untouched, though he made some alterations to the house.

During the winter of 1815–16 the Elgin Marbles lay sheltered in a large shed in the courtyard of Burlington House, next door to Albany. Lord Elgin, while British Ambassador in Constantinople, had bought them from the Turkish Government and removed them from the Parthenon.

Parliament was now debating whether they should be bought for the nation, and fierce controversy raged about their merits. Some authorities expressed doubt of their artistic value, others praised them. Eventually they were bought for the nation by Act of Parliament for £36,000, about half what they had cost Lord Elgin, and were removed to the British Museum.

In 1819 Lord George Cavendish built in his grounds, to the west of his house, a 'covered promenade from Piccadilly into Cork Street', with shops on either side and rooms above. This was Burlington Arcade. The reason for its building was said to be 'the great annoyance to which the garden is subject from the inhabitants of a neighbouring street throwing oyster-shells, etc. over the wall'. The new building would prevent this nuisance and would also block the houses' view into the garden.[1]

Lord George was evidently determined to preserve his privacy and to keep his garden clean, for on 14 August 1819 the Trustees authorized a letter to be sent to all Proprietors and Inhabitants on the west side of Albany, saying that there had been repeated complaints from Lord George Cavendish of 'annoyance proceeding from Dirt, broken Bottles, Water etc. thrown over into his Garden'. They told the inhabitants that if these practices were continued, Lord George would have the windows stopped up which looked into his garden. A year later (in August 1820) the Trustees were writing to Mr. Samuel Ware, Lord George's architect, who was also the architect of Chesterfield House and had made the plans for Burlington Arcade, trying to prevent him building a high wall along the very edge of the garden, which would block out all light and air from that side of Albany. They persuaded him to modify his plan, but a lesser wall was built down the garden behind the whole length of Albany.

V

A Contract was accepted in May 1818 for lighting Albany with gas for £190 per annum, 'one or more Rates to be made on the Proprietors' to raise the sum. The Trustees also considered a suggestion, made at the request of various inhabitants, by the Grand Junction Water Works Company to lay the Company's water to Albany. But in spite of the Company's offer to pay all expenses of laying it on, with the bonus of 'a stand Fire Pipe with a leathern Hose . . . in case of Fire', and an assurance that 'from the largeness of their Main and force of their Steam Engine' they could 'raise Water above the highest House', the Trustees decided against it, and the Night Porter con-

[1] *Gentleman's Magazine*, September 1817.

A PRINT OF 1804 SHOWING THE NEW ENTRANCE TO ALBANY FROM PICCADILLY WITH SHOPS DESIGNED BY HOLLAND ON EITHER SIDE. THE EAGLES SUPPORTING THE BALCONIES CAN BE SEEN

THE NORTH ENTRANCE TO ALBANY DESIGNED BY HOLLAND, WITH THE COVERED WAY LEADING TO THE BACK OF THE MANSION

LORD BYRON
*A drawing by Count d'Orsay, in the
possession of John Murray, Esq.*

tinued to pump the water for the cisterns attached to each set of chambers by hand. (It was not until 1853 that water was supplied by the high-pressure system.)

One of these water tanks was the cause of a tragedy in March 1820. At the 164th Meeting of the Trustees it was reported that a man was to be prosecuted for 'stealing a Piece of Lead that had been cut from one of the Tanks in the New Buildings'. At their next meeting they heard that 'John Johnson had been tried at the Old Baily Sessions and was convicted for stealing Lead from the Tank H. Albany and Sentenced to 7 Years' Transportation.'

VI

A precedent was established by the Trustees in 1824 when they refused to allow an auction sale which had been advertised of the late William Osgoode's effects in A.4. The Trustees ruled that 'a Sale never had been permitted in Albany and if sanctioned by the Trustees in this instance would be the means of Establishing a Precedent that would occasion considerable annoyance to the Proprietors and Inhabitants of Albany'. Their edict was challenged, but when they announced their intention 'to oppose the entrance of the Public into Albany for the above purposes' the administrators of the estate had to give way and were forced to alter the place of sale. Sales in Albany are still prohibited.

CHAPTER V

IN THE DAYS OF GLADSTONE
AND LYTTON

I

*A*T THE *237th Meeting of the Trustees in Albany House on the 29th November 1832 the Consent of the Trustees was given to the Rev. Francis Brownlow to sell and convey the Chambers L.2 Albany to John Gladstone, Esq.*

These rooms were taken for his son, William Ewart Gladstone, who moved into them in the following March. Three months earlier, a few days before his twenty-third birthday, he had been elected Member of Parliament for Newark, and it was only just over a year since he had achieved a double first at Oxford.

'I am getting on rapidly with my furnishing,' he wrote to his father, 'and I shall be able, I feel confident, to do it all, including plate, within the liberal limits which you allow. I cannot warmly enough thank you for the terms and footing on which you propose to place me in the chambers, but I really fear that after this year my allowance in all will be greater not only than I have any title to, but than I ought to accept without blushing.'[1]

In addition to his new Parliamentary duties, he was not unmindful of the obligations of social life. He enjoyed musical parties, where he could use his fine singing voice, and he sometimes made as many as fourteen social calls in an afternoon. He went to public concerts, too, and to dinner parties, but he was a regular church-goer and would never dine out on Sunday, even with Sir Robert Peel, the leader of his party.

[1] John Morley, *Life of Gladstone*, Vol. I, p. 98.

Before the opportunity of standing for Parliament had suddenly arisen and when he had finally decided not to go into the Church, he had planned for himself on coming down from Oxford 'a good many years of silent reading and inquiry'. This was now clearly not to be, but he entered at Lincoln's Inn and during the six years that he spent in Albany he dined fairly frequently in hall, while then, as at all times in his long life, he found happiness and refreshment in reading. Wordsworth was still his favourite poet. He had read his poems to quieten his mind during the four days of the mathematical examination at Oxford, and had proclaimed their effect far more soothing than the draughts against over-excitement given him by a doctor. A pocket Wordsworth had been his companion, too, when he travelled back to the University by coach to take his degree.

In spite of these other interests he was a diligent Member of Parliament. The first few words officially spoken in the House of Commons by that rich voice which was to be so memorable in its history were uttered just a month after moving into Albany. But his first speech proper, lasting fifty minutes, was delivered two months later, in defence of the system of slave labour, answering an attack on his father, as a West Indian plantation proprietor, in the debate on the Government's proposals for the gradual abolition of slavery.

Like other inhabitants of Albany, he kept a journal, though only in note form. Nevertheless it is possible through it for us to have a glimpse of his life during this first year of his life in London and in Parliament, and to wonder at the industry which filled his leisure moments. '*July* 21, 1833, Sunday.— . . . Wrote some lines and prose also. Finished Strype. Read Abbott and Sumner aloud. Thought for some hours on my future destiny, and took a solitary walk to and about Kensington Gardens. *July* 23.—Read *L'Allemagne*, *Rape of the Lock*, and finished factory report. *July* 25. Went to breakfast old Wilberforce introduced by his son. He is cheerful and serene, a beautiful picture of old age in sight of immortality. Heard him pray with his family. Blessing and honour are upon his head. *July 30.—L'Allemagne*. Bulwer's England. Parnell. Looked at my Plato. Rode. House. *July 31.*—Hallam breakfasted with me . . . Committee on West India Bill finished . . . German lesson. *August 2.*—Worked German several hours. Read half of the *Bride of Lammermoor*. *L'Allemagne*. Rode. House. *August 3.*—German lesson and worked alone . . . Attended Mr. Wilberforce's funeral; it brought solemn thoughts, particularly about the slaves. This is a burdensome question.'[1] The following Sunday he attended services at St. James's, Piccadilly, in both morning and afternoon. He read the Bible to himself and a sermon aloud, and wrote a paraphrase of part of the eighth chapter of the Epistle to the Romans.

That autumn he spent away from London, at his father's new estate in Scotland, and after a short stay at Oxford returned to London for the Parliamentary session in the New Year, where he was cheered by Peel's kindness to him. His second year in Parliament was uneventful. He continued to play his part in Parliamentary committees, attended concerts, and read enormously—books on theology, philosophy, politics and history, plays, poetry and speeches. In July, being very anxious to speak on the Universities Bill, he was 'tortured with nervous anticipations' but 'could not get an opportunity'. A month later he spoke for thirty-five minutes on this subject, 'with more ease than I had hoped, having been more mindful or less unmindful of Divine aid'. Peel was among those who congratulated him on his speech.

A few months later, in December 1834, King William had dismissed Melbourne's Government and Peel was posting back in haste from Rome to England—a twelve-day journey by carriage—to kiss hands as First Lord of the Treasury. Gladstone, now twenty-five years old, re-

[1] Quoted Morley, op. cit., Vol. I, pp. 106–7.

ceived a letter from his leader which had taken four days to reach him at his father's home in Scotland. Booking the first available place in the mail-coach, he hastened south with his father's advice to take any position involving work and responsibility.

It was a privation not to be able to read in a coach. He could not even concentrate. 'The mind is distracted through the senses, and rambles. Nowhere is it to me so incapable of continuous thought.' They arrived at Newcastle that evening, and during a brief stop at York at six next morning he ran to peep at the minster 'and bore away a faint twilight image of its grandeur'. Next day— 'Arrived safe, thank God, and well at the Bull and Mouth $5\frac{3}{4}$ A.M. Albany soon. To bed for $2\frac{1}{4}$ hours. Went to Peel about eleven.'[1]

Sir Robert received him kindly and offered him a seat on either the Admiralty or the Treasury Board. The latter was chosen. It was said that he was 'about the youngest lord who was ever placed at the treasury on his own account, and not because he was his father's son'. But hardly had he taken up his post than Peel promoted him to be Under-Secretary for the Colonies. This was all the more remarkable, in view of the fact that he had only been in Parliament for two years and had no family connections to help him. But his enjoyment of office was not to last long. Peel's Government being defeated he resigned after only a few months in power and Gladstone, after this brief experience of office, returned with renewed vigour to his indefatigable programme of reading and study. That autumn (1835) his mother died, after a long and painful illness. Her youngest son had visited her every day when she was in London, and would read the Bible to her or amuse her by news of his own doings. Her death was a great blow to him, but her fortitude in suffering and her unfaltering faith inspired and consoled him.

[1] Gladstone's Diary, quoted Morley, op. cit., Vol. I, p. 119.

The following summer he had the pleasure of entertaining Wordsworth on several occasions in his rooms in Albany. The veteran poet, whom he so much admired, breakfasted and dined with him and they met, too, during his London visit, at other houses, with Sergeant Talfourd, Mr. Hallam and Samuel Rogers. Gladstone found his conversation 'very pleasing', though a few months before Moore had said that he was 'according to his usual fashion, very soliloquacious'. He had described to Moore what happened on the rare occasions when he dined out with neighbours in the country. 'The conversation,' Wordsworth said, 'may be called *catechetical*; for, as they do me the honour to wish to know my opinions . . . they ask me questions, and I am induced to answer them at great length till I become quite tired.' Moore said it was impossible to edge in a word in a *tête-à-tête*, till he did get tired.[1] The conversation at Rogers's house was about copyright, and when the host produced an American poem Wordsworth proposed that Gladstone should read it to them. After the young man first and then Rogers had both declined to do so, Wordsworth read it aloud himself, 'in good taste, and doing it justice.'

On one occasion Wordsworth arrived for breakfast at Albany before the time arranged. Gladstone asked him to excuse him while he had his servant to prayers, but 'he expressed a *hearty* wish to be present, which was delightful.'[2] Wordsworth later gave it as his opinion that Shelley had the greatest native powers in poetry of all the men of the age, but regretted in him the lowest form of irreligion, though he saw a later progress towards better things. He was vehement against Byron. Gladstone found Wordsworth a most agreeable man, 'always amiable, polite and sympathetic'. Only once did he jar upon him, when he spoke slightingly of Tennyson's *Juvenilia*. When Wordsworth left after dinner he would change his silk stockings

[1] *Diary of Thomas Moore*, Vol. VII, p. 70.
[2] Morley, op. cit., Vol. I, p. 136.

in the anteroom and put on a pair of grey worsted before he ventured outdoors.[1]

In June 1837 King William IV died, and according to the old law prescribing a dissolution of Parliament within six months of the sovereign's death, the country was soon plunged into a general election. Gladstone was returned once again for Newark, but his party was still in opposition. He remained an active Member, but a great deal of his time outside the House he devoted to writing a book on a subject which he had long been considering—the relationship of State and Church. Too much reading had strained his eyes and before the book was published, his doctors told him that it was absolutely necessary for him to abstain from reading or writing, and advised him strongly to take a holiday abroad. With his sister he went first to Ems in Germany, where he disobeyed his doctors by working hard on the proofs of his book which followed him there. After this they travelled on to Italy and Sicily.

While he was in Catania Gladstone heard news that his book had been published. From there he went on to Naples, where he passed a great deal of his time with Sir Stephen Glynne and his two sisters. After Christmas with them in Rome he returned to London at the end of January (1839) when his book had been out for several weeks. Its emphasis on the desirability of the State giving exclusive support to the Established Church, and its vision of the nation united in the communion of the Church of England were naturally popular with Anglicans and particularly the clergy, but his friends trembled for the effect on his political career. Yet though he made few converts to his own ideas and received a good deal of criticism,[2] in the political field his progress was unchecked.

His physical vitality was superb, his versatility of mind and interests astonishing. Concentration, he said,

---

[1] Morley, op. cit., Vol. III, pp. 483–4.

[2] Most notable was an unsigned review by Macaulay in the *Edinburgh*.

was the master secret. With his grave temperament and brilliant intellect, toil seemed his natural element. Already, in these early days, promise of the greatness to come was clearly visible to his contemporaries. It was said of him at the time that he could do in four hours what it would take another man sixteen to do, and Gladstone worked for sixteen hours a day. In oratory an astonishing command of words and bold fine gestures were enhanced by a voice of great depth and power and an impressive appearance.

Contemporaries described him as he looked during those early years in Albany. His pale complexion was slightly tinged with olive, beneath a fine head of jet black hair. He held himself alertly erect and his rather sombre expression was redeemed by his 'falcon's eyes'—imperious, clear and quick, the eyebrows dark and prominent. Lord Malmesbury thought that he looked like a Roman Catholic ecclesiastic, but found him very agreeable. Of himself at this time Gladstone wrote that the dominant tendencies of his mind were those of a recluse, and, said that he might in most respects have accommodated himself with ease to the education of the cloister. In spite of his intellectual brilliance and powers of oratory he was slow to learn the ordinary aptitudes of the man of the world. For years, he said, he considered actions simply as they were in themselves, and did not take into account the way in which they would be taken by others. 'All the mental apparatus requisite to constitute the "public man" had to be purchased by a slow experience and inserted piecemeal into the composition of my character.'[1]

But before his vigorous public personality had finally formed, while he was still a purposeful and confident young member of Her Majesty's opposition, he left Albany to marry Miss Catherine Glynne, one of Sir Stephen Glynne's two sisters, of whom he had seen much in Italy during his enforced holiday the previous year. 'A deranging incident

[1] Morley, op. cit., Vol. I, p. 198.

has occurred,' he wrote to Samuel Rogers, excusing himself from an appointment. 'I am engaged to be married.'

There was a double wedding at Hawarden, when Catherine's sister at the same ceremony was married to Lord Lyttelton, and shortly afterward the Gladstones moved into 13 Carlton House Terrace, John Gladstone having transferred to his sons his Demerara properties. 'This increased wealth, so much beyond my needs, with its attendant responsibility is very burdensome,' said Gladstone, 'however on his part the act be beautiful.' But he took a great interest in the arrangements of his new home and helped his wife to engage a cook 'after a long talk on religious affairs'.[1]

So we leave him, as he quits Albany for a marriage that will bring him more than fifty-eight years of affectionate companionship. He is to be four times Prime Minister, one of the greatest finance ministers and most brilliant orators of his age. He will dominate the House of Commons by his ardour, eloquence and gifts of exposition. Years of power, untiring industry and brilliant effort lie before him and through them all his lofty religious ideals will be the basis of his daily life. He leaves Albany, aged twenty-nine, still a Tory, still in opposition, a brilliant young man with an astounding life before him.

II

It seemed almost as though the chambers which Lord Byron had occupied were dedicated to men whose greatest misfortune proved to be marriage. To them in May 1835 there came Mr. Edward Bulwer, a handsome, fair-haired man of thirty-two, who concealed behind the appearance of 'the complete dandy' a passionate absorption in his career as a writer. He came to Albany in retreat from an unhappy married life, in search of quiet and peace in which to work

[1] Georgina Battiscombe, *Mrs. Gladstone*, p. 41.

without disturbance—a sad ending to a marriage embarked on with courage and chivalry in the face of violent opposition.

Edward was the youngest of three brothers and his mother was sole heiress to Mr. Lytton of Knebworth. His father, General Bulwer, had died when he was four years old. He was the youngest son, delicate and precocious, thought by his schoolmasters to be a genius. His elder brother inherited their father's property in Norfolk and the second had been brought up by their maternal grandmother, who was counted on to leave him a handsome fortune. Edward alone was without independent means, save for two hundred pounds a year which his father had left to him. Nevertheless his prospects were bright. It was thought he would inherit Knebworth and a fortune from his mother, who doted on her handsome, foppish youngest son.

At Cambridge he published a small volume of verse, won the Chancellor's Medal for a poem on Sculpture, spoke frequently at the Union debates, and fell in love with Caroline Lamb. He had written her a poem at fifteen, and his boyish admiration had pleased her. As an undergraduate he adopted the Byronic pose of the man whose life has been blighted at an early age by love. The romance had been with a beautiful young girl whom he had known when he was sixteen years old and still at school. After vows had been exchanged between them she was married to another man, and died soon afterwards. In the summer vacation from Cambridge Bulwer made a pilgrimage to the Lake District, where she was buried, and kept vigil over her grave all through the night. At the end of the vacation he accepted an invitation to stay a few days at Brocket with Lady Caroline and immediately fell under her spell.

'Lady Caroline Lamb was then between thirty and forty,' he wrote later, 'but looked much younger than she was; thanks, perhaps, to a slight rounded figure and a childlike mode of wearing her hair (which was of a pale golden colour) in close curls. She had large hazel eyes . . . exceedingly good teeth, a pleasant laugh, and a musical intonation of voice, despite a certain artificial drawl, habitual to what was called the Devonshire House Set. Apart from these gifts, she might be considered plain. But she had, to a surpassing degree, the attribute of charm, and never failed to please if she chose to do so.'[1] Her conversation dazzled the young man. 'Now sentimental, now shrewd, it sparkled with anecdotes of the great world, and of the eminent persons with whom she had been brought up, or been familiarly intimate.' He listened spellbound to her stories of Byron and listening, fell in love. She seemed to return his feelings and they kept up a sentimental correspondence when he returned to Cambridge.

But already Lady Caroline was looking for new excitement. Her restless imagination must constantly be stimulated by the subjugation of a new admirer with the old weapons of coquetry, sentiment, and stories of her fatal love for Lord Byron. Once vanquished the new idol would soon lose his grasp and he in turn would be supplanted. It was small wonder that Bulwer noticed later that her husband 'was particularly kind to me. I think he saw my feelings.' When she was ill she sent for him to sit by her bedside, but once recovered she told him that she acted wrong in loving him, and that she was endeavouring to overcome it. She wished he should be like her son, the dearest of her friends, but not her lover. 'She talks sentiment exceedingly well . . . of course she talked me over. I left her, half pleased, half piqued . . . and more in love with her than ever.'

But the romance was soon to end. Bulwer came from Cambridge to join a party at Brocket for a ball to be given by Lady Cowper, William Lamb's sister, at nearby Panshanger. It did not take him long to see that he had been

---

[1] *Life and Letters of Edward Bulwer, Lord Lytton* by his Son, Vol. I, p. 328.

supplanted by 'a fashionable beau, extremely handsome, but dull, insipid and silly'. It was a Mr. Russell, natural son of the Duke of Bedford. She took Mr. Russell in her carriage to the ball and spent the evening with him. Bulwer threatened to leave next morning, was reassured that Mr. Russell was an old friend, but was finally rendered miserable by seeing his rival seated opposite him at the dinner table wearing a ring which he had often worn himself. It was the one which Lady Caroline said Lord Byron had given her, to be worn only by those she loved.

When dinner was ended he threw himself upon a sofa. Music was playing. 'Lady Caroline came to me. "Are you mad?" said she. I looked up. The tears stood in my eyes. I could not have spoken a word for the world. What do you think she said aloud? "Don't play this melancholy air. It affects Mr. Bulwer so that he is actually weeping!" ' Edward Bulwer was a proud young man and this cruel remark wounded him deeply. He 'sprang up, laughed, talked and was the life of the company'. He left Brocket next morning very early, feeling only an intense aversion and contempt for Lady Caroline.

After this his mother was easily persuaded to let him pay a visit to France and gave him a handsome allowance. A charming and intelligent Englishwoman, somewhat older than himself and then living in Paris, soon became his principal confidante. This Mrs. Cunningham was a lively, clever and kindly woman, with a gift for quick repartee, who wrote 'beautiful poetry almost impromptu'. Her knowledge of the world was of great value to Bulwer. She introduced him to her French friends and he found himself welcomed in the salons of the old *noblesse* in the Faubourg St. Germain. Brilliant *soirées*, literary gatherings and 'the feverish excitement of the gambling house'—he enjoyed them all. But then, in a mood of dejection and aversion to society, he would retire to Versailles, to solitary reading, to writing poetry or taking violent exercise. Mrs. Cunningham addressed him as Childe Harold, and evidently tried to prevent him taking too gloomy a view of his blighted life.

'What beautiful letters you write,' he replied from Versailles. 'I admire your prophetic wisdom, when you so safely contradict me about love, and tell me I shall think differently of it at thirty. I began the world at sixteen. That is five years before anyone else . . . *J'ai vécu beaucoup en peu d'années. Et c'est le chemin des passions qui m'a conduit* . . . to a state resembling that silence after storm in which we shrink from the turbulence of emotion, and covet the repose of insensibility.'[1] He evidently still saw himself as the tragic Byronic hero. At twenty-two he had already adopted a very exaggerated style of dress and manner, and his 'beautiful curls' were a joke among his new friends.

But the time came with the spring when he must go back to London and there, on the evening of his return, he met his fate. Staying in London with her uncle, Sir John Doyle, was a beautiful Irish girl, Rosina Wheeler, who confessed to 'a great engoument for literary celebrities', and lost no opportunity of collecting an invitation to houses where she would be likely to meet them. Her first acquaintance was with Miss Landon, who writing as 'L.E.L.' had made a name as an authoress. At one of Miss Landon's literary parties she made friends with another woman writer, Miss Spence, who in imitation of Mme de Staël always twirled a sprig of some plant in her fingers. Writing years later Rosina compared poor Miss Spence, whom she had used and then discarded, to the immortal Mr. Collins of *Pride and Prejudice*. 'She never harpooned anyone for her parties without the peroration "if they would condescend to honour her humble abode". And if Mr. Collins had his Lady Catherine de Burgh always ready, as a social battering-ram, wherewith to pulverize his inferior acquaintance into awe and admiration, in like manner did

[1] Bulwer, op. cit., Vol. II, p. 48.

Miss Spence bring up her great gun Lady Caroline Lamb.'[1]

Miss Wheeler had soon monopolized the 'great gun'—
or rather she had become Lady Caroline's disciple. Among
the 'literary menageries' which they both frequented,
where the authoresses were mostly plain, eager and
usually turbaned, were the parties given by Miss Benger,
who specialized in historical works. To her house, on the
evening of his return from Paris, young Edward Bulwer
escorted his mother.

According to Rosina's own account of the evening she
had a heavy cold and was already hoarse from having read
aloud to her uncle 'a book that all the world was mad
about—*Vivian Grey*'. While she was sitting as near as
she could to the fire and talking to Miss Landon, she saw
a richly, but dowdily dressed woman appear at the door,
accompanied by a handsome young dandy. Edward Bulwer
wore a 'cobweb cambric shirt, a triumph of lace and
embroidery . . . A perfect galaxy of studs glittered . . .
down the centre of this fairy-like *lingerie*. His hair, which
was really golden, glitteringly golden, and abundant, he
wore literally in long ringlets, that almost reached his
shoulders.'[2] Rosina, observing him, thought him 'un-
mistakably gentlemanlike-looking, indeed, according to
his then surroundings, too patrician-looking . . . Looking
round at . . . the literary gentlemen, in gold nose-pinchers
. . . and the literary ladies, who were darting about like
galvanized rag-bags, a man who . . . would have created
a smile and riveted a stare even at Devonshire House or
Almack's, certainly *did* explode upon that literary *Folk-
mote* like a sort of sartorial shrapnel!'

Rosina was speedily informed that old Mrs. Bulwer was
very rich, that this, though her youngest, was her favourite
son, and that he had written the Poem which had won the
Chancellor's Medal at Cambridge that year. It is hardly
surprising that in this meeting of middle-aged and dowdy

[1] Louisa Devey, *Life of Rosina, Lady Lytton*, p. 43.
[2] Devey, op. cit., pp. 50, 51.

people, Edward should at once have singled out the beautiful Irish girl with her dark, braided hair and ivory skin, 'lively, vivacious, with a ready, if not brilliant, word to say to every member of the assembly—displaying marvellous grace in all her movements . . . her abundant hair fell over the whitest of shoulders . . .'[1] She must have known, before Miss Benger told her, that he had never taken his eyes off her.

Before the end of the party Rosina had been invited by Mrs. Bulwer to her house on the following evening, and when Rosina's carriage was announced rather early, the son 'darted across the room to offer me his arm to take me downstairs, and packed me up as carefully as if I really had been something of value . . . The night was rainy. I begged of him not to come out, but he *would* put me into the carriage, and regardless of the little cataracts that were falling from the servant's umbrella, still stood, hoping that I would honour his mother on the following evening.'[2]

Rosina went to Mrs. Bulwer's party and by then she had found out more about her hostess—that she was the only daughter of Mr. Lytton of Knebworth, who had left her his house and a substantial fortune. As she was an heiress, all her sons had been given the name of Lytton as their last Christian name. When her father had died, two or three years after her husband, General Bulwer, from whom she was separated, she had re-taken her maiden name, calling herself Mrs. Bulwer Lytton, while her son remained Mr. Edward Lytton Bulwer.

There were powdered footmen at Mrs. Bulwer's house in Upper Seymour Street, and pineapples amongst the refreshments in the room to which her son soon guided Miss Wheeler. She was pleased to see that his dress that evening was less exaggerated. After some playful talk she suggested that as no one else had yet come to the refreshment-room they should return upstairs. Her host

[1] S. C. Hall, *Retrospect of a Long Life*, Vol. I, p. 264.
[2] Devey, op. cit., p. 59.

demurred. 'It does seem such sacrilege to see you among those old fossils,' he said—a remark not very flattering to his mother's guests. Mrs. Bulwer, who must have suspected what was happening, soon removed him to make up a table of whist, but she was too late. Her son was in love.

He spent much time at Knebworth that summer, but his friendship with Rosina Wheeler ripened. He frequented the society where he knew he would meet her, and with her he would often find her patroness and adviser, Caroline Lamb. He wrote to Mrs. Cunningham in Paris: 'Talking of Byron and poets, I have lately been much amongst the Blue Stockings. I go to town every fortnight for two or three days; and the evenings of those days, instead of being spent at balls, are generally consumed in the *soirées* of the savants, and the learned and literary ladies.' There followed a more significant note. 'Pray did you ever hear in Paris of a Mrs. Wheeler? Do find out about her. Reasons in my next. I believe she is a Liberal and the widow of a Col. Wheeler—tell me all you can find out.'[1]

His relationship with the beautiful Irish girl had rapidly warmed into love. Caroline Lamb asked nothing better than to assist in the drama of a love affair which she must have had no doubt would be unwelcome to Edward's mother. But that Edward, once her boyish admirer, should now be in love with her penniless *protégée* must have titillated her taste for romance, and the two were able to meet frequently, and without supervision, at Brocket. So far the course of their love had run smooth. Each loved and was loved. But Edward realized that opposition from his mother lay ahead, and it was even more violent than he had feared. He had to tell Rosina that his mother refused to consider the possibility of their marriage while he was still financially dependent upon her.

[1] *Life of Edward Bulwer, 1st Lord Lytton* by his Grandson, Vol. I, p. 163.

She considered him too young to be married. Let him make a name for himself first. '*Distinguish yourself*, and I will ask from you no consequence reflected from your wife.' But apart from her insistence on his first succeeding in public life, she soon made clear that she did not consider Rosina, the penniless daughter of a mother who she had heard was dangerously free-thinking, a suitable wife for her son.

Rosina did not relish the idea of waiting for an indefinite period for Edward to have achieved sufficient success in life to satisfy his mother. An engagement of unknown duration was much less attractive to her than a quick marriage to the handsome, clever son of a rich old lady. They talked together at Brocket and they parted with tears. Edward was torn between Rosina's reproaches that he could not love her and his mother's flat refusal to countenance his marriage. Miserably they broke off their engagement. It seemed that Mrs. Bulwer had won. Edward wrote to Mrs. Cunningham[1] that his fate had nearly been altered and forever, but the die had been cast differently and he was still unchanged. He was now going to throw himself into a new life, enter the House of Commons, devote himself to society. He had evidently accepted the fact that his romance with Rosina Wheeler was ended.

But she had not. While Edward, handsome, talented and rich (as long as he was prepared to humour his mother), could turn to new worlds and interests, her only future seemed to be to return to the literary parties, where she would be pointed out as the beautiful Miss Wheeler who had nearly married Mr. Bulwer. She did not enjoy the prospect. Within a month the news was brought to Edward that she was ill and sad and longed to see him. His heart was touched and forgetting all that reason had urged against a marriage without his mother's consent, he rushed to Rosina's side, full of love and contrition. She had often heard him talk proudly of his honour. Whether she

[1] 25 October 1826.

deliberately planned what came about we cannot know. In the joy of their reconciliation they became lovers, and from the moment of her surrender Rosina had conquered Mrs. Bulwer.

Edward's sense of honour and chivalry towards this defenceless girl, who had no father or brothers to protect her, urged him unceasingly towards marriage. In vain his mother raged and argued. He was adamant. He was now not only infatuated, he was also strengthened by the promptings of his conscience. After eleven months of angry scenes and embittered correspondence, he told his mother that he could no longer wait, in the hope of reconciling her to the idea of his marriage, he must fix the date of the wedding. In a last effort to satisfy her in some small degree he promised, firm of faith in Rosina's word, that if his mother could produce proof of her accusation that Rosina had lied about her age, and was really two years older than she said, he would not marry on the day arranged. It seems a strange concession, but in the event Mrs. Bulwer's agents failed. Rosina had been born in November 1802. She was not quite twenty-five years old when they were married.

'The bride,' wrote the *Morning Post* next day, 'is remarkably beautiful. The happy pair, partaking of a cold collation at the house of Colonel Doyle, in Montagu Square, set off for their seat, Woodcot House, in Oxfordshire.' This was the house near Pangbourne which Bulwer had leased. His allowance from his mother had ceased that morning. His own fortune consisted of £6,000 left to him in his father's will, and his bride brought only £80 a year with her. But his exorbitant pride made him determined not to reduce in any way his style of living. To avoid this he had only one weapon—his pen—backed by tremendous industry.

Rosina quickly proved herself a very bad manager. She had no idea of making the money her husband gave her go as far as possible. They kept a carriage and two or three saddle horses and they entertained a good deal. Edward 'liked his house to be decent and graceful, his table well served, and his establishment efficient and orderly'. He was careful about money and kept detailed accounts. Rosina was entirely different. She said that a woman who is always occupied about the management of her house cannot properly attend to other things. 'For my part, I know I should be sorry to spend more than half an hour every morning on the management of the largest establishment that ever was . . . I have nothing to do all day but cultivate my mind, and I never suffer myself to be troubled, if I can help it, with the vile details of household affairs.'[1] Already she began to show an inordinate affection for dogs. She had a Blenheim spaniel named 'Fairy' and had tiny visiting cards printed for it, which she left with her own on their neighbours.

Ten months after their marriage a daughter was born. Bulwer wrote to his mother but she remained unrelenting. He was working desperately to pay for his house, his wife's pleasures and now a family. Excessive pride, which was one of the most powerful traits in his character, compelled him to provide everything possible for his wife. When one would have expected him to be careful of expenditure, with the object of amassing some capital, so that he should not always have to work at such pressure, he reacted in exactly the opposite way, showering Rosina with expensive presents, encouraging her to extravagance in clothes, and maintaining an unnecessarily lavish household. The world must be shown, beyond a doubt, that Edward Bulwer's wife lacked nothing.

Words poured from his pen. Ephemerals, keepsakes, newspapers, monthly reviews, all published contributions from him—mostly anonymous. In the same month that his daughter was born, his first novel, *Pelham*, appeared. He had begun it two years before. For two months after its publication he read the notices gloomily—only three good

[1] Bulwer, op. cit., Vol. II, pp. 157-8.

reviews, the rest were crushing. But during the third month its sales began to rise and continued to do so, until it became the most popular novel of the day. Its picture of the dandy, with a serious nature hidden beneath the surface frivolity, was taken to be a self-portrait, but this Bulwer denied. In December of the same year another novel, *Disowned*, was published. He had received £500 for *Pelham*. For his second book he was paid £800.

At last his mother allowed herself to be reconciled to her son, but she still refused to meet his wife. The young couple left the country and took a house in Hertford Street. His mother restored his allowance and Bulwer, after endless arguments, persuaded her to abandon the feud, and to accept Rosina as a member of her family. She paid a call in state on her daughter-in-law, but the visit was not a success. Rosina did not attempt to conceal the resentment she felt. Her mother-in-law thought that she was conferring a great favour by calling, and was furious that she was not met with a fitting show of gratitude on the threshold.

Poor Bulwer. His mother did not wait to complain of her reception, and when he defended Rosina, made the wounding rejoinder that she could surely expect a better reception from his wife whom she 'maintained'. Bulwer's sensitive pride was deeply wounded. He immediately renounced the allowance which he had received. He pointed out that he had made, during nearly three years, from his own exertions, over £1,000 a year, though 'only by labour, confinement and great mental anxiety',[1] and that he had felt that his health had been overstrained. Without his mother's offer to renew his allowance he would not have felt justified in giving himself any relaxation. 'But . . . I did not consider this . . . in the light of a "maintenance". Maintenance I required from no human being. My own exertions had, and my own exertions yet could, maintain me and mine in all we required.'

[1] Bulwer, op. cit., Vol. II, p. 226.

From this proud line he would not be moved. Though his mother and wife eventually became fairly friendly, he turned doggedly back to the unremitting labour of writing, from which he had hoped to gain a respite. Time had not made Rosina any cleverer with the money he toiled so hard to earn. 'As for poor me,' she said, 'why, ten thousand a year would not be a penny too much for my living in London, and three thousand required all the management I can bestow upon it.'[1]

'It is . . . the husband's [part] to provide, to scheme, to work, to endure, to grind out his strong heart at the miserable wheel,' Bulwer made one of his characters say. The intensity of the toil to which he resolutely dedicated himself made him increasingly difficult and irritable and abnormally sensitive—'like a man who had been flayed, and is sore all over'.

For three years they lived in Hertford Street, during which time Bulwer continued to publish novels and articles as fast as he could write. After a year he added to his labours by being elected to Parliament. The young couple's relationship steadily deteriorated, in spite of the birth of a son. Rosina by now saw very little of her husband. When he was at home he would remain shut away in his room at his desk. When he left his work his one desire was for company and change, so that he liked to entertain large parties to dinner—parties of the fashionable world mingled with writers, whom Rosina found very dull.

He had always enjoyed society. 'What with parties at home and parties abroad, I am quite worn out,' wrote Rosina. 'We have another large dinner at home on the 5th June, among the literary part of which we shall have Master Tommy Moore, young D'Israeli—the author of *Vivian Grey*, Washington Irving, Mr. Galt . . . It is astonishing what bores I find all authors excepting my own husband, and he has nothing author-like about him,

[1] To Miss Greene, February 1832.

for this reason, that his literary talents are his very least.'[1]

As a friend of old D'Israeli, Bulwer helped to launch the son in the social world of London, for his house was almost unique in that there writers and noblemen and politicians met on equal terms. Young Benjamin, in green velvet trousers and canary-coloured waistcoat, with lace at his wrists and his black hair in ringlets, was a frequent visitor at Hertford Street, and it was there that he first met his Mary Anne. Mrs. Wyndham Lewis, whose husband was then still alive and the Member for Maidstone, asked that he should be presented to her. Disraeli recorded his impressions: 'A pretty little woman, a flirt and a rattle; indeed, gifted with a volubility I should think unequalled . . . She told me that she liked "silent, melancholy men". I answered "that I had no doubt of it".'[2] He little realized that in a few years' time he would be writing to her, 'I wish to be with you, to live with you, never to be away from you—I care not where, in heaven or on earth, or in the waters under the earth.'

Edward Bulwer rapidly became very friendly with Benjamin Disraeli and did his best to see that he was not opposed as Parliamentary candidate for Wycombe in 1832, when he was unsuccessful. A few months later they went together to Bath and Disraeli wrote to his sister: 'I like Bath very much. Bulwer and I went in late to one public ball, and got quite mobbed.' On their return to London he dined with Bulwer *en famille*. 'His mother-in-law, Mrs. Wheeler, was there; not so pleasant, something between Jeremy Bentham and Meg Merrilies, very clever, but awfully revolutionary. She poured forth all her systems upon my novitiate ear, and while she advocated the rights of women, Bulwer abused system-mongers and the sex, and Rosina played with her dog.'

[1] *Life of Edward Bulwer, 1st Lord Lytton* by his Grandson. Vol. I, p. 253.

[2] W. F. Monypenny, *Life of Benjamin Disraeli*, Vol. I, p. 204.

As Bulwer and Disraeli were returning together from Bath to London where the former was to speak in the House of Commons, Disraeli said that though the world might wonder at his *ambition*, it was really *pride* which prompted him to struggle. 'They shall not say I have failed.' Bulwer felt that this expressed his own sentiments and turning to him, he pressed his arm and said, 'in a tone the sincerity of which could not be doubted: "It is true, my dear fellow, it is true. We are sacrificing our youth, the time of pleasure, the bright season of enjoyment—but we are bound to go on, we are *bound*. How our enemies would triumph were we to retire from the stage!" '[1]

Edward Bulwer was living his life at a feverish pace and there seemed less and less place in it for his wife, save as a recipient of presents and as hostess at his dinner-table. Sometimes she would not see him alone for days on end, except for a few minutes in the early hours of the morning. But no human frame could stand for ever the violent strain which he was putting on his mind and body. His health suddenly collapsed, and the doctors advised a complete change of scene. Together they set off for Italy, in September 1833, leaving their children and Rosina's beloved dog with her old friend, Miss Greene. The mother's letters from Milan, Florence, Venice and Rome were unenthusiastic about her travels. She was 'so knocked up with sight-seeing'. She sent no message to the children, but her dog was never forgotten; it was referred to by affectionate pet names and endearments in every letter. 'Pray tell pretty, darling, darling Faizey that I never kiss or even pat these dogs . . . but I have written to Faizling by Mrs. Leigh—darling, darling little dog.'

In Naples Rosina found a new happiness. She, who had been so meek and kind in the first years of her marriage, had become resentful at being left so much alone, and jealous of her husband's friendships with other women. In Naples she found herself in gay, congenial society and

[1] W. F. Monypenny, op. cit., Vol. I, p. 235.

while Bulwer, who had seized immediately on the idea of a novel about Pompeii, spent hours exploring its streets and houses, she was soon the object of flattering attentions from a Neapolitan prince.

It was sweet to be admired, to be treated with tenderness. It was not long before she was convinced that she was in love with him. But her happiness did not last long. On an impulse she confessed her love to her husband, perhaps during one of their quarrels. His reaction was violent. In a passion of rage he had their luggage packed immediately and they set off at once for England. All the way home they quarrelled violently, and he told her that he would never live with her again as a husband, unless she could tell him that the confession was untrue and would reaffirm her love for himself. Rosina, resentful and furious at being snatched away from her admirer and the happy life she had been leading in Naples, refused to do so and they arrived unheralded at their house in Hertford Street, worn out with bitter and mutual recriminations.

Both sent immediately for Miss Greene. Directly she saw Bulwer he struck her as 'looking very fierce and odd. His hair and whiskers had grown to a most ridiculous length and there was a fiery expression fixed in his eye, which I had never before seen.'[1] Rosina, on the other hand, she found 'frightened and subdued', but before she left them she saw her 'for the first time . . . turn upon him with violence and throw back whatever he said. And at last he rushed out of the room saying, "We never then meet again except upon our mutual death-beds".' They both seemed exhausted with rage, but she persuaded Bulwer to let his wife stay another day under his roof, and in the end arranged for her to come with her son and his nurse to stay with her at Hounslow, until he had found a house for them.

Bulwer's mother now took a hand and invited them together to Knebworth, in an effort at reconciliation, while

[1] Michael Sadleir, *Bulwer: A Panorama*, p. 384.

Miss Greene went off to visit friends in Gloucester, taking their little daughter, Emily, with her. She soon found herself involved in their troubles again. The reconciliation ended in the worst and most violent scene of all, when Bulwer lost all control and treated his wife so brutally that, overcome with an agony of shame and humiliation at his own behaviour, he rushed out of the house, went off to a hotel at Richmond and talked of leaving England for ever.[1]

Even after this last violent scene they did not finally separate. Bulwer left for Ireland and Rosina retired to Gloucester, taking her little son and his nurse to join her daughter and Miss Greene in a furnished lodging. This sensible woman found herself powerless to check Rosina's extravagance or to interest her in her children. Miss Greene was devoted to Emily, who had been left in her charge while her parents were abroad, and now she became almost the mother of both children. Their own mother took no pleasure in their company and struck up a friendship with a Scottish lady of whom Miss Greene could not approve, a lady who had been disowned by her relations because of her love of brandy. It was here that Rosina first began to drink too much.

'Whilst we were thus getting over our time in Gloucester,' wrote Miss Greene in her journal, 'Rosina was receiving the most clever and bitter answers to her letters of the same kind in which she taunted him in the most violent manner with everything terrible she had ever said or thought of him. However, he kept supplying her with money in the most surprising manner, which she spent in a most wasteful and unprofitable way upon clothes, etc.'[2]

The Last Days of Pompeii had been published about a month after the Bulwers' quarrel and achieved an immediate and sensational success. That autumn the Melbourne

[1] Devey, op. cit., p. 84. A. W. Frost, *Bulwer Lytton*.
[2] *Life of Edward Bulwer, 1st Lord Lytton* by his Grandson, Vol. I, p. 289.

Ministry fell, and Bulwer fought and won his seat in Parliament. The long-distance marriage-by-letter continued. Sometimes the correspondence was embittered, on her side by hysterical and wounding recrimination, on his by lofty, and as she thought, hypocritical reproach and self-justification. Sometimes a momentary shadow of the love they had felt for each other would soften them. It was on one of these occasions that Bulwer, at Rosina's urgent request, travelled down from London to visit her at Gloucester.

They had not met for nine months, but her fickle temper had changed by the time that he arrived. She received him 'with coldness and hauteur' and after several days of incessant quarrelling he 'rushed downstairs in violent anger, drank two glasses of brandy, sent for a post-chaise and drove towards London', with the intention of arranging a legal separation. Miss Greene was sent after him by Rosina, to say that she was ill and unhappy at his departure and longed for a reconciliation. She overtook him at Cheltenham. He was persuaded to return and this time was received with warmth and affection. He stayed there with her on good terms for a little while and on his return to London wrote to his mother, 'I think things are now so smooth as to promise more favourably than I had ever anticipated. I am therefore going to hire a house near town, and I hope to be able to let this, and have only some little chamber near Parliament.'[1] For his wife and children he leased a house at Acton, called Berrymead Priory. At the same time he took for himself the chambers in Albany which had once been lived in by Lord Byron.

During May 1835 his family moved into the house at Acton. Rosina seemed pleased with it. She wrote 'delightful accounts of the beauty of the house and of the great kindness and affection of her husband' to Miss Greene. During the early summer their improved relationship continued. But she was soon complaining again. He had

[1] *Life of Edward Bulwer, 1st Lord Lytton* by his Grandson, Vol. I, p. 305.

taken an old-fashioned, uncomfortable house for her, while he had 'furnished his chambers sumptuously for himself'. She said that 'on arriving at this damp, dreary, desolate place, she found she had not even a bed to lie on; but the housekeeper told her . . . that a very sumptuous one of crimson damask, lined with white silk, had been put up the day before, but the upholsterer had returned in a great hurry, saying he had made a mistake, as that bed was for the chambers at Albany.'[1]

Bulwer must have rejoiced in the tranquillity and repose of his chambers. *Rienzi* was published the year that he moved in,[2] and there he must have written the first two volumes of *A History of Athens, Its Rise and Fall*, which he never completed; another novel, *Godolphin*, and the first of two novels which were afterwards combined as *Ernest Maltravers*. In addition to these works, surely enough for a two years' stay, he wrote a play which he dedicated to Macready, *The Duchess de la Vallière* which sold two editions very quickly after it was published, but failed when it was later produced by Macready at Covent Garden.

The improved relationship with his wife was not to last long. Two months after her move to Acton, Rosina heard gossip connecting her husband with another woman. At last she, who had been unreasonably jealous of his previous friendships with women, had true cause for jealousy. Bulwer, with his abnormal sensitivity and vanity, must have felt emotionally bruised and exhausted by the dance she had led him and he had found elsewhere the devotion, admiration and affection which were so necessary to him, and which for the last two years his wife had denied him. He had formed an attachment which was to last for some years to come. Five years later he wrote in his diary: 'I am loved, I believe, honestly, deeply and endearingly, by one who is indeed to me a wife . . . Had we but been married,

[1] Devey, *Nemesis*, p. 90.
[2] December 1835.

we should have been cited as models of domestic happiness and household virtues.'

Rosina immediately dashed him off 'a letter of insult and abuse in words so outrageous as to put an end for ever to any possibility of their permanent reconciliation'.[1] What Bulwer's feelings must have been when he opened this letter in his chambers in Albany it is better not to speculate, but it decided him finally to take action, to communicate with Rosina's only close relation, Sir Francis Doyle, and to arrange an agreement for a legal separation.

Rosina, with her usual irresponsibility, was now terrified of the consequences of her action. After agonized appeals for advice to Sir Francis and Miss Greene, she wrote a heart-rending letter of self-abasement and apology to her husband. What torture it must have been to Bulwer then, and for years to come, to find a letter addressed to him in that hand, to force himself to open it and to read what new trials his wife intended for them both. On this occasion she implored forgiveness 'for that horrid letter', took all blame to herself, reproached him with nothing. 'All that I ever was to you I will be to you and more, if you will but try me again . . . I will study every hour of my life to make you so happy and contented that you shall have no room to recollect it.' Such humility, and perhaps a sense of his own guilt, touched Bulwer's heart and once again he relented. But Rosina was incapable of holding to her resolves.

'Mr. Bulwer came but seldom to visit us,' wrote Miss Greene of the house at Acton, 'but expecting him and preparing for him was his poor wife's greatest pleasure and amusement. Yet I was often provoked to find that, notwithstanding, we would not have sat down to dinner five minutes, before she would say the most insulting things to him. These I often saw him try to bear, and when they

---

[1] *Life of Edward Bulwer, 1st Lord Lytton* by his Grandson, Vol. I, p. 309.

at last produced the effect of putting him in a rage, she was sorry.'[1]

Bulwer, wearied of these constant scenes and recriminations, left before Christmas for a holiday in Paris. From there he wrote that his mind was made up finally and irrevocably. They must part. 'For more than two years I have had at your hands harsh unkindness, bitter taunts, constant bickering, accusation and complaint . . . You shall no longer complain that I keep you in a "county jail". Take your own residence where you will . . . Learn now only that my resolution is unalterable, and no threats, no violence, on the one hand, no unreal and mocking attempts at reconciliation on the other, can shake it . . . The Priory is at your service till it suits your convenience to change it for a more agreeable residence . . . I will take . . . care to secure you an honourable independence.'

Yet again Rosina managed to avoid the issue. In four broken letters, addressed to him in Paris, she wrote of her lacerated body and mind, her torturing pain and a cough that would kill a Hercules. 'I crawl about the room with great difficulty. I can do nothing but sit down and cry when I think of finally leaving this place, incapable as I am of any exertion, and not a human being to exert themselves for me . . . God must effect the separation you so pant for very soon, as permanently as you can desire.'[2] In a final *cri de coeur* she reverted to the dog-endearments of their old love-letters: 'My dearest Pups . . . Forgive poor old sick, dying Poodles, and try him again . . . If I die before you return to England, will you give an order to have poor darling Fairy sent to Lady Westmeath, as she is the only person I know who would love her enough . . . God bless you, Pups, prays poor old Poodle.'

These pathetic letters weakened Bulwer's resolution and he wrote to her before he left Paris, abandoning the

[1] *Life of Edward Bulwer, 1st Lord Lytton* by his Grandson, Vol. I, p. 315.
[2] Ibid., p. 323.

idea of a complete separation, and telling her to stay at
Acton. The Parliamentary session would begin soon after
his return. He would stay in his chambers at Albany during
the week. After making this decision he wrote wearily to
his mother, with two prophecies for the future which were
both to come true. 'I am just where I was . . . Rosina . . .
runs on so much about her health and dying and so forth
that it puts me in a most harsh and brutal point of view
to insist while she affects to be so ill and miserable—
especially as my letters are all likely I think to be published. So I am quite at a nonplus . . . I have forgiven
again and again . . . My career is blighted; my temper
soured; my nerves shattered; and if I am to go on for ever
this way because she insists on continuing to force herself
upon me, God knows what I shall do at last . . . If the
separation cannot be effected before I return I must again
be the victim. For what can I do if she comes to the
Albany, throws herself on the ground and declares she
won't leave till it is made up? I cannot have scenes in a
place like that.'

His last fear was curiously prophetic. A few weeks after
his return, weeks during which they had exchanged kindly
letters, Rosina did come to Albany and made just such a
scene as he had dreaded. According to Rosina her husband had promised to dine with her that February[1] evening
at The Priory. At nine o'clock a groom appeared with a
note to say that he was ill and unable to leave his chambers.
Rosina, according to her own story, immediately started
for London in alarm, taking medicines with her. (One
wonders what medicines?) She arrived at the door of Bulwer's chambers in Albany at eleven at night. She 'rang
and rang'. Bulwer had been expecting a friend, Frederick
Villiers, who had not appeared. His servant was out.
When Bulwer opened the door, with a dressing-gown
thrown over his shoulders, he must have shown his annoyance at her unlooked-for appearance. She, through the

[1] 1836.

open door, glimpsed a 'cosy salver with tea for two on it' and immediately decided that her husband was entertaining a woman in his rooms. Before he could protest at her arrival she made a violent scene of jealousy in the hall of Albany, accusing him shrilly of deceiving her.

The scene which Bulwer had dreaded was only ended by her being removed, still screaming, from Albany. Thence she rushed off to Mrs. Wyndham Lewis's house, to pour out her story and to dash off a violent letter to her husband. It may have been there that she first coined the phrase: 'I went to visit my husband in his rooms, which he kept in order to have undisturbed communion with the Muse. I found the Muse in white muslin seated on his knee.' The story spread all round London and Bulwer, whose manners had always been too affected and proud to make him a popular man, must have winced to read the paragraphs in the Press.

Publicly humiliated and ashamed, Bulwer had a deed of separation drawn up, wherein he covenanted to pay her £400 a year for life and £50 a year for the maintenance of each of her children, so long as he consented to their being with her. This document was signed by them both and on Rosina's behalf by her cousin, Sir Francis Doyle, and another trustee. None of those who signed with her escaped Rosina's virulent reproaches later on for the inadequacy of the allowance. In the meantime she was not without friends and her side of the story was vividly presented. One of her champions was Mrs. Wyndham Lewis, and it was at her house in London that Rosina put her signature to the deed of separation. It was still more than three years before Mrs. Wyndham Lewis, by then a widow, was to marry Benjamin Disraeli.

The day after the deed of separation was signed Bulwer wrote to Mrs. Wyndham Lewis:

'My dear Madam, 'April 20, 1836. *Albany*.

You must permit me to place strongly before you what

I venture to consider grounds for a certain caution on your part relative to the situation of Mrs. Bulwer and myself. Paragraphs have appeared in more than one newspaper containing a very grave calumny upon me, namely that Mrs. Bulwer found some person in my rooms and that our separation is in consequence of that discovery. Similar rumours have been industriously propagated. On tracing the origin of them, I think it right frankly to say that many of those who spread them sheltered themselves under your authority—in fact they assert that you told them such was the fact. You are perfectly aware that this is not the truth. You yourself told me, that Mrs. Bulwer was convinced of the injustice of her suspicions. The real grounds of my separation are these: violent provocation on her part, over a series of years, frequently forgiven by me; the last act of coming to my rooms and without the smallest excuse making a scene, going then to your house and writing to me from thence a letter which if I published it would justify fifty separations. Fully persuaded that you would not do me the wrong, Mrs. Bulwer the injury, or bring on yourself the consequences of accusations against me which you know to be false, you will be cautious in the statements you make of my affairs.'[1]

Mrs. Wyndham Lewis after this letter was more careful in her championship of Rosina, but it is understandable that when she was Disraeli's wife in later years, her influence should have been exerted against Edward Bulwer's advancement.

On the 14th June 1836 Bulwer must have sighed with relief. For on that day his turbulent wife left Berrymead Priory and took the children to Ireland, to live with Miss Greene and her widowed sister near Dublin. So he must have had one year's enjoyment of a quiet life in Albany, time for the wounds to his pride to heal a little, while he attended the House of Commons and worked like a demon.

[1] Sadleir, op. cit., pp. 406, 407.

'MONK' LEWIS BY H. W.
PICKERSGILL
*From the National Portrait
Gallery*

'TITA' FALCIERI, THE
VENETIAN GONDOLIER
ENGAGED BY MONK
LEWIS AS HIS MAN-
SERVANT. HE AFTER-
WARDS ENTERED
BYRON'S SERVICE, WAS
WITH HIM IN GREECE
WHEN HE DIED AND
SUBSEQUENTLY WORKED
FOR DISRAELI AND HIS
FATHER
*In the possession of the National
Trust at Hughenden*

W. E. GLADSTONE, AGED 29.   PAINTED BY W. BRADLEY IN
THE YEAR WHEN GLADSTONE LEFT ALBANY TO BE MARRIED
In the possession of C. A. Gladstone, Esq., at Hawarden Castle

The following year he left his chambers for a house in Charles Street, so he was no longer a resident of Albany when his wife quarrelled with Miss Greene and departed to Bath, leaving the children behind her. All his life she was to persecute him, publishing a book, *Chieveley or the Man of Honour*, of which he was only too clearly the villain, sending letters to him and his friends, of which the envelopes were covered with obscene inscriptions, harassing him with lawsuits, and pouring out her woes to anyone who would listen.

More than twenty years after their separation she appeared at Hertford, where he was being returned to Parliament in an unopposed election, having just been appointed Colonial Secretary in Lord Derby's Government. She pushed her way through the crowd, calling in a loud voice, 'Make way for the member's wife!' Then she denounced him violently from his own platform. 'How can the people of England submit to have such a man at the head of the Colonies, who ought to have been in the Colonies as a transport long ago,' she shouted. After this Bulwer lost his head and had her certified as insane, and placed in the charge of a doctor at a home in Brentford. The Press took up her cause and after a public outcry she was released. Bulwer paid all her debts, increased her allowance to £500 a year, and their son, now grown up, took her away to France. But she soon quarrelled even with him, and lived on, hysterical and suspicious and always regarding herself as the innocent victim of persecution, until her eightieth year, nine years after Bulwer's death.

Never can a man have paid more dearly for marrying against his mother's wishes!

III

The Chambers A.14 once had a strange inhabitant who brought the respectable name of Albany into the newspapers and the law-courts. Mr. Gundry, 'a man of fortune, traveller and linguist', was a man of violent temper. On 7 March 1841, the readers of *The Sunday Chronicle and People's Weekly Advertizer* were regaled with a front page story headed 'Desperate Affray with the Police at The Albany'. Mr. Gundry had been charged with having beaten his cab-boy, struck his cook, 'and kept the police at bay, with sword and pistol'. Even in court he admitted to carrying a double-barrelled pistol, capped and loaded, but agreed to give it up until the case was over. Throughout the proceedings he 'assumed a very lofty bearing, almost amounting to a swagger' and when the police complained that he had assaulted an officer in the execution of his duty he attempted a counter-charge against the police.

The constable's story was that he had served the summonses on Mr. Gundry and that they were not attended to. He went in the evening to Albany and being told that Mr. Gundry was within, waited until eight o'clock when he emerged. The constable went up to him and told him that he had a warrant against him. 'Mr. Gundry called him a rascal and appeared as if about to get away.' The constable laid hold of him, but was immediately thrown down and Mr. Gundry pulled out a double-barrelled pistol, and threatened to shoot him. When the constable called for help Mr. Gundry ran up the stairs to the top of the house and threatened to blow out the brains of any policeman who attempted to touch him. 'A gentleman named Kinnaird reasoned with Mr. Gundry and a promise having been given to the Inspector the police were taken off.'

Mr. Gundry's reply to these accusations was to say that he had been frequently annoyed by the police. 'There are things gentlemen won't submit to. Blood will be shed.' He wished to make a most serious charge 'as to the manner in which the police executed the warrant. The affair must be carried to the highest tribunal; when, if a punishment of one, two, nay, three years at the tread-mill is not inflicted,

it shall not be my fault . . . I thought by not attending to
the summons I had merely incurred some small fine or
so; but he—yes, that fellow—seized a gentleman. I
dragged him instantly up the steps, and he fell with fright.
He took out his staff and pursued me. I had a sword-stick
in my hand, and in the scuffle the sheath came off. I dare say
he thought I was going to pierce him . . . I stood with
my pistol in my hand to prevent the police from beating
me with their staves and trampling on me.'

Other inhabitants of Albany must have found him a very
trying neighbour. Sometimes he would stand in the hall
and insult everyone who tried to pass him. At others he
would take it into his head to break all the windows. Or
he would have a cab in Albany courtyard and sit in it for
hours together, looking at the heavens, and obstructing
the passage of anyone who wished to enter the building.

Whenever Mr. Gundry caught sight of one unfortunate
employee, who had incurred his displeasure, he pelted
him with pieces of fine china and glass and on one occasion
fired a pistol at him. Eventually he had to answer another
charge of assault at Marlborough Street.

As a precaution a solicitor's clerk stood by his side 'to
restrain those ebullitions of temper to which he is wont to
give vent'. Mr. Cox, the plaintiff, gave evidence that two
years before he had accidentally touched Mr. Gundry
when he entered the Opera-house, just as the performance
had begun. At the end of the first act Mr. Gundry had
reviled him in the rudest terms. Two years after this incident, as he walked in Hyde Park Mr. Gundry had ridden
past him, then suddenly dismounted and struck him with
his cane. Mr. Gundry's counsel argued that his client had
merely acted 'as a gentleman would who wished to compel
another to meet him and arrange a quarrel'. The magis-
trate said that an assault had been committed with a view
to provoke a duel. He agreed to treat the affair summarily
and fined Mr. Gundry 20s. and costs, and ordered him to
find bail to keep the peace for six months.

Perhaps the strain was too great. A year later 'mind aberrations' were alleged against him before the Commission of Lunacy, and in February 1843 the Trustees gave their consent to those acting for 'Daniel Gundry, formerly of Albany, but now residing at Brislington House, in the County of Somerset Esq<u>re</u> a Lunatic' to assign the Lease of the Chambers A No. 14 Albany . . . to John Ramsbottom Esq<u>re</u> M.P.'

IV

In 1848 a novel appeared written by Marmion Savage and entitled *The Bachelor of the Albany*. In it we find this description of Albany and its inhabitants at that date:

'You know the Albany—the haunt of bachelors, or of married men who try to lead bachelors' lives—the dread of suspicious wives, the retreat of superannuated fops, the hospital for incurable oddities, a cluster of solitudes for social hermits, the home of homeless gentlemen, the diner-out and the diner-in, the place for the fashionable thrifty, the luxurious lonely, and the modish morose, the votaries of melancholy, and lovers of mutton-chops. He knoweth not western London who is a stranger to the narrow arcade of chambers that forms a sort of private thoroughfare between Piccadilly and Burlington Gardens, guarded at each extremity by a fierce porter, or man-mastiff, whose duty it is to receive letters, cards, and parcels, and repulse intrusive wives, disagreeable fathers, and importunate tradesmen.'

CHAPTER VI

IN THE DAYS OF MACAULAY

I

LET US STROLL down the long covered way, which seems
always to echo with the sound of departed feet. Between the two cream-painted, stucco-covered rows of
buildings we make our way, until, on the left, we see the
entrance to the staircase labelled E. Here, on the ground
floor, in the set of chambers known as E.1, lives for five
years a man who has never married. But do not imagine that
he is a lonely bachelor. He finds life in Albany much to his
taste, reminding him of his happy days at Cambridge. After
five years he leaves his rooms at E.1, only to move to
larger chambers at F.3,[1] on the second floor by the gate
which leads into Vigo Street, where he finds more room
for his constantly increasing library. His most intimate
friends lived, some of them, more than two thousand years
ago. To him they are more real and far more interesting
than the people he meets every day.

By the time that he comes to live in Albany at the age of
forty-one, he has already achieved success as an author,
politician and Indian administrator. He is a great walker
and paces through crowded London streets or country
lanes, with his eyes always fixed upon a book, 'walking as
fast as other people walked, and reading a great deal
faster than anybody else could read.'[2] He is short and stout

---

[1] Consent was given to the executors of Henry Sanford Esqre. to
let F.3 to The Right Honorable Thos. Babington Macaulay at the
364th Meeting of the Trustees on 17 December 1846.

[2] *Life and Letters of Lord Macaulay* by Sir George Otto Trevelyan,
p. 87.

and untidily dressed, but holds himself erect. His only concession to dressiness is an apparently inexhaustible supply of handsome embroidered waistcoats, and when going out, a pair of dark kid gloves. But he is so clumsy with his hands that he can never get his fingers more than half-way into them. His head is massive, his face rugged but good-humoured.

'I have taken a very comfortable suite of chambers in the Albany,' wrote Thomas Babington Macaulay to his friend Mr. Thomas Flower Ellis, on 12 July 1841, 'and I hope to lead, during some years, a sort of life peculiarly suited to my taste,—college life at the West-end of London. I have an entrance hall, two sitting-rooms, a bedroom, a kitchen, cellars and two rooms for servants,—all for ninety guineas a year; and this in a situation which no younger son of a Duke need be ashamed to put on his card. We shall have, I hope, some very pleasant breakfasts there, to say nothing of dinners. My own housekeeper will do very well for a few plain dishes, and the Clarendon is within a hundred yards.'

Macaulay had come far, and by his own efforts, when he was able to pen those words. As a child he had been precocious, with an astonishing facility for absorbing and remembering everything that he read from the earliest age. His father, Zachary Macaulay, had the same extraordinary memory, and had crammed it with facts and statistics. A fervent Evangelical, he was a leading member of what was known as the Clapham Sect, a group of remarkable men with strong Low Church convictions, whose passion was to rid the world of slavery and who founded most of the English Bible and Missionary Societies.

Zachary Macaulay's fund of knowledge was so extensive and exact that when Wilberforce needed information or accurate statistics he used to say, 'Let us look it out in Macaulay.' The son inherited his father's gift for absorbing information and secreting it in his memory, ready to be produced when it was required, perhaps years later. But his interests became wider than his father's, especially after he had taken up residence at Trinity College, Cambridge. Where the father was grave, stern, methodical and precise, the son was impetuous, untidy and careless of dress. Above all he loved to talk. 'So long as a door was open, or a light burning, in any of the courts, Macaulay was always in the mood for conversation and companionship.'[1]

He said of himself at Cambridge that whenever anybody enunciated a proposition, all possible answers to it rushed into his mind at once. He liked to walk rapidly up and down the room as he talked and although his manner was vehement and self-confident, and his rush of words was uttered in a loud voice, his friends never found him over-bearing or anything but good-humoured. His 'abomination' of mathematics led him to fail twice before he achieved his Tripos, but he twice won the Chancellor's Medal for English verse, and in 1821 a Craven University Scholarship. At the age of twenty-three he was awarded the honour which in his eyes was the greatest that Cambridge could give and became a Fellow of Trinity. By this he was assured of £300 a year for seven years, providing that he did not marry, and this became extremely important to him when he learned, before leaving the University, that his father, by imprudent investments, had lost the greater part of his fortune.

Although Macaulay was called to the Bar, he never seriously intended to make the law his profession. From the first his interests were literature and public affairs, and within a year of beginning to practise on the Northern Circuit he was spending more time in the House of Commons than in the Law Courts.

His impact on public life came very early. Before his twenty-fifth birthday his articles on Milton in the *Edinburgh Review*—then at the height of its fame and influence, and the spearhead of the Whig attack on the Tory Govern-

[1] Sir G. O. Trevelyan, op. cit., p. 56.

ment—brought him instant recognition. John Murray
declared that 'it would be worth the copyright of *Childe
Harold* to have Macaulay on the staff of the *Quarterly*'.
Invitations arrived from London hostesses for the brilliant
young author. (It is strange to see how many of these
writers who lived in Albany found themselves famous
overnight.) His family had moved from Clapham to a
house in Great Ormond Street when their fortunes had
declined so suddenly. The son was now largely responsible for their financial support and for the next five years,
until he was nearly thirty, his pen 'ran like fire'. Until he
was twenty-nine he lived at home and even then, when he
moved to chambers in Gray's Inn, he would take his two
youngest sisters, Hannah and Margaret, who were ten and
twelve years younger than himself, for long afternoon
walks whenever he could. They would wander round the
City, Islington, Clerkenwell and the Parks. 'What anecdotes he used to pour out about every street, and square,
and court, and alley!'

Some of his new acquaintances in society thought his
conversation too informative. Sydney Smith called him 'a
book in breeches' and said 'if he could forget half what he
reads, he would be less suffocating than he is'. But his sisters adored him and would listen eagerly as he re-lived for
them the parties he had attended and the famous people
he had talked with (or perhaps to), depicting for them a
world very different from their own austere home, where
he was sternly rebuked by his father when, poor as
he was, he wrote an article for 'a worldly magazine'.

At twenty-nine he was elected to Parliament, where his
speeches were immediately successful. The Reform Bill
was the battle of the hour and Macaulay's eloquence and
learning made him one of the most prominent of the
young reformers. He entered with zest into the life of the
House of Commons and the excitement of those stirring
times. For three seasons he dined out almost every night.
He was a welcome guest at Holland House, and at

Samuel Rogers's breakfasts in St. James's Place, and never failed to recount to his sisters every detail that would interest them. He was a perfect brother and brought to them the excitement and glamour of the outside world. He would read his articles aloud for their approval and would even alter phrases which they protested were too unkind.

Besides the more serious books which he read and discussed with them, he was equally fond of novels, which they read and re-read and whose dialogue was absorbed by that tireless brain as thoroughly as the classics. Their conversation would be carried on in the words or manner of Jane Austen's Mrs. Elton or Mr. Collins, or they would use quotations from *Sir Charles Grandison* or *Evelina* to describe their own friends. Macaulay said that he thought he could re-write *Sir Charles Grandison* from memory.

Other less classical authors were equally popular with them. A prolific writer named Mrs. Meeke, in whose romances the impoverished young hero invariably turned out to be a Duke's son, was a great favourite, and Macaulay knew almost all her works by heart. Not only was his memory superb, but he had also an extraordinary facility for composing verse on the spur of the moment. 'Games of hide and seek, that lasted for hours, with shouting and blowing of horns up and down the stairs and through every room, were varied by ballads, which . . . he composed during the act of recitation.' These verses, which he produced so rapidly for home consumption, he invariably attributed to a being known as 'The Judicious Poet'.

But this carefree young man, playing happily with his younger sisters and brothers, showed a very different side of his character to the outside world. His Cambridge Fellowship had ended, and although he had since become a Junior Minister and yet found time for a succession of long reviews for the *Edinburgh Review*, he was constantly worried about his financial position. His sensitive conscience made him fear that he might be suspected of hanging on to office because he was in the unusual position of having no private means.

Already he felt the contrary attractions of the two lives which he was trying to combine—the politician and the writer. At one moment he would be carried away by party zeal and enthusiasm for the Whig cause. At another he would feel that he was wasting his time in politics, that his family depended on him and that he should be working for them in some less hazardous profession. In the first mood he described the passing of the second reading of the Reform Bill by one vote, 'We shook hands, and clapped each other on the back, and went out laughing and crying and huzzaing into the lobby,' or wrote 'the news in rhyme' to his sisters:

'We gained a victory last night as great as e'er was known.
We beat the Opposition upon the Russian loan.
They hoped for a majority and also for our places.
We won the day by seventy-nine. You should have seen their
    faces . . .
Though not his friend, my tender heart I own could not but
    feel
A little for the misery of poor Sir Robert Peel.
But hang the dirty Tories! and let them starve and pine!
Huzza for the majority of glorious seventy-nine!'

Yet less than a year later he was writing to his sister, Hannah: 'I begin to wonder what the fascination is which attracts men, who could sit over their tea and their books in their own cool, quiet rooms, to breathe bad air, hear bad speeches, lounge up and down the long gallery, and doze uneasily on the green benches till three in the morning. Thank God, these luxuries are not necessary to me. My pen is sufficient for my support.'[1]

He was not anxious for great wealth, but he longed to have what he described as 'a competence' with which he

[1] 17 June 1833.

could support his family, now almost entirely dependent on him financially. 'If I left my place in the Government, I must leave my seat in Parliament too. For I must live: I can live only by my pen: and it is absolutely impossible for any man to write enough to procure him a decent subsistence, and at the same time to take an active part in politics.' Yet the alternative of living entirely by his pen did not appeal to him. 'The thought of becoming a bookseller's hack; of writing to relieve, not the fulness of the mind, but the emptiness of the pocket . . . of filling sheets with trash merely that the sheets may be filled . . . is horrible to me.'[1]

At this moment of perplexity a solution offered itself to all his troubles—a solution which, after a few years away from home, brought him back to England with a modest fortune and enabled him to lease a set of chambers in the comfort of Albany. The newly passed India Bill stipulated that one of the members of the Supreme Council, which was now to govern India, must not be a member of the East India Company. The position, an extremely important one carrying with it a salary of £10,000 a year, was offered to Macaulay. He was advised that he could live 'in splendour' in Calcutta for half that sum, yet with his peculiarly strong attachment to his family, he felt his exile would be unbearable unless his sister, Hannah, would share it with him. Once her assent had been given he was in no doubt about his decision. He would lose a few years of English politics, but he would return at the age of thirty-nine with enough money saved to make him henceforth independent. And there was useful work to be done in India.

So he and Hannah had sailed for India and there, within a few months, she met a young civilian, Charles Trevelyan, and all her brother's plans were overturned. Whether Macaulay had wished to marry or not, it had become impossible from the moment when he had accepted respon-

[1] 5 December 1833.

sibility for the maintenance of his family and the payment of his father's debts. He had concentrated all his
affection on his two little sisters. Margaret had married a
year before they left England and now Hannah, whom he
had persuaded to accompany him by saying, 'I can bribe
you only by telling you that, if you will go with me, I will
love you better than I love you now, if I can,' Hannah, too,
would leave him. Another man was to come first in her
affections.

Trevelyan was an active, ardent man of twenty-seven,
completely lacking in social graces. From twenty to
twenty-five he had lived in a remote province of India,
where his whole time was divided between public business
and field sports. He had no small talk. 'His topics, even
in courtship,' said Macaulay, 'are steam navigation,
the education of the natives, the equalization of sugar
duties, the substitution of the Roman for the Arabic
alphabet.'

In spite of these restricted conversational abilities,
Macaulay soon saw that Hannah returned Trevelyan's
love. He knew it, he believed, before she did herself. 'I
could most easily have prevented it by merely treating
Trevelyan with a little coldness, for he is a man whom the
smallest rebuff would completely discourage.' Thus he
wrote to Margaret, the only person to whom he could
express his feelings. 'I would as soon have locked my dear
Nancy up in a nunnery as have put the smallest obstacle in
the way of her having a good husband . . . What I have
myself felt it is unnecessary to say. My parting from you
nearly broke my heart. But when I parted from you I had
Nancy: I had all my other relations: I had my friends: I had
my country. Now I have nothing except the resources of
my own mind, and the consciousness of having acted not
ungenerously . . . Whatever I suffer I have brought on myself. I have neglected the plainest lessons of reason and
experience. I have staked my happiness without calculating
the chances of the dice . . . I must bear my punishment as I

can and, above all, I must take care that the punishment does not extend beyond myself.'[1]

It must have helped Macaulay to pour out his true feelings about his sister's marriage to the only person who could understand. But before his letter had arrived in England Margaret was dead. Under the shadow of this tragedy, the news of which reached them on their honeymoon, the Trevelyans set up house with Macaulay in Calcutta, and there they lived with him until they all returned to England together, bringing with them their baby girl who had already found a place in her uncle's heart.

Macaulay's anodyne for unhappiness was two-fold—work and books. 'What a blessing it is to love books as I love them;—to be able to converse with the dead, and to live amidst the unreal!'[2] he said. 'Literature has saved my life and reason. Even now, I dare not, in the intervals of business, remain alone for a minute without a book in my hand.'[3]

As President of the Committee of Public Instruction, whose duty was in fact to construct a plan for the education of the whole Indian people, Macaulay found an outlet for his intense industry. The work occupied him for a time completely and the liberal system of education which was adopted throughout India was largely shaped by his mind. But this was not his only lasting contribution to the welfare of India. When he returned home in 1838 he left behind him the draft of a Penal Code, which, over twenty years later, after the Indian Mutiny, was with only slight revisions passed into law. Under this system the administration of criminal justice was 'entrusted to a very small number of English magistrates, organized according to a carefully devised system of appeal and supervision'. The disappearance of large-scale organized crime, which revo-

[1] 7 December 1834.
[2] Letter to Ellis, 8 February 1835.
[3] Ibid., 30 December 1835.

lutionized the life of the mass of the Indian people, was brought about by a few hundred civilians governing the continent according to the regulations laid down by the Indian Penal Code. The years that Macaulay spent in India brought immense and accumulating benefits to her people.

The homeward voyage, with the Trevelyans and their baby daughter, took nearly six months. (Macaulay employed the time in learning German.) Old Zachary Macaulay died just before his son and daughter reached England.

Before Macaulay had been home a twelve-month he had refused the position of Advocate-General and been elected M.P. for Edinburgh. The following September (1839) Lord Melbourne made him his Secretary at War with a seat in the Cabinet. He was immediately subjected to a violent attack, lasting several months, from *The Times*, faithful supporter of Peel, for heading the letter to his constituents, announcing that he had taken office, from Windsor Castle where he was staying. This attack (*The Times* referred to the new Minister always as 'Mr. Babbletongue Macaulay') affected him little. What cheered him immeasurably was the deferment, perhaps for ever, of the Trevelyans' return to India. Hannah's husband was that autumn appointed to the Assistant Secretaryship of the Treasury and for a year Macaulay took a house in Great College Street and insisted on their all living together.

'He is certainly more agreeable since his return from India,' said Sydney Smith. 'His enemies might perhaps have said before . . . that he talked rather too much; but now he has occasional flashes of silence that make his conversation perfectly delightful.' He seemed to have put aside all idea of writing and devoted himself to his official work. But in June 1841 Parliament was dissolved, Macaulay was returned unopposed and found his party in opposition. It was at this moment that the Trevelyans moved to

Clapham and that he began a residence which was to last for fifteen years in Albany.

'I own that I am quite delighted with our prospects. A strong opposition is the very thing that I wanted. I shall be heartily glad if it lasts till I can finish a History of England, from the Revolution, to the Accession of the House of Hanover. Then I shall be willing to go in again for a few years.'[1]

With every day that passed he felt happier in the turn his life had taken. His chambers were very comfortable and every corner of them was soon to be a library. In the quiet of his rooms, so like Cambridge, he found himself at last with his time to dispose of as he willed. To another man it might have seemed that he had earned a little leisure. To Macaulay it meant that he could turn happily to the beginning of a life's work.

'I can truly say that I have not, for many years, been so happy as I am at present,' he wrote soon after he had moved into E.1. 'Before I went to India, I had no prospect in the event of a change of Government, except that of living by my pen, and seeing my sisters governesses. In India I was an exile. When I came back, I was for a time at liberty; but I had before me the prospect of parting in a few months, perhaps for ever, with my dearest sister and her children. That misery was removed; but I found myself in office, a member of a Government wretchedly weak, and struggling for existence. Now I am free. I am independent. I am in Parliament, as honourably seated as a man may be. My family is comfortably off. I have leisure for literature; yet I am not reduced to the necessity of writing for money. If I had to choose a lot from all that there are in human life, I am not sure that I should prefer any to that which has fallen to me. I am sincerely and thoroughly contented.'[2]

He was soon happily at work on his *History*. 'I have at

[1] Letter to Ellis, 12 July 1841.
[2] Letter to M. Napier, 27 July 1841.

last begun my historical labours,' he wrote from Albany
in November 1841; 'I can hardly say with how much interest and delight . . . I shall not be satisfied unless I
produce something which shall for a few days supersede
the last fashionable novel on the tables of young ladies.'[1]
No English historian had ever had such an ambition.

But long before he had completed the first volume of his
History he had produced what he called a 'little volume' of
poems which, to his astonishment, was received with
acclamation by an enormous public. One of Macaulay's
idiosyncrasies was a delight in ballads and broadsheets,
both of his own day and of times past. His favourite occupation was to go for long rambles round London and particularly the back lanes of the City. His nephew said that
Macaulay knew the location and the stock-in-trade of
every bookstall in London. He bought from them not
only books but 'every half-penny song on which he could
lay his hands; if only it was decent, and a genuine, undoubted poem of the people'. He liked to tell the story of
how he was followed from one bookstall, where he had
bought a parcel of ballads, by a crowd of children whom
he heard discussing whether or not he was about to
sing.

He believed that the story of Romulus and Remus and
other similar legends derived from ballads of the early
Romans, which had since disappeared, and while he was in
India he had amused himself with trying to re-create
some of these long forgotten poems. Now, while embark-
ing on his life's work, he found time to complete and correct them. At his express wish his 'little volume' was published without any preliminary publicity. There was to be
'no puffing of any sort'. He meant to leave it 'as the
ostrich leaves her eggs in the sand'. To his surprise the
Lays of Ancient Rome were highly praised, even by his
erstwhile adversaries, in the Press. They sold like Walter
Scott's most popular poetry. Their swinging rhythm,

[1] Letter to M. Napier, 5 November 1841.

their stories of patriotism and courage stirred the blood of Englishmen. When Macaulay wrote them he had not been trying to write great poetry, but to give the effect of history sung in verse. In this he succeeded admirably, and lines from his ballads have lingered in the minds of Englishmen of every succeeding generation.

The tremendous success of the *Lays of Ancient Rome* must have been one of the reasons why his publishers began to press him for permission to re-publish in book form his reviews written for the *Edinburgh Review*. Macaulay had already refused this suggestion only a few months before. But it was exasperating to learn that no fewer than three unauthorized editions of his essays had been published in America, and as copyright laws stood then, he not only received no money for these pirated editions, but had also the provocation of seeing 'trash, of which I am perfectly guiltless', inserted among his writings. Nevertheless he had, up to this moment, steadily refused to have his essays re-published in England.

'The public judges,' he said, 'and ought to judge, in-dulgently of periodical works. They are not expected to be highly finished. Their natural life is only six weeks. Sometimes their writer is at a distance from the books to which he wants to refer. Sometimes he is forced to hurry through his task in order to catch the post . . . All this is readily forgiven if there be a certain spirit and vivacity in his style. But, as soon as he republishes, he challenges a comparison with all the most symmetrical and polished of human compositions . . . in that form they would be compared, not with the rant and twaddle of the daily and weekly Press, but with Burke's pamphlets, with Pascal's letters, with Addison's *Spectators* . . . What the Yankees may do I cannot help; but I will not found my pretensions to the rank of a classic on my reviews.'[1]

If the decision had been left to Macaulay alone, the famous *Essays*, so widely read and often quoted, would

[1] Letter to M. Napier, 25 April 1842.

never have been re-published. But the unscrupulous behaviour of the American publishers forced him to change
his mind. Finding that there was a widespread demand for
these writings in England, they began to send their
editions across the Atlantic in large numbers. 'The question now is merely this,' wrote Macaulay from Albany in
December 1842, 'whether Longman and I, or Carey and
Hart of Philadelphia, shall have the supplying of the
English market with these papers.' In these circumstances
he reluctantly decided to re-publish and spent the first
few weeks of 1843, in his ground floor rooms in Albany,
revising his *Essays* and writing a preface to them.

Thus this celebrated book was sent forth, to meet with
instant success, to be read and enjoyed by succeeding
generations, even by those who disagree with the author's
inflexible historical prejudices. Macaulay had determined
that the great *History of England from the Revolution to the
Accession of the House of Hanover* was to be the crowning
work of his life and the achievement on which he would
base his claim to be a great writer and historian. It is
ironical that the readers of the *History* are now few, in
comparison with the multitude who know Macaulay
through his *Essays*, which he called 'hasty and imperfect',
and did not wish to re-publish, and the *Lays of Ancient
Rome*, of which he wrote 'the success of my little book has
far exceeded its just claims'.

Of this conclusion Macaulay had no suspicion. Gradually he gave up even his reviews for the *Edinburgh*, so that
he might concentrate completely on the *History*. There
were people, he said, who could carry on twenty works at
a time. 'Southey would write the History of Brazil before
breakfast, an ode after breakfast, then the History of the
Peninsular War till dinner, and an article for the *Quarterly
Review* in the evening.' But he was of a different temper.
He preferred never to write until his subject had for the
time driven every other out of his head. When he turned
from one work to another he found that he lost time in the

transition. 'I must not go on dawdling, and reproaching myself, all my life.'[1]

Macaulay's conception of 'dawdling' was certainly different from that of most people. Every day in Albany he set himself to complete his 'task'. This was the minimum amount of writing that he was determined to do. It consisted of six pages of foolscap, which would make two pages of print. But reading and study were behind every line. Thackeray wrote of his prodigious memory and vast learning, of 'the wonderful industry, the honest, humble, previous toil of this great scholar. He reads twenty books to write a sentence; he travels a hundred miles to make a line of description.' There was truth in what sounds like flattery. He was willing to take almost incredible pains to achieve accuracy, and yet ironically much of the reading and travelling in search of truth was wasted. Truth in his writing was distorted by the unyielding prejudice of his own opinions, which were formed early in his life and never altered. Facts were tailored to fit these preconceived ideas. Walter Bagehot summed up this fatal weakness by applying to him the words used of the younger Pitt: 'He never grew, he was cast.'[2]

Nevertheless, few historians can have been more conscientious. When the first two volumes of his *History* had been published, he laid down his future programme in his journal:

'I will first set myself to know the whole subject:—to get, by reading and travelling, a full acquaintance with William's reign. I reckon that it will take me eighteen months to do this. I must visit Holland, Belgium, Scotland, Ireland, France. The Dutch archives and French archives must be ransacked . . . I must see Londonderry, the Boyne, Aghrim, Limerick, Kinsale, Namur again, Landen, Steinkirk. I must turn over hundreds, thousands, of pamphlets. Lambeth, the Bodleian and the other Oxford

[1] Letter to M. Napier, 18 January 1843.
[2] Walter Bagehot, *Literary Studies*, Vol. II.

Libraries, the Devonshire Papers, the British Museum, must be explored, and notes made: and then I shall go to work.'[1]

But Macaulay's mind was not entirely engrossed by his academic work. Mrs. Trevelyan used all her influence to persuade him to accept an occasional invitation. Few of those who met him on these social occasions, she thought, and enjoyed his 'animated conversation' could guess how much rather he would have remained at home or what difficulty she had to prevent his becoming a recluse. His devotion to his sister was now extended to her children, to whom he was 'Uncle Tom', the perfect uncle.

Every Easter he would take the whole Trevelyan family on a tour of two cathedral towns, spending Good Friday in one and Easter Sunday in the other, and return to London on Monday. Each year he would choose different towns—York and Lincoln, or Salisbury and Winchester, varying their travels by a trip to Paris or the great churches of the Loire. Their party just filled a railway carriage, in which Macaulay would keep up a never-ceasing flow of jokes, rhymes and puns. In the evenings, back at the hotel after their sightseeing, he would read aloud, or they would play games of capping verses or making impromptu rhymes.

In London he was equally fond of the children's company. He was never bored by them. Often he would walk to Clapham, or later to Westbourne Terrace, book in hand, and finding his sister out, would spend the rest of the morning playing with her children. With them he was so merry and unassuming that, as they- grew up, they found it difficult to realize that their uncle was, to the rest of the world, a famous man. When they were very young he would build a den of newspapers behind the sofa from which he would emerge as a tiger, a game which terrified yet fascinated them. When they were away he would write them long letters, carefully adjusted to the age of

[1] 8 February, 1849.

the recipient, and childish poems which he would pains-
takingly print in capital letters. These verses and the
rhymed Valentines which his nieces received on St. Valen-
tine's Day he attributed with such conviction to his old
colleague, 'the Judicious Poet', that in spite of some of
them appearing amazingly apt to the immediate event,
it was a long time before the children realized that he was
the author.

Perhaps the days he enjoyed most—he was always
trying to make them more frequent—were those when he
entertained his two nephews and his niece in his rooms at
Albany before taking them sight-seeing—to the Zoo, to
the Colosseum in Regent's Park,[1] to Madame Tussaud's
Chamber of Horrors, or for long walks through the back
ways of the City, when he would tell them thrilling tales
of the people who had lived and died there. 'Fanny brought
George and Margaret with Charley Cropper,[2] to the
Albany at one yesterday,' he wrote in January 1845. 'I
gave them some dinner; fowl, ham, marrow bones, tart,

[1] The Colosseum stood about two hundred yards north of Park
Square, looking west over Regent's Park. It was a very large building,
surmounted by an immense dome made entirely of glass, and fronted
by a grand portico. In form it bore some resemblance to the Pantheon
in Rome. Inside there were many attractions, grottoes, a Gothic
aviary, classical ruins, a stalactite cavern and a Swiss chalet with real
water running through the mountain scenery. But its most famous
and popular feature was the Great Panorama of London. The visitor
viewed this from two galleries, one higher than the other, intended
to correspond with the galleries in the dome of St. Paul's Cathedral.
Below him a framework, made in exact imitation of the outside of the
dome, gave him the illusion of looking out from the top of St. Paul's,
with the sky overhead and a magnificent view of the whole city spread
out below him. This enormous panorama, which was said to cover
more than an acre of canvas, was painted from the sketches made by
an intrepid Mr. Horner, who in 1821 had himself slung in a crow's
nest on the top of the Cross on St. Paul's Cathedral, so that the views
should be accurately presented. The Colosseum opened in 1829 and
was demolished in 1875.

[2] Mrs. Trevelyan's two children and the son of Macaulay's dead
sister, Margaret.

ice, olives, and champagne. I found it difficult to think of any sight for the children: however, I took them to the National Gallery, and was excessively amused with the airs of connoisseurship which Charley and Margaret gave themselves, and with Georgy's honestly avowed weariness. "Let us go. There is nothing here that I care for at all." When I put him into the carriage, he said, half sulkily: "I do not call this seeing sights. I have seen no sight today." '

Some months after this outing, in December 1845, Macaulay was nearly drawn back into active political life. He had lately been content to make speeches only on subjects of which he had special knowledge, while his party were in opposition. Sir Robert Peel, faced with the prospect of famine and riots in Ireland, had decided that the Corn Laws which his party had been elected to maintain, must be repealed. He resigned and Lord John Russell called a consultation of Whigs—a shadow Cabinet of five, which included Macaulay.

On 19 December Lord John Russell was sent for by the Queen. The following day ·Macaulay wrote to his sister from Albany that it was an odd thing to see a Ministry making. He had never witnessed the process before. 'Lord John has been all day in his inner library. His ante-chamber has been filled with comers and goers, some talking in knots, some writing notes at tables. Every five minutes somebody is called into the inner room. As the people who have been closeted come out, the cry of the whole body of expectants is, "What are you?" ' Macaulay was called in almost as soon as he had arrived. Lord John told him that he had been trying to ascertain his wishes and believed that he wanted leisure and quiet more than salary and business. He therefore offered him the Pay Office, which Macaulay at once accepted. It would mean, he explained to his sister, that he would have to attend Parliament more often than he had of late, but he would have two thousand pounds a year and his mornings would be as much his own as if he were out of office. Some other arrangements promised to be less satisfactory. Palmerston would hear of nothing but the Foreign Office and Lord Grey therefore declined taking any place.

Macaulay's forebodings were rapidly justified. That evening, as he was undressing late at night, a knock came at the door of his chambers. A messenger had come from Lord John with a short note. The quarrel between Lord Grey and Lord Palmerston had made it impossible to form a Ministry. Unlike most of his colleagues, Macaulay was not really regretful at the *débâcle* of Whig hopes. He went to bed and slept soundly. Next morning he was inclined to think that things had turned out for the best. 'Perhaps the pleasure with which I have this morning looked round my chambers, and resumed my History, has something to do in making me thus cheerful.'[1]

Nevertheless, only six months later, in June 1846, he found himself once more in office in a Whig Government. As Paymaster-General of the Army he was re-elected for Edinburgh, after a spirited display on the hustings, beating his opponent by two to one at the poll and returning to Albany in triumph. He told his sister that he had become somewhat effeminate in literary repose and leisure. She would not know him again now that his blood was up. He soon found that the duties of his office were even less onerous than he had expected. As a Minister he had to be present at the House of Commons in the evenings but, apart from this and attendance at an occasional Board Meeting at Chelsea Hospital, he had little else to do for his £2,000 a year. His new position in no way prevented work on his *History*; he was soon immersed in the story of Monmouth's rebellion.

It was in December 1846 that Macaulay moved from the chambers E.1 to the much larger second-floor apartment, F.3, in the tall brick building which Holland had

[1] Letter to Ellis, 20 December, 1845.

designed to end the stuccoed row of chambers on the west side of Albany. Here he could house his enormous collection of books in the lofty sitting-room, with its large window looking north up the length of Savile Row, and its double doors opening at the opposite end into a fine dining-room. His nephew said that every corner of these chambers was library. They were 'comfortably, though not very brightly furnished. The ornaments were few, but choice:—half a dozen fine Italian engravings from his favourite great masters; a handsome French clock, provided with a singularly melodious set of chimes, the gift of his friend and publisher, Mr. Thomas Longman; and the well-known bronze statuettes of Voltaire and Rousseau (neither of them heroes of his own), which had been presented to him by Lady Holland as a remembrance of her husband.'[1]

The charming northern entrance to Albany, with the old lamp overhead and the porter's lodge inside the spiked gates, was close to the entrance of the staircase to Macaulay's new rooms. The story has been told[2] that these iron gates were hurriedly erected after he had received an anonymous letter, warning him that Albany would be broken into the following night by a gang of thieves. It was later revealed, this story goes on, that the letter was a hoax played on him by his niece, Margaret Trevelyan, afterwards Lady Knutsford, but the spiked iron gates have been retained to this day.

There is no published authority for this story and Professor G. M. Trevelyan, Lady Knutsford's nephew, can-

[1] Some confusion has been caused by Macaulay's nephew and biographer writing that when his uncle moved to Albany it was to 'a commodious set of rooms on a second floor in the Albany', of which he gave the description quoted above. The reason for the mistake must be that Macaulay headed his letters only 'Albany, London' and that his biographer, having often visited F.3, but being only 8 years old when his uncle left E.1, assumed that his uncle had always lived in the rooms which he knew so well.

[2] H. Furniss, *Paradise in Piccadilly*.

not either confirm or contradict it. Evidently it was not a
family story, as he had never heard it, but 'Margaret was
on such terms with her beloved uncle, that her playing
him such a trick is not unlikely'.[1]

Macaulay made only five speeches during the sessions
of 1846 and 1847, but whenever he was to speak the House
filled well beforehand, and one of these speeches he afterwards said was his very best. It was in support of the Ten
Hours' Bill, which sought to regulate the hours of work by
law. Macaulay made an effective comparison with the
benefits of the Sabbath.

'Man, man is the great instrument that produces
wealth . . . we are not poorer, but richer, because we
have, through many ages, rested from our labour one day
in seven. That day is not lost. While industry is sus-
pended, while the plough lies in the furrow, while the Exchange is silent, while no smoke ascends from the factory,
a process is going on quite as important to the wealth of
nations as any process which is performed on more busy
days. Man, the machine of machines, the machine compared with which all the contrivances of the Watts and the
Arkwrights are worthless, is repairing and winding up,
so that he returns to his labours on the Monday with
clearer intellect, with livelier spirits, with renewed cor-
poral vigour. Never will I believe that what makes a
population stronger, and healthier, and wiser, and better,
can ultimately make it poorer.'

In political, literary, and social circles Macaulay was
admired and respected, but he was now to receive a rebuff from the people of Edinburgh. A General Election
came in the summer of 1847. Until this moment election to
Parliament had always been easy to him—it was merely a
question of whether he would choose to stand as a candidate. But for some time he had been becoming increasingly unpopular in Edinburgh. His constituents believed,
perhaps rightly, that he cared more for his *History* than

[1] Letter to the author.

for them. He did not answer their letters promptly, and his replies, when received, were found to be so brief that they were thought contemptuous. Even more important, when a deputation came all the way to London to enlighten him with their views, they would no sooner enter their member's chambers than they would be swept away by a flood of eloquence and would find themselves leaving, some time later, having had no opportunity to acquaint him with their own opinions.

They had their revenge. After a short, sharp contest of days, Macaulay was defeated. While the crowds celebrated their noisy triumph in the streets of Edinburgh he sat in his hotel room and wrote to his sister, Hannah, 'I hope that you will not be much vexed; for I am not vexed, but as cheerful as ever I was in my life. I have been completely beaten . . . I will make no hasty resolutions but everything seems to indicate that I ought to take this opportunity of retiring from public life.'[1]

A few quiet days and nights among his books in Albany soon restored Macaulay's strength and spirits, but he felt that his future had been decided for him. A week after polling-day he wrote to his unmarried sister, Fanny, 'I am here in solitude, reading and working with great satisfaction to myself. My table is covered with letters of condolence, and with invitations from half the places which have not yet chosen members. I have been asked to stand for Ayr, for Wigton, and for Oxfordshire . . . I did not know how great a politician I was till my Edinburgh friends chose to dismiss me from politics. I never can leave public life with more dignity and grace than at present.'

He felt no temptation to accept the offers of other constituencies. His mind was made up. No longer would he be torn between the rival magnets of public life and literature. 'Having once been manumitted, after the old fashion by a slap in the face, I shall not take to bondage

[1] 30 July 1847.

again.'[1] He settled down to a programme of unremitting work.

By the following summer (1848) the first two volumes of his *History* were in the publishers' hands. Even then he would not allow himself to relax, and insisted on correcting every smallest error and re-polishing every unbalanced sentence. But he could still find time for his niece. He wrote to his sister that Margaret had passed a pleasant day with him. They had a long walk, a great deal of chat, a very nice dinner, and a quiet, happy evening. That was his only holiday in the week. He was working 'with scarcely any intermission from seven in the morning to seven in the afternoon' and would continue to do so during the next ten days. Then his labours would become lighter and in about three weeks would cease completely. There would still be a fortnight before publication.

On 18 November 1848 he began to keep his diary again.

'*Albany.*—after the lapse of more than nine years, I begin my journal again. What a change! I have been, since the last lines were written, a member of two Parliaments, and of two Cabinets. I have published several volumes with success. I have escaped from Parliament, and am living in the way best suited to my temper. I lead a college life in London, with the comforts of domestic life near me; for Hannah and her children are very dear to me . . . To-day I enjoyed my new liberty, after having been most severely worked during three months in finishing my History and correcting proofs. I rose at half after nine, read at breakfast Fearon's *Sketches of America*, and then finished Lucian's critique on the bad historians of his time . . . Ellis came to dinner at seven. I gave him a lobster curry, woodcock, and macaroni.'

He had armed himself with all his philosophy for the event of a failure, but he need not have worried. Within three days of its publication the *History's* first edition of

[1] Letter to Ellis, 30 July 1847.

three thousand was nearly sold out and a second was preparing. The book was published in large editions in America, Paris and Brussels. It was read in England by people who had never read history before and its effect was widespread. A meeting near Manchester passed a vote of thanks to Mr. Macaulay 'for having written a history which working men can understand'. The Chancellor of the Exchequer said all members of Parliament had read it. This startled Walter Bagehot. 'What other books could ever be fancied to have been read by them?' he asked. 'A county member . . . hardly reads two volumes *per* existence. Years ago Macaulay said a History of England might become more in demand at the circulating libraries than the last novel. He has actually made his words true.'[1]

This must perhaps have been one of the happiest periods in Macaulay's life, living book in hand, rambling through the City streets, exploring the contents of bookstalls and print-shops or taking his long Sunday walks from Piccadilly to Clapham and from Clapham to Richmond or Blackwall.

His presence was still sought for every kind of social occasion, but he went little into the world. His sister, Hannah, and her family were always first in his affections, but he had also a small number of intimate friends who enjoyed long discussions of historical and literary subjects. They had to be both quick and determined to make their opinions heard when Macaulay was present.

'Never were such torrents of good talk as burst and sputtered over from Macaulay and Hallam,' wrote one of them, Lord Carlisle, in his journal. On 12 February 1849—'Breakfasted with Macaulay. There were Van de Weyer, Hallam, Charles Austin, Panizzi, Colonel Mure, and Dicky Milnes, but he went to Yorkshire after the first cup. The conversation ranged the world; art, ancient and modern; the Greek tragedians; characters of the orators,—

[1] Walter Bagehot, op. cit., Vol. II.

how Philip and Alexander probably felt towards them as
we do towards a scurrilous newspaper editor. It is a re-
freshing break in common-place life. I stayed till past
twelve. His rooms at the top of Albany are very liveable
and studious-looking.'

On 25 May Lord Carlisle breakfasted with Rogers in
St. James's Place, where Macaulay seems to have maintained the conversation on more intellectual topics than
were usual in that house. 'It was a beautiful morning, and
his house, view, and garden looked lovely. It was extremely
pleasant. Mahon tried to defend Clarendon, but was put
down by Hallam and Macaulay. Macaulay was very
severe on Cranmer. Then we all quoted a good deal;
Macaulay (as I had heard him before), four very fine lines
from the Tristia, as being so contrary to their usual
whining tone, and of even a Miltonic loftiness of sentiment . . . I think we must have rather shot beyond
Rogers sometimes.'

Lord Carlisle's diary also recalls a dinner at his own
house in October. 'The evening went off very cosily and
pleasantly, as must almost always happen with Macaulay.
He was rather paradoxical, as is apt to be his manner, and
almost his only social fault. The greatest marvel about
him is the quantity of trash he remembers. He went off at
score with Lord Thurlow's poetry.' Of another evening he
wrote, 'Macaulay's flow never ceased once during the
four hours, but it is never over-bearing.' The conversation
at a breakfast in Macaulay's chambers 'got upon moral
obligations, and was so eagerly carried on by Hallam,
Whewell and Macaulay, though without the slightest loss
of temper, that not one sentence could any of them finish.'[1]

With his friends he discussed Junius and expounded
'the irresistible proofs for Sir Philip Francis'. But not
everyone took as much pleasure in Macaulay's memory.
Thomas Carlyle, an equally formidable conversationalist,
met Macaulay at Lord Ashburton's, and was bored by his

[1] Sir G. O. Trevelyan, op. cit., pp. 478–80.

arguments. 'As if it could matter the value of a brass farthing to any living human being who was the author of Junius!'

His nephew has described Macaulay's appearance during these discussions which he so much enjoyed. He would sit bolt upright, with his hands resting on the arms of his chair or folded over the handle of his walking-stick, his great eye-brows knit if the subject was one which had to be thought out as he went along. His voice was pleasant and sonorous and his language was always admirably clear. 'To get at his meaning people had never the need to think twice, and they certainly had seldom the time.'

His memory remained fantastic. It seemed to retain indefinitely everything that he had ever read. When challenged he repeated at once the names of the owners of all the carriages that went to Clarissa Harlowe's funeral, and wrote on the spot a full list of the Senior Wranglers at Cambridge, with their dates and colleges, for the hundred years during which their names had been recorded in the University Calendar. On another occasion he was asked if he knew his Popes and confessed that he always got wrong among the Innocents. Could he say his Archbishops of Canterbury? 'Any fool,' said Macaulay scornfully, 'could say his Archbishops of Canterbury backwards,' and off he went at speed, 'drawing breath only once to remark on the oddity of there having been both an Archbishop Sancroft and an Archbishop Bancroft', until he was stopped at Cranmer.[1]

Even in Royal circles he now felt sufficiently at ease to talk as much as he did elsewhere. When he had first dined at the Palace ten years before, he had been sufficiently intimidated to attempt to adjust his voice to the near-whispers of the courtiers. When presented to the Queen he 'had the honour of a conversation with her of about two minutes, and assured her that India was hot, and that I

[1] Sir G. O. Trevelyan, op. cit., p. 484.

kept my health there.' But in the years that followed, during which he dined frequently, both as a Cabinet Minister and as a private guest, he apparently lost his inhibitions. He was observed to be 'very interesting to listen to; quite immeasurably abundant in anecdote and knowledge', and on at least one occasion he went so far as to correct the Queen when, talking of his book, she remarked that she had nothing to say for her poor ancestor, James the Second. 'Not Your Majesty's ancestor, Your Majesty's predecessor,' said Macaulay. 'I meant it as a compliment and she seemed to take it so.'[1]

But he was never deflected by social life, in however grand a milieu, from the work which was so precious to him, and rebuked himself in his private journal for any backslidings. On the morning of 26 March 1849, he received a letter from his publisher, Longman, to tell him that the third edition of his book was sold out 'to the last copy'. Then came a call from a friend 'with whom I had much good talk which occupied most of the morning. I must not go on in this dawdling way. Soon the correspondence to which my book has given occasion will be over; the correcting of proof-sheets will be over; the mornings will be mild; the sun will be up early; and I will try to be up early too. I should like to get again into the habit of working three hours before breakfast. Once I had it, and I may easily recover it. A man feels his conscience so light during the day when he has done a good piece of work with a clear head before leaving his bed-room.'

His *History* was now the prime object of his life. When summoned to the Palace by Prince Albert and, to his astonishment, pressed to accept the Professorship of Modern History at Cambridge, he was resolute in refusing it. 'It would be strange,' he wrote in his journal that evening, 'if, having sacrificed for liberty a seat in the Cabinet and £2,500 a year, I should now sacrifice liberty for a chair at Cambridge and £400 a year. Besides, I

[1] *Journal*, 9 March 1850.

never could do two things at once. If I lectured well, my History must be given up.'[1]

In the summer he took a month's holiday from his work, the first fortnight in Ireland, for which he prepared himself by looking through Swift's Correspondence and a shelf-full of Irish novels, and reading more carefully Moore's *Life of Sheridan*, the *Life of Flood* and the *Memoirs of Wolfe Tone*. On the express train from London to Holyhead he read the *Lives of the Emperors* from Maximin to Carinus in the Augustan History. Deprived of a reading light, he whiled away the crossing of the Irish Channel, sitting in his great coat on deck in the starlight, by reciting *Paradise Lost* to himself. He had repeated about half when he saw the lights of Dublin Bay.

Back at Albany his daily entry in his journal begins or ends with the words: 'Did my task'; 'My task, or something over'; 'Wrote my regular quantity,—six foolscap pages of my scrawl, which will be about two pages in print'; 'Wrote fast, and long . . . I have got far beyond my task'; 'I sate down doggedly, as Johnson used to say, and did my task, but somewhat against my will'; 'Not quite my whole task; but I have a grand purple patch to sew on, and I must take time.'

We have a good idea of Macaulay's personal appearance at the time when he was working so hard in his second set of chambers in Albany. On 19 February 1850, he took his sister to George Richmond's studio to see his portrait, and she pronounced it an excellent likeness. Macaulay, too, was pleased with it. 'I am no judge of the likeness; but the face is characteristic. It is the face of a man with considerable mental powers, great boldness and frankness, and a quick relish for pleasure. It is not unlike Mr. Fox's face in general expression. I am quite content to have such a physiognomy.'

From the artist's studio he went home to amuse himself by counting his books. In the front of the shelves he

[1] 1 July 1849.

EDWARD BULWER, 1ST
LORD LYTTON, FROM A
PORTRAIT BY H. W.
PICKERSGILL IN 1831
National Portrait Gallery

ROSINA BULWER AND
HER DAUGHTER, EMILY
*From a miniature at Knebworth
painted 1831-2 in the possession
of Lady Hermione Cobbold*

DESPERATE AFFRAY WITH THE POLICE

AT THE ALBANY.

MR. GUNDRY KEEPS THE POLICE AT BAY. THE FRONT PAGE OF "THE SUNDAY CHRONICLE AND PEOPLE'S WEEKLY ADVERTIZER", MARCH 7, 1841

calculated that there were about six thousand one hundred books, with several hundreds more, mostly novels, behind them. 'I might call the whole collection at least 7,000. It will probably amount to 10,000 by the time that my lease of these chambers expires; unless, indeed, I expire first, which I think very probable.' Thoughts of the passing of his life occurred to him again a few months later. 'My birthday. I am fifty. Well, I have had a happy life . . . I have not children of my own, it is true; but I have children whom I love as if they were my own, and who, I believe, love me. I wish that the next ten years may be as happy as the last ten. But I rather wish it than hope it.'[1]

He had always been a generous man, giving freely, not only to his relations, but to many in distress who were unknown to him. Now with the enormous success of the volumes of his *History* already published and the continuous demand for his other works, ('even the hasty and imperfect articles which I wrote for the *Edinburgh Review* are valued by a generation which has sprung up since they were first published'), he felt he could afford a little personal luxury. As usual, he walked from Piccadilly to Westbourne Terrace, to talk the matter over with his sister, Hannah, and together they decided that he should set up a brougham. 'The cost will be small, and the comfort great. It is but fair, too, that I should have some of the advantages of my own labour.'

So at half-past seven on 16 January 1851, Macaulay, just returned to Albany from a visit to Windsor, could have been seen stepping into his brougham to dine with Lord John Russell, 'pleased and proud, and thinking how unjustly poor Pepys was abused for noting in his diary the satisfaction it gave him to ride in his own coach. This is the first time I ever had a carriage of my own, except when in office.'

On the 1st of May he left Albany to see the Opening of the Great Exhibition in Hyde Park. At first he wandered

[1] *Journal*, 25 October 1850.

along the Serpentine admiring the spectacle. There were immense crowds on both sides of the water—near three hundred thousand people in the Park. Through the green boughs he could see boats and little frigates darting across the lake. The flags, the music, the guns, the good temper of the multitude—all delighted him. 'There is just as much chance of a revolution in England as of the falling of the moon.' At last he made his way into the great building —'a most gorgeous sight; vast; graceful; beyond the dreams of Arabian romances. I cannot think that the Caesars ever exhibited a more splendid spectacle. I was quite dazzled, and I felt as I did on entering St. Peter's.'

When he got home he settled down, as always, to read —this time to finish *Persuasion*. 'I have now read over again all Miss Austen's novels. Charming they are; but I found a little more to criticize than formerly. Yet there are in the world no compositions which approach nearer to perfection.'[1]

A few months later, in January 1852, when Palmerston had just been removed from the Foreign Office, Lord John Russell invited Macaulay to join the Cabinet, but he refused, pleading his literary habits and reputation, his health, temper and tastes. He was happy in his life of work and reading, interspersed with breakfasts and dinners with 'good talk' at a few favoured houses. He rarely went now to bigger parties. Yet even his steady determination to let nothing deflect him from his task was not proof against the astonishing, unsolicited tribute which now came to him from his former constituents in Edinburgh. Ashamed, apparently, of their previous treatment of him, they decided to show their esteem by electing him —without asking him to go there, or to give any pledges, or even any opinions, on political matters. All he was asked was to say that, if he was chosen on those terms, he would sit as their Member. Macaulay was not at all pleased by this prospect. Though he was resolved not, in

[1] *Journal*, 1 May 1851.

any case, to accept office, it might mean postponing the appearance of his next two volumes by a year, or even two. But he did not feel that he could in duty decline the invitation, which he saw as a vindication of the freedom of conscience of parliamentary representatives. 'They should not expect slavish obedience from men of spirit and ability' was still his opinion.

In these singular circumstances he was elected by a handsome majority. But there had already been ominous signs of a decline in his health. He had complained of feeling faint, out of sorts, languid and depressed. He felt himself unable to undertake the long journey to Edinburgh and a public appearance. His doctor was sent for and found that the action of his heart was seriously deranged. From that time Macaulay was a semi-invalid. He appeared twenty years older in a week. Bronchitis and then asthma afflicted him—no more long walks, unmindful of wind or weather. But he still would not surrender without a fight. He refused the doctor's advice to apply for the Chiltern Hundreds. He went but seldom to the House of Commons, but when he did, and the words 'Macaulay's up!' were heard again after so many years, they emptied committee rooms, as in the old days they had emptied clubs.

For the summer months he now very often leased a small house outside London, but the winters were hard for him and he felt he must conserve what strength he still had for his *History*, 'a work which is the business and the pleasure of my life'. He knew now that he would never finish it to the grand design that he had planned, but he was determined to complete William's reign. So he worked on in his library in Albany, weeks at a time passed by the fireside, unable to face the steep stairs outside. 'I am a prisoner to my room, or nearly so. I do nothing but write or read.' Government crises meant little to him, though he grieved over Gladstone's lamentable account of affairs in the Crimea. He was thankful that his illness absolved him from voting and was only prevailed on to

continue as their Member by earnest and repeated solici-
tations from his leading supporters in Edinburgh.

'Odd,' he wrote in his journal, 'that here, within a
few yards of all the bustle of politics, I should be as quiet
as a hermit; as quiet as Cowper was at Olney . . . buried
in old pamphlets and broadsides; turning away from the
miseries of Balaklava to the battle of Steinkirk, on which
I was busied today . . . Hannah, Margaret, Alice, Trevelyan and George are as kind as possible. I want no
more; but I have other very kind visitors. I cannot think
that this can go on long. But I hope that I shall bring out
my two volumes.'[1]

By November 1855 he was at last correcting the proofs,
both morning and afternoon, only leaving his desk when
the lamp was brought in, to draw his easy chair on to the
hearth-rug, with a favourite book in his hand. It was to
this room, which he rarely left in these winter days, that
Longman came, first to tell him that 25,000 copies had
been printed of the two new volumes, then, the day before
publication, to say that they must print more.

No such edition had ever been printed of so large a
work and its success was greater even than that of the
previous volumes. As the New Year dawned he was able
to say that though his health was very indifferent, he was
happy in fame, fortune and family affection. He amused
himself by reading 'miscellaneous trifles' from the back
row of his books, and one day he even gave a breakfast
party, with Jowett and his old friend, Ellis, his sister and
niece and two young Fellows of Trinity, Vaughan Haw-
kins and Montague Butler. 'After long silence and solitude I poured myself out very freely and generally. They
stayed till past one; a pretty good proof that they were
entertained.'[2]

It was in this month (January 1856) that Dean Milman
and the Duchess of Argyll combined to urge him to move

[1] 29 January 1855.
[2] *Journal*, 4 January 1856.

to a charming country villa which was for sale on Campden Hill. His friends must have felt, since the onset of his illness, that chambers on the second floor were no longer the ideal residence for a man with asthma and a weak heart. At Campden Hill he would be able to step from his library windows on to the lawn. It seemed to offer more comfort to a tired man, whom the steep stone stairs of Albany had lately kept prisoner in his room. Nothing, he said, would at one time have reconciled him to the thought of leaving Albany. But now he saw that his friends were right. He bought the house on Campden Hill and began to move his furniture and to empty his book-shelves.

One more happy event was to take place in his chambers. 'Longman came, with a very pleasant announcement. He and his partners find that they are overflowing with money, and think that they cannot invest it better than by advancing to me, on the usual terms of course, part of what will be due to me in December.' In short the publisher had come to present to Macaulay a cheque for £20,000. 'What a sum to be gained by one edition of a book!' exclaimed the gratified author.

Before leaving for his new home, where he was to spend the last three years of his life, becoming in turn a peer, and High Steward of the Borough of Cambridge, an office dear to him because it had been held by Bacon, Cromwell and Clarendon—before he leaves Albany for ever he entertains his friend, Ellis, to one last dinner, and makes a last entry in his journal.

'May 1, 1856.—The change draws very near. After fifteen happy years passed in the Albany I am going to leave it, thrice as rich a man as when I entered it, and far more famous; with health impaired, but with affections as warm and faculties as vigorous as ever . . . I do not at all expect to live fifteen years more. If I do, I cannot hope that they will be so happy as the last fifteen. The removal makes me sad, and would make me sadder but for the extreme discomfort in which I have been living during the last week. The books are gone, and the shelves look like a skeleton. Tomorrow I take final leave of this room where I have spent most of the waking hours of so many years. Already its aspect is changed. It is the corpse of what it was on Sunday. I hate partings. To-day, even while I climbed the endless steps, panting and weary, I thought that it was for the last time, and the tears would come into my eyes. I have been happy at the top of this toilsome stair. Ellis came to dinner;—the last of probably four hundred dinners, or more, that we have had in these chambers. Then to bed. Everything that I do is coloured by the thought that it is for the last time. One day there will come a last in good earnest.'

II

In December 1853, there were rumours of the sale of Burlington House, and the Trustees had to consider whether anything could be done to protect the rights of Albany proprietors to light and air.

Burlington House with its gardens was sold to the Government in 1854 for £140,000, double the price given by Lord George Cavendish in 1815, but for several years it was doubtful for what purpose it would be used. It was suggested that a member of the Royal Family might eventually live there, and the University of London was allowed the temporary use of the mansion. Then a plan was made to rebuild on the whole site, with two great courtyards and a street running through them from Piccadilly to Burlington Gardens, the buildings to be divided between the Royal Academy and various learned societies.

The Trustees had obtained Counsel's opinion, which they found with distress to be that the owners of the Burlington House garden were entitled to obstruct the light and air from the windows of Albany, and might build upon their own ground 'as close as they please to the Albany Chambers'. So when the grand plan was proposed for re-building on the whole site they wrote to Lord John Manners, then Chief Commissioner of Works, hoping that he would 'kindly stipulate that any building which the Academy may intend to erect on the site may be so planned . . . that the Gentlemen residing on the West side of Albany may not be prejudiced in their enjoyment of light and air.'

A change of Government caused all these plans to be put aside, and Lord Palmerston's Ministry proposed to build premises for a National Gallery on to the back of the house. But the House of Commons refused to allow the pictures to be moved from Trafalgar Square, and the next Government, under Lord Russell, made arrangements for buildings to be erected at the far end of the garden facing Burlington Gardens, to house the University of London.

In the same year (1866) Lord Derby's Ministry leased the house to the Royal Academy, and also the ground be-tween the house and the University buildings at the end of the garden, on which to build picture galleries. In September of that year the old garden wall was knocked down and the foundations of the new University buildings were laid. At the beginning of 1867 work was begun on the new galleries for the Royal Academy, in the garden immediately behind the house, and the following year the East wing, the stables and the colonnade in front of the house were pulled down and the long wall on Piccadilly destroyed, to make way for buildings to house the learned societies.

All this activity next door must have made Albany much less peaceful for a time. It had also kept the Trustees busy. The new building in Burlington Gardens was planned to come 'within 13 feet of Albany'. A deputation waited on Lord John Manners, who was again in charge. He 'ex-pressed himself very favourably and appeared willing to meet the views of the deputation but referred them to the Architect . . . much to the regret of the deputation as they feared that unless His Lordship decided the question nothing satisfactory would be done by way of compromise.'[1]

Their fears proved unfounded. An agreement was reached about the residents' right to light and air; part of the garden wall might be pulled down behind blocks D, E and F, and certain windows might be opened in that direction on payment of 5s. a year for each window. This dealt only with the new buildings for the University of London. Another agreement would be made on the same lines for 'the land allotted by the Government for the Royal Academy'.[2]

The Trustees must have sighed with relief at such a satisfactory outcome of their long efforts, and those residents of Albany who today inhabit the chambers on the west of the Rope Walk should bless their memory.

III

It is odd how few references to world events find their way into the decorous minutes of the Trustees' Meetings. There is nothing to remind us of Nelson's victory and death in 1805, of Napoleon's exile to Elba, nor his return and defeat at Waterloo.

One of the few reflections from the outside world is found in the minutes of the Trustees' 440th Meeting on 13 May 1856, when the Secretary produced estimates 'for a Gas Illumination on the occasion of the General Illumination in celebration of the peace with Russia'. It was agreed to erect a seven-foot star illuminated by gas. All materials, including the star itself, would be returned to the contractor 'so that the expense shall not exceed 5 guineas'.

The Crimean War was over.

[1] Minutes of Trustees' Meeting, 12 November 1866.
[2] Ibid., 14 May 1867.

CHAPTER VII

IN THE DAYS OF
'THE SATURDAY REVIEW'

I

FOR NEARLY forty years after its first issue *The Saturday Review* was edited from G.1, Albany. The capital for the new paper was provided by Mr. Beresford Hope, a Peel-ite and High Churchman, who was also joint-editor, but the real managing editor at the outset was Douglas Cook.

Cook was a remarkable young Scot who had gone out to seek his fortune in India and, after quarrelling with his employers, returned to England, doing a large part of the journey, or so he claimed, on foot. No one took this story literally, as he was an incurable and fluent romancer, and had been known to weep after dinner in G.1 with several of his contributors, at the sad tale of his own adventures in the tropics at a time when his listeners were well aware that he had been at work in Albany. He had a violent temper, was a man of little education, and was never seen to read a book. But he had a *flair* for recognizing a good writer, and in his fifteen years as editor he collected a very distinguished list of contributors, among them Sir William Harcourt, John Morley, Froude and Walter Bagehot. Other great names were added after his retirement— Andrew Lang, George Saintsbury, W. E. Henley and Edmund Gosse. *The Saturday Review* paid only two or three pounds for an article, never allowed one to be signed, and the proprietor disapproved so much of his contributors writing for other periodicals that, in the early days, he

187

parted with several writers for this reason. Still, the prestige of becoming a contributor was great.

A prominent writer in *The Saturday Review* was George Stovin Venables, who in a fight at Charterhouse had broken Thackeray's nose, disfiguring him for life, but nevertheless numbered him, with Tennyson, among his closest friends. He was a strikingly handsome man, who made a large income at the Bar, but enjoyed writing for *The Saturday Review*. In spite of the enforced anonymity Venables' style was unmistakable. He wrote in a series of brief, similarly constructed sentences, whose effect Sir William Harcourt, another *Saturday* writer, described as like watching a flock of sheep browsing along the Downs, dropping little round 'observations', all of the same form and size, as they went. Venables wrote literary criticisms and claimed to be one of the first to have recognized the genius of his friend, Tennyson, and later of Swinburne.

Another lawyer who wrote regularly for *The Saturday Review* was James Fitzjames Stephen, who afterwards became a High Court Judge and first editor of the *Dictionary of National Biography*. His speciality was the 'middle', originally an article not necessarily on a political subject which grew into 'a sort of lay sermon'.

The Saturday Review was proud of its independence and intolerance of popular humbug. It was outspoken—Bright called it 'The Saturday Reviler'. One of its favourite butts was a Dr. Cumming, who had rashly prophesied that the world would come to an end in 1865. It became known for its vigorous Toryism and attacked Gladstone violently on his Irish policy.

It was never like other periodicals, perhaps because it was edited from such unusual premises. Everyone in *The Saturday* was presumed to be a gentleman and was treated as such. The long room in G.1 was no ordinary office, and the editor and his assistant lunched in the little room, often with their writers as guests, in a friendly, social atmosphere. The resemblance to a private house was increased by the presence of a well-trained man-servant, Wilson by name, who lived in the little room at the top of the building. He opened the door to callers, served luncheon, acted as messenger between editor and anyone actually writing on the premises, carried proofs to the printer and generally looked after 'the *Saturday* gentlemen'.[1]

On make-up day a brougham would carry the editor and sub-editor with the proofs of the paper from Albany to Messrs. Spottiswoode, the printers, and would bring them home again in comfort and dignity.

There was an annual function, *The Saturday Review* Dinner, which was first held at Oatlands Park, once the home of Albany's previous owner, the Duke of York, now a hotel, and later at a riverside inn at Greenwich. The rule was that anyone who had contributed even a single article during the year must be invited.

Towards the end of its life in Albany *The Saturday Review* declined in importance, and in 1893 it was sold and left for offices elsewhere, changing at the same time its personality. But the connection of the chambers G.1 with the world of English letters was to continue without a break.

II

In January 1878, General Johnston complained of the annoyance he experienced from the noise made over his head by the two children of Mr. Styan, the tenant of A.4, during the holidays. The Trustees determined 'that on all future lettings of rooms the Tenants be informed that the Consent of the Trustees will be given only subject to the understanding that Children are not admitted to live in the rooms'.

This disposed of the threat from children. Two months

[1] H. Furniss, op. cit., pp. 90–92.

later an attack from a different quarter was repulsed. A Mr. Benson had left his Chambers—B.2—to Miss Sarah Benson, Spinster. The Secretary was instructed to write 'asking for information regarding the station in life of Miss Benson and whether she intended to occupy the Chambers herself . . .' The Secretary was authorized 'to intimate that the Trustees could not give their consent without an assurance that Miss Benson did not intend to occupy the rooms'. It was apparently acceptable for a lady to own Chambers, so long as she did not live in them.

III

Innovations were coming, even in Albany. In January 1879, the Secretary was authorized by the Trustees to provide an Inverness Cape for the use of the night porters, and in November 1881, a Mr. Alexander Henderson, tenant of G.2, asked for leave 'to put up a Telephone Standard for the purpose of communication with the Comedy Theatre'.

The Trustees resolved that they had no power under the terms of their trust to agree to the application. This was hardly surprising as the telephone had not been invented when the Trust was formed. They refused again, three years later, in April 1884, when Major Baldwin of L.2 asked if he could bring a telephone wire from the Piccadilly entrance to the courtyard and over the Mansion, bringing it down outside the house. At the same meeting there was a request from Mr. Baker to be allowed 'to lay a 2-inch pipe from the Main in Piccadilly to A.14 in order to feed a hydraulic machine for blowing the Organ'.

The first man to succeed in gaining the Trustees' permission 'to have a telephone wire conveyed to his Chambers' was a Mr. E. M. Posen, owner of E.6, who was granted it in January 1889, on the understanding that the wire would be run from the Bristol Hotel, in Burlington Gardens 'to an attachment on E.6, Albany, be led

down by covered wire and taken in at the W.C. window ...
and that it will not cross Albany at any point'. The ice
was broken, but as late as 1897 the tenants of K.5 and H.6,
Ernest Crawley and A. Holford Gower, were only given
permission 'provided that the Telephone Co. brought
their wire direct into the . . . rooms without making any
attachment on to the Chimneys or Roofs of Albany'.

Other innovations have been allowed. Mr. O'Hagan
of A.14 introduces 'the Electric Light' to his rooms in
November 1887, and correspondence begins with the
London Electric Supply Corporation a year later about
lighting Albany by electricity. Language is changing, too.
In the Minutes of the Trustees' Meeting in April 1885, it
is recorded that new Trustees are elected 'in the place of'
others. Up to this date they had always been described as
being elected 'in the room of' the retiring or deceased
Trustees.

IV

In June 1885, Mr. Stephen Tucker, tenant of A.3 and A.6,
was given permission 'to place an Illumination of V.R.I.
in front of his own window and the porch of the Mansion
on the occasion of the celebration of the Queen's Birthday'. But the Trustees warned that this was not to establish
a precedent in future years.

CHAPTER VIII

IN THE DAYS OF THE BODLEY HEAD

I

ALBANY, WHICH has been the home of so many writers, is now to become the centre of the literary world of the 'nineties. A set of chambers is to be used, not by one distinguished author, but by a company of young, revolutionary writers and artists whose work in a few years changes the taste of their times.

The fashion of interior decoration is changing, too, no doubt as much in Albany as in private houses elsewhere. Though the 'nineties are *fin de siècle* they seem to be more like the opening years of a new era than the last of an old century. The Landseers are being swept from the walls to make room for the works of Rossetti and Burne-Jones, and art serge is draping the chimney-pieces. There is a tremendous vogue for oriental *objets d'art*. Japanese prints and silken fans are everywhere, and so is oriental porcelain —ginger jars and tall vases decorated with blossom. It is the hey-day of poker-work and beaten bronze, and Mr. Liberty in Regent Street is selling hundreds of yards of materials in richest hues for draperies of every kind.

Vigo Street was still a quiet little thoroughfare off Nash's cream-coloured Regent Street, its way barred to carriages or hansoms, with their jingling bells, by posts which stretched across its width just beyond Savile Row, and prevented vehicles from passing the back entrance to Albany. A little bookshop appeared in this street in 1887, a shop which specialized in rare and limited editions, and outside there hung the sign of the Bodley Head.

John Lane, the moving spirit in the new venture, was a small man, thirty-three years old at this time, 'alert, well-groomed, debonair, his eyes with a twinkle in them, his hair well brushed, his auburn-sandy beard neatly trimmed to a point.' He was talkative, sympathetic and boundlessly ambitious. At fourteen he had been given a place as clerk in the Railway Clearing Office, and his mother had brought him to London from the farm where they lived in Devon to settle him in suitable lodgings. Wandering about the streets of London when he was free from work, poring over the contents of junk-shops in Holborn and Charing Cross Road, he developed a passion for old books, prints and china. He was a gregarious young man and made friends who had similar interests. He seemed to have an extraordinary *flair*, and soon began to act as unofficial agent for some of his new friends. Whether it was books or mezzotints or historical documents, somehow little John Lane always seemed able to find what the collector wanted.

In taking *The Bodley Head* as the name for the new business Lane had been inspired by the sign of the Rembrandt Head Galleries in the same street. He and his partner, Elkin Mathews, were both Devon men and Bodley one of the most notable sons of Devon. 'Bodley, the most pious of founders!' said Lane. 'Who could so fittingly be enshrined as patron?'[1]

Mathews had been persuaded by Lane to leave his bookshop in the Cathedral Yard at Exeter and to bring his stock with him. For the first few years, while Lane remained in the background, continuing to work as a clerk at the Railway Clearing Office, Mathews was happy. He would have been quite content to remain all his life in the little Vigo Street shop, with its sixteen-foot-square room, lined from floor to ceiling with old books, partly his own from Exeter and partly books found by Lane in the second-hand bookshops which he haunted in his spare

[1] Lane's account from his reprint of *Life of Sir Thomas Bodley*.

hours. Mathews would have been happy to confine himself to selling rare books, but Lane's restless ambition drove his partner unwillingly forward and he soon found himself committed to publishing books as well as selling them.

From the first publication, a volume of poems by an unknown young man, Richard le Gallienne, who had just come to London from Liverpool, their books were a success. Lane had a genius for titillating the appetite of the collector. The volume was beautifully printed on hand-made paper, with untrimmed edges, and bound in blue-grey with a white panelled back. The edition was limited to 250 copies and fifty more were printed on large paper. Lane, who was interested in everyone, had by now made many friends among the book-collectors of London, and he used all his enthusiasm and charm to sell his books.

To these friends he showed advance copies of Le Gallienne's little volume of poems. He described the poet as 'a young man of undoubted genius, who was bound to set the Thames on fire, and whose face was the face of a Greek god'.[1] He assured them with infectious enthusiasm that before long the book would be worth far more than its original price. He had no difficulty in selling the whole edition quickly and a succession of other volumes followed. The books were all beautifully but simply produced, usually in limited editions, and all were charming to look at.

Word went round literary circles that at last there had appeared a publisher who *liked* to publish poetry, who was willing to pay for it and who could actually sell it. 'To Messrs. Elkin Mathews and John Lane almost more than to any other, are the thanks of the grateful singer especially due'; wrote the *St. James's Gazette*, 'for it is they who have managed, by means of limited editions and charming workmanship, to impress book-buyers with the belief that a volume may have an aesthetic and commercial value.'

[1] J. Lewis May, *John Lane and the '90s*, p. 33.

SOME PERSONS OF THE NINETIES: BY MAX BEERBOHM, INCLUDING MANY CONTRIBUTORS TO THE YELLOW BOOK. BACK ROW; L. TO R.: RICHARD LE GALLIENNE, WALTER SICKERT, GEORGE MOORE, JOHN DAVIDSON, OSCAR WILDE, W. B. YEATS. IN FRONT: ARTHUR SYMONS, HENRY HARLAND, CHARLES CONDER, WILL ROTHENSTEIN, MAX BEERBOHM, AUBREY BEARDSLEY

The Ashmolean Museum

THE ROPE WALK, WITH VIGO STREET AND THE NORTH
ENTRANCE TO ALBANY IN THE DISTANCE. THE ENTRANCE
TO THE CHAMBERS B.1, 2, ETC. CAN BE SEEN ON THE LEFT
AND THAT TO THE BLOCK L, WHERE GLADSTONE LIVED, ON
THE RIGHT

*From a photograph in the possession of Captain C. H. Adams, Secretary
of Albany*

MACAULAY, AGED 50, BY GEORGE RICHMOND
THIS IS THE DRAWING REFERRED TO IN MACAULAY'S DIARY
ON FEBRUARY 19TH, 1850, WHEN HE TOOK HIS SISTER TO THE
ARTIST'S STUDIO TO SEE IT. SHE SAID IT WAS "AN EXCELLENT
LIKENESS"

E. H. NEW'S DRAWING OF THE ENTRANCE TO G. I. WHICH
WAS ADMIRED BY WHISTLER AND USED BY JOHN LANE FOR
THE COVER OF HIS CATALOGUE

Distinguished figures could now be seen pausing, in well-cut frock coats and curly-brimmed top hats, to look into the little bay window of the shop where the painting of Sir Thomas Bodley swung over the door. So successful was it that Lane felt justified in abandoning his steady job and joining his name to the firm, which now became 'Elkin Mathews and John Lane: Publishers, and Vendors of Choice and Rare Editions in Belles Lettres'.

From that moment the partnership became increasingly uneasy. Lane, enthusiastic and daring, was continually pushing Mathews to go further than he wanted. Mathews exasperated his partner by his slowness, caution and lack of initiative. Within two years they realized that they could no longer work together. In March 1894 John Lane moved across the street, taking the Bodley Head sign and most of his authors with him, while Mathews remained for a time in their little shop and moved after a few years to Cork Street.

Then began an extraordinary chapter in the history of Albany. *The Bodley Head* became the place where the writers and artists of the new movement foregathered—it was the almost unchallenged centre of literary London. John Lane, with characteristic originality and taste, had conceived the idea of running his business from Albany. He took the remainder of Mr. Beresford Hope's lease of G.1, the ground floor set of chambers on the east side of the north entrance, and obtained the Trustees' permission to convert the bay window of the dining-room into an entrance opening directly on to Vigo Street.[1]

In November 1894 the Trustees considered another request in a letter from him. They had been 'kind enough to grant . . . a licence for converting the Dining-Room into a publisher's office with an entrance from Vigo Street'. He has used the address 'Vigo Street which name is labelled on the wall facing Savile Row, and as there is no number which I can adopt have made use of the name "The

[1] Trustees' Meeting, 24 January 1894.

Bodley Head" as the name of my house. Of course the
Albany address with its literary traditions would confer
much more distinction, but out of consideration for the
tenants of Albany, many of whom are my friends, I have
refrained from using it, pending your permission, to affix
on my rail in Vigo St. a plate bearing the words "John
Lane" . . . and by the affixing of a wrought iron grille
designed by Mr. Nelson Dawson in the light or centre
panel over the door with the name of my house viz. "The
Bodley Head Vigo Street" in copper.'[1]

The changes, as with everything he did, were made
with great taste, and a drawing of the new entrance was
used as a cover for his catalogue. This black and white
drawing was done by a young artist, E. H. New, who
afterwards illustrated Lane's editions of White's *Selborne*
and Walton's *Compleat Angler*. He stayed with Lane in
G.1, while he was working on the drawing in July 1895,
and found himself at once in the atmosphere which made
The Bodley Head in many ways more like a club than a
publisher's office.

John Lane liked personal contact with his authors. He
had the tastes and instincts of an artist and his poets and
writers were his friends. Although a keen business man
and not yet by any means well off, Lane was willing to
help anyone he believed in, when he could, and his spare
rooms in Albany were almost always being used by his
many friends. In fact William Watson is said to have
occupied a guest room for nearly twenty-five years. One
of his poets wrote to him that he had only £1 10s. in the
world. Another had pawned his dress trousers and, need-
ing them urgently, posted the ticket to Lane, imploring
him to redeem them and forward them immediately.

'I shall always remember those visits to G.1,' wrote
Edmund New to Lane, 'and my first introduction into the
Literary and Artistic circles of London, with peculiar
pleasure . . . I think of your charming little sitting-

[1] Trustees' Meeting, 29 November 1894.

room and the notable men and women whom you receive there.'[1]

While he was staying there, New made brief entries in his diary:

'Thursday 25th July 1895.

Began again drawing front of "Bodley Head" from opposite side of Vigo Street, for Catalogue cover . . . Tea at 5.0 in Lane's room. Met "Mrs. Devereux" again, Wilfrid Ball, James Welch, who told us of the fall of Le Gallienne's mulberry tree at Brentford, Arthur Symons, Dr. and Mrs. —(very beautiful), Cunninghame-Graham, Pauline Johnson, "Teka-Lionwake", the Canadian-Indian poet, Miss Gertrude Prideaux-Brune, etc. Dined with Lane and William Watson at the "Cheshire Cheese", . . . and then had a lovely walk along the Embankment to Watson's rooms at Westminster, under the Abbey.
'26th.

Beardsley to breakfast: brought wonderful design of Venus (proof), T. C. Gotch—very pleasant man. Professor Sylvanus Thompson (delightful person), Mr. Millard, of publishing firm of Chicago, and Laurence Housman, dined at the Hogarth Club with us. George Moore, Greiffenhagen, Bell, Professor Raleigh, and H. G. Wells (it was their first meeting) returned with others for smoke and talk. Miss Netta Syrett (Grant Allen's niece) in to tea. At Bodley Head drawing all day . . . Captain Dunne took me to Fly Fishers' Club to see book on Fishes, for "Walton". Couldn't sleep, either of us, so we
'(27th) came down at 1.0 and I went on with drawing for cover of Catalogue until 2.0, and finished it before breakfast next day.'[2]

This was the drawing that Whistler admired so much. Talking to Lane at the Hogarth Club, where both were

---

[1] J. Lewis May, op. cit., p. 63.
[2] Ibid., p. 209–10.

breakfasting, Whistler at this time living at Long's Hotel in Bond Street, he asked if he might have a proof. The two men returned to G.1 together, where Whistler to his delight was given a copy of the drawing on Japanese vellum.[1]

Lane would praise a new poet or essayist to the skies, and had a wonderful gift of being able to make other people talk about them, too. He believed in them and worked with boundless enthusiasm to sell their work. This propensity for discovering genius was the subject of a witty verse by Canon Ainger. One of Lane's earlier publications was an edition of Thomas Lovell Beddoes's letters edited by Edmund Gosse. Unfortunately a misprint in one paper advertised it as 'edited by Edmund Goose'. Canon Ainger wrote to Gosse:

> 'Heed not this last *bêtise*
> of John's;
> We know that all his geese
> Are Swans.'

Le Gallienne said that Lane was a father and a brother to his poets. So many of the poets and artists of the 'nineties who worked for *The Bodley Head* were doomed to early death. Francis Thompson, an opium addict, Ernest Dowson, Charles Conder and Beardsley were all consumptives. They seemed to live with feverish intensity, as though they knew they had little time.

Reaction had set in against the stern Victorian ideals of discipline and duty. A new doctrine had crept across the Channel, a revolt against convention and hypocrisy, a determination by artists to live life daringly and without regard to the deadening hands of authority and tradition. Pater, as author of a book on the Renaissance, was virtually the founder of the aesthetic movement in England, whose young followers were constantly 'exhorting each other to "burn always with this hard, gem-like

[1] H. Furniss, op. cit., p. 106.

flame" and to maintain that ecstasy which is the true success in life.'[1] They applauded the artist's absorption in his own sensations. Sin played a great part in their thoughts and conversation, and it was fashionable amongst them to pose as mysteriously wicked. They were impatient of restraint, determined to wring from life, at whatever cost, its richest experiences and satisfactions. They were serious about Beauty. Their movement was a protest against Victorian ugliness, a reaction from everything they considered 'respectable'.

In these years of the 'nineties there was an amazing outburst of creative energy, and Lane, by his selection of artists and writers, and his talent for getting his protégés accepted and admired, helped very largely to create the new fashions in art and literature.

In *The Book of the Rhymers' Club* he published poems by twelve poets, most of them young, unknown and newly arrived in London. The members of this Club met informally at odd times at each other's houses or in an upper room at the Cheshire Cheese in Fleet Street. Arthur Symons described it later. 'Long clay pipes lay . . . on the wooden tables between tankards of ale; young poets, then very young, recited their own verses to one another with a desperate and ineffectual attempt to get into tune with the Latin Quarter.'[2]

Here Ernest Dowson, a frail figure with a haggard, sensitive face, first recited *Cynara*, 'fresh from his pen'—a poem which is perhaps one of the most characteristic of the 'nineties movement. This poem and W. B. Yeats's *Innisfree* were first published in Lane's *Book of the Rhymers' Club*. 'Of course, they had their weaknesses and affectations, these Rhymers of our youth,' wrote Arthur Waugh, fifteen years after the Club had petered out. 'They were none of them above riding their Pegasus through the public streets, and some even assumed a Viking air of

[1] R. le Gallienne, *The Romantic '90s*, p. 74
[2] J. Lewis May, op. cit., p. 119.

conquest in flowing locks and wide gesticulations. But, after all, they did care. They did care very much for poetry, and there was something infectious about their enthusiasm, for they made other people care as well.'[1]

Lane was the first to apply the new artistic ideals to publishing. One could tell *Bodley Head* books at a glance. There was a new distinction and luxury about them. But his influence on the period was most strikingly shown by the *Yellow Book*, which seemed to embody the ideals of the aesthetic or 'decadent' movement.

Vigo Street was most conveniently situated for writers, artists or members of a richer circle who were interested in books and writing. It was in the centre of West London, and for the more bohemian it lay conveniently between the Café Royal in Regent Street, with its Second Empire décor, its red plush and its marble-topped tables, and the Hogarth Club, a favourite haunt of Lane's in Dover Street. It was at the Hogarth Club that the *Yellow Book* was born. After a public dinner one evening Lane repaired to the Club, accompanied by Aubrey Beardsley and Henry Harland. Lane had already noted with interest a drawing of Salome, which had been used to illustrate an article on Beardsley's work in the first number of a new art magazine, *The Studio*. He had seen at once that here was the artist to illustrate the English version of Wilde's play which he was about to publish. Beardsley's illustrations made a sensation, quite eclipsing the interest in the letterpress. He was then only twenty-one.

Henry Harland was an American who had lived in Paris and become more French than any Frenchman. He was in his early thirties, with long black hair, a dark goatee beard and a pallid complexion. He was endlessly talkative, witty and enthusiastic, and thought art the only thing in life worthy of interest. He liked to hint at mysterious parentage, Russian blood or the strange paternal interest taken in him by the Emperor Franz Joseph.

[1] J. Lewis May, op. cit., p. 93.

REYNAL & COMPANY, PUBLISHERS

221 EAST FORTY-NINTH STREET • NEW YORK 17, N. Y.

REVIEW COPY

TITLE   PEACE IN PICCADILLY

AUTHOR   Shelia Birkenhead

PRICE $4.00

PUB. DATE   September 16, 1958

Kindly send us two clippings of
your review of this book.

At the Hogarth Club these three met George Moore, Frank Harris and M. H. Spielmann. Moore and Harris began a discussion by saying literary criticism simply did not exist in England. Lane denied it, citing the names of Richard Garnett, Andrew Lang, Saintsbury, Archer, Gosse, Arthur Waugh and others. Beardsley said there were almost no art critics of worth, and all agreed that there was no good review.

'Why don't *you* start a really first-rate, up-to-date review?' they said to Lane. Before leaving the Hogarth Club that evening Lane had undertaken to bring out a new and daring review. Beardsley was to be art editor and Henry Harland literary editor. It was to be 'representative of the most cultured work which was then being done in England, prose and poetry, criticism, fiction and art, the oldest school and the newest side by side, with no hall-mark except that of excellence and no prejudice against anything but dullness and incapacity'.[1]

Within a few days it had been decided that the cover should be yellow, a stroke of genius, for yellow has come to be thought the colour of the 'nineties. Aubrey Beardsley and Harland were all for making the new review a revolutionary publication. Lane was a restraining influence. His was the business intelligence, but even he enjoyed the idea of the shock which their review would be to the reading public. The whole window of the old Bodley Head bookshop was filled with a blaze of yellow on the day of publication. (It was a few months before Lane moved across the road to Albany.) People paused at the window and gazed at 'the flaming cover of yellow, out of which the Aubrey Beardsley woman smirked for the first time'.[2]

Lane and his two editors may have taken an impish delight in the prospect of shocking middle-class complacency, but the immediate reaction of the Press startled even them. *The Times* described the new review as 'a com-

[1] J. Lewis May, op. cit., p. 73.
[2] R. le Gallienne, op. cit., p. 170.

bination of English rowdyism with French lubricity', and called Aubrey Beardsley and Walter Sickert 'advanced and riotous representatives of the new art'. *The Westminster Gazette*, referring to some of Beardsley's drawings, suggested 'a short Act of Parliament to make this kind of thing illegal', and of Max Beerbohm's contribution it wondered 'how any editor came to print such pernicious nonsense'.

Looking through the first issue of the *Yellow Book* now, it is hard to see what roused such passionate disapproval. Harland was a clever editor. He had gathered together many new writers, Beerbohm, Arthur Symons, Hubert Crackanthorpe, John Davidson and George Moore. But Lane, who even then was nervous of giving his two editors a free rein, had insisted on the inclusion of some well-established, 'respectable' names such as Henry James, A. C. Benson, Waugh, Garnett and Gosse. In spite of these precautions the immediate impression was undoubtedly made by the strong personality of Aubrey Beardsley. His strange drawings, with their troubling suggestions of a world of artificiality and vice, seemed to permeate the book with the very spirit of decadence.

The public felt immediately that there was something at once fascinating and repellent about the new quarterly. There seemed amongst the contributors a collective enthusiasm which made each work more vigorously towards his own ideal. Nothing like it had been seen before. It was in vain that Lane pointed out that, even on the artistic side, which was more revolutionary than the literary, he had included two studies by Sir Frederick Leighton. Sir Frederick himself appeared at *The Bodley Head* and complained that his friends had reprimanded him with the utmost severity for having contributed to such a review. But the startled disapproval of the Press and public naturally did nothing to reduce the sales, and the *Yellow Book* quickly became the symbol of a new movement in art.

Lane was kept busy supervising both his editors, but

particularly Beardsley. Aubrey Beardsley was now twenty-two. Tall and emaciated, with a face of almost transparent pallor, he wore his hair cut in a flat fringe on his high forehead. His hands were incredibly long and delicate. He dressed in a dandified way in a tail-coat and top hat, and usually carried a black portfolio of his drawings under his arm, which someone said made him look like 'the man from the Pru'. Yet, although uncannily thin and frail-looking, he gave an impression of extraordinary power and nervous strength. Wilde described him—'a face like a silver hatchet, with grass-green hair'.[1]

In spite of his brilliance he was alarmingly irresponsible and a constant worry to Lane. He refused to be serious, and was always trying to slip some indecency into his drawings, well hidden from any but the closest scrutiny. Lane 'used to go over them with a microscope and submit them to a jury of his friends' before he dared pass them for publication.[2] Even so, one issue went to press before a particularly audacious impropriety was discovered and the whole binding had to be replaced. Another of Beardsley's playful habits was to introduce portraits of well-known people into his drawings. He took an impish delight in this game of hide-and-seek with Lane.

His employment in an insurance office had accustomed him to drawing at night, and he continued the habit. He liked to make himself a figure of mystery. He must darken the room before he could begin his work, and drew by the light of candles set in two tall ormolu candlesticks. The *Yellow Book* made Beardsley famous. Not to have heard of him was to show yourself a philistine. But Beardsley and the *Yellow Book* had soon to part company.

Lane used to boast that every book published by *The Bodley Head* had been placed with a leading American publisher, until the time (in 1896) that he opened a branch of his own business in New York. A year after the appear-

---

[1] R. le Gallienne, op. cit., p. 173.

[2] Ibid., p. 172.

ance of the *Yellow Book* he made his first visit to New York. Wilde had just lost the libel action that he had brought against Lord Queensberry, and his prosecution was about to begin. As Lane stepped ashore in New York he was horrified to see enormous headlines in the Sunday papers: 'Arrest of Oscar Wilde, *Yellow Book* under his arm.' It was a terrible shock. 'It killed the *Yellow Book* and it nearly killed me,' Lane used to say, not quite accurately, as the *Yellow Book* survived for two years longer. The book under Wilde's arm turned out to be *a yellow book—Aphrodite.*[1]

Oddly enough Wilde, although in his flamboyant personality seeming to personify its ideas, had never contributed to the *Yellow Book.* This may have been partly because, while Lane had published his plays, they had never liked each other, but was mostly owing to Beardsley's strong dislike for Wilde. Unfortunately, to the public, their names were linked. They were thought to be 'birds of a feather'. Crowds assembled in Vigo Street. Stones were thrown through the windows of G.1. Six of Lane's principal authors cabled an ultimatum to him that they would withdraw their books, unless Beardsley's work in the fifth volume of the *Yellow Book* was suppressed and Wilde's name omitted from the *Bodley Head* catalogue.

Lane wrote letter after letter home, begging for copies of the English papers, saying that nothing had appeared in the American Press which could justify such an action. He quoted Kipling, Le Gallienne and Tree as thinking it would be a great injustice to Beardsley. He surmised that something disagreeable must have happened, unknown to him, to have caused such a proposal.

The editor of the *New York Times* had told him that the English papers were giving ten or twelve columns to the case every day. 'If Beardsley is attacked,' he wrote, 'I hope someone will suggest that he has been the modern Hogarth in pointing out and, as it were, lampooning the period and

[1] J. Lewis May, op. cit., p. 80.

its customs and *chiefly in the T.B.*' The business man was
not going to miss the chance of free publicity. He cabled a
further protest, but saw that all he had achieved might be
swept away by the wave of hatred and reaction. 'This is
where your new ideas will lead us to,' cried the outraged
forces of respectability. Lane in New York decided to
leave the decision to members of his staff who were on the
spot, and the terms of the ultimatum were agreed.

Beardsley, still only twenty-three and suffering from a
return of consumptive symptoms, bitterly resented being
made a scapegoat for the recklessness of a man he had
never liked. The *Yellow Book* had been his main source of
income, but luckily he found a substitute in a commission
for a series of drawings for a new magazine, *The Savoy.*
His life burned inexorably away. Before the end he
was received into the Roman Catholic Church and died
at the age of twenty-five. The *Yellow Book,* when it lost
the fantastic genius of Beardsley, lost at the same time its
sense of being a symbol of something new and strange. It
lasted for two more years, a very good review with excellent short stories, but the romance had vanished from the
venture.

Lane's rooms in Albany were perhaps familiar to a
wider circle, and a more distinguished one, than any others
in its history. Authors have used their rooms in Albany
as a quiet oasis in the bustle of London, where they can
think and write without disturbance. Politicians have
found them a useful base for Westminster, easy to return
to after late sittings of the House. To actor-managers,
such as Herbert Tree and Squire Bancroft, Albany was
convenient for the theatre. But Lane's rooms were never
quiet and he was almost never alone in them. He was one
of those fortunate men whose work is also their favourite
hobby, and *The Bodley Head* was his life. He did not
grudge an hour devoted to its advancement. His energy
and enthusiasm were irresistible. He liked nothing better
than to act as his own 'traveller'. He enjoyed the task of

convincing people that his new author was a writer of superlative merit and he usually returned from his journeys with big orders for his latest publication. It was not only that he believed in his authors, or even that he was anxious to enlarge his market. He enjoyed selling books, and took as much trouble to place a copy or two in some village shop in Devon as in selling thousands to the circulating libraries.

His only other pleasures, and both were related to his business, were people and collecting. Some people called him a lion-hunter, and in a way he was. At his gatherings at *The Bodley Head* he liked to have people well known in the worlds of fashion, art or letters—money or titles were not interesting to him, unless they could be related in some way to the work of *The Bodley Head*. Sir John Squire said that he was 'an antiquary, a connoisseur, a *raconteur*, and one who displayed an infinite curiosity about human character'. These qualities made him an ideal host, and his rooms were a half-way house, where the fashionable and the artistic worlds of London could meet, and both feel at their ease.

The 'teas' held at G.1 from four to six o'clock were famous in their day. There one could meet distinguished and beautiful women (Lane was very fond of women's company, and one wit christened him 'Petticoat Lane'), amongst them the boyish, bird-like 'E. Nesbit' and the lovely Olive Custance, afterwards Lady Alfred Douglas. Lady Randolph Churchill was often there, always wrapped in becoming furs. In the evenings his gatherings were exclusively masculine and included 'not only writers and artists, but generals and literary lords who collected bookplates and old china, and venerable scholars mysteriously learned'.[1] The more observant noticed that these apparently incongruous guests had been chosen because Lane was aware of mutual interests which made them agreeable to each other.

[1] R. le Gallienne, op. cit., p. 124.

At these parties he had always some new 'find' to show, something which he had bought for very little in one of the antique shops which he was constantly searching. He had a passion for collecting *objets d'art* and liked nothing better than to show them off to a congenial gathering. Book-plates, prints, samplers, china, glass, furniture, silver, pewter, fans, books and, as he got older, above all pictures were amongst his finds. He was particularly proud of his collection of old glass, with which his rooms at Albany were perilously crowded, 'so that one was afraid to turn about for fear of bringing some precious thing with a crash to the floor; particularly on those genial evenings when guests as heterogeneous as the *objets d'art* which surrounded them would drop in for animated talk on their particular hobbies, with the usual humanizing accompaniments of tobacco and whisky-and-soda.'[1]

The Westminster Gazette described life in G.1 in those days with some verses beginning:

> 'There's a street that men call Vigo,
> Whither scribblers such as I go,'

and referred to John Lane under the pseudonym of Sir Thomas Bodley.

> 'There's a sign we know as Bodley
> Whither wander folk ungodly;
> All the writers, all the scribblers,
> All the critics, all the quibblers,
> Smoking pipes and drinking whisky,
> Telling tales of matter risky—
> "This is business, this is commerce,"
> Thinks their doughty host, Sir Thomas—
> Steers with skill the conversation
> Till to *him* it hath relation.
> (an it please you, he's the fellow
> Owns a certain Book that's Yellow)—
> 'Neath the sign we know as Bodley
> Business greeteth friendship oddly.

[1] R. le Gallienne, op. cit., p. 124.

'There's a room in Number G.1
Where this publisher can see one;
Femininity invades it,
Scent of many flowers pervades it:
Here are violets—and a sonnet
(Writer wears a witching bonnet);
Here's a novel—and a lily
(One is pure—the other silly);
Here's a drawing wrapped in roses
(Its creator yonder poses):
'Tis a matter most astounding
All these geniuses abounding;
Over tea and bread and butter
Many compliments they utter.
"This is pleasure, though it's commerce,"
Chuckles wicked old Sir Thomas,
Ah! that jolly room in G.1
Is the place he loves to see one.'

Richard le Gallienne was often a lodger in Lane's rooms. He enjoyed expeditions with his host to explore what seemed to be unpromising heaps of rubbish and returning to Albany with treasure trove. One evening they could have been seen on the pavement in Vigo Street, Le Gallienne looking just as a poet should, with his handsome face, thick mane of hair, green velvet jacket and loosely flowing tie, and Lane a small, dapper figure with sandy, pointed beard, each carrying his hat in his hand, and balancing on his head a Sheraton chair, oblivious of the smiles of passers-by.

Of course the 'Nest of Songbirds', as someone had christened *The Bodley Head*, was a good subject for parody and satire. Amongst other verses ridiculing Lane and his poets there was one by Owen Seaman (afterwards editor of *Punch*) addressed to 'A Boy-Poet of the Decadence'.

'The erotic affairs that you fiddle aloud
Are as vulgar as coin of the mint;
And you merely distinguish yourself from the crowd
By the fact that you put 'em in print.

For your dull little vices we don't care a fig,
It is this that we deeply deplore,
You were cast for a common or usual pig,
But you play the invincible bore.'

The unexpected result to the author of these lines was an invitation to dine with Lane, when he found himself in the company of several of the victims of his satire.

Punch described the scene:[1]

'. . . He went. The air was thick with brains,
The language loud and tall;
Some wore their locks like lions' manes,
And some had none at all.

Who should his neighbours be? He scanned,
Trembling, the dinner list;
A decadent (consumptive) and
A blatant atheist!

Both victims! Wedged between the bards,
He spilled, with furtive shame,
A large *hors-d'œuvre* across the card's
White face that bore his name . . .'

To his surprise he was greeted warmly, and in a short time Lane had arranged to publish a collection of his satirical verse, which was not only a great success but provided an excellent advertisement for the *Bodley Head* books.

It was not long after this that Lane married an American widow from Boston, of German extraction, whose father was Director of the Boston Conservatory of Music. She was very musical, spoke four languages and also had literary interests. Her first husband, when he died, had left

[1] 6 March 1897.

her very well off, and she was looking round for someone to publish her work. In John Lane she found both a publisher and a husband. Her money helped Lane in his business and he came to place great reliance on her literary judgment.

Lane's entertaining now became very much more formal, and mostly took place at their house in Lancaster Gate Terrace. Mrs. Lane usually dressed 'in light-grey silk, which, shining like steel, gave her a war-like appearance'.[1] She was evidently rather a formidable woman and the parties in her drawing-room on Sunday afternoon, although attended by many brilliant people, lacked the easy, bohemian atmosphere of the gatherings in Albany. Part of his by this time enormous collections of glass, china, fans and pewter now lay grouped round the rooms of his house, while the walls were covered with pictures and prints, but there was still more than enough left to fill G.1. An attic at the top of the building was often lent by him to friends who needed a bed, when the other rooms in G.1 were full. After climbing ninety-odd steps to this haven, they would find that they had to share it with the overflow of Lane's library and old glass which lay around on the floor.

The list of authors whose work was published by *The Bodley Head* is an extraordinary one, particularly when one remembers that John Lane was born the son of a Devonshire farmer and had come to London at the age of fourteen, with no advantage of wealth or connection to help him. His place of business in Albany, so unlike an ordinary office, lent it an atmosphere of romance. His choice of name for his business and the sign above the door showed his genius for advertising. 'The very intonation which he gave to the words "Bodley Head" when he spoke them in conversation,' said Sir John Squire, 'betrayed an honest pride, not only in the success of the business which he had built up, but in its quality. So

[1] J. Lewis May, op. cit., p. 166.

famous had *The Bodley Head* become, that even its founder spoke of it with awe and admiration.'[1]

He published books by Wilde, Max Beerbohm, J. A. Symonds, Kenneth Grahame, Saki, H. G. Wells, Chesterton and Arnold Bennett, besides thirty volumes written by W. J. Locke and translations of André Maurois's work. Perhaps his most famous translation was the complete English edition of the Works of Anatole France. When this idea was first suggested Lane, accompanied by his wife, crossed the Channel to interview the Master. They did not make an entirely favourable impression. A friend who was with France described Lane as staring about him through his *pince-nez* 'as though he had come to value the furniture'. Mrs. Lane, with American earnestness, persistently asked the Master's opinion of a series of English writers of whom he had probably never read a word, as he spoke no English, 'till the old man was nearly forced to cry for mercy.'

Nevertheless, Lane came back to London with an agreement in his pocket. The books were beautifully produced. There were end-papers by Aubrey Beardsley, initials by Henry Ospovat, red cloth covers, gilt lettering, uncut edges to the paper—and all for six shillings a volume.

A visit to London by the Master had been discussed for over a year, when he suddenly announced that he would appear in a week's time. A reception committee was hurriedly formed, of which John Lane was a leading member. The veteran author's impetuosity led to the abandonment of some of the more ambitious plans which had been proposed. The American Ambassador, Whitelaw Reid, had promised a reception at Dorchester House, but he was unfortunately out of England. There had been talk of another reception at 10 Downing Street, but this dwindled to a tea-party with Mrs. Asquith.

However he was taken to the National Gallery, where Lane managed to have several rooms, which had been shut

[1] J. Lewis May, op. cit., p. 216.

because of suffragettes' activities, opened for his inspection. He saw more pictures at Bridgewater House, and of course a party was given for him at the Lanes' house in Lancaster Gate Terrace. Mrs. Lane carefully put on one side the glove she had worn, which had been made sacred by its contact with the Master's hand. Unfortunately the relic was later inadvertently sent to the cleaners.

Then naturally there followed a visit to Albany.

'On entering my room,' wrote Lane, 'he came face-to-face with his own portrait by Guth, which he greeted as an old familiar friend. On the opposite wall hung the picture by Miss Gertrude Hammond entitled *"The Yellow Book"*,[1] which he greatly admired, as Whistler had often done before him. The picture . . . represents a young man, *Yellow Book* in hand, from which he is reading to a blushing girl. I said, "You will observe she is blushing." "Why?" said he, to which I replied: "He is evidently reading your story to her." '[2]

The translations of the Works of Anatole France were thought by Edward Garnett to be 'the most important . . . since Tolstoy's works were translated'.

Let W. J. Locke have the last word on John Lane and his achievement. Lane had published every one of Locke's books, and when he died Locke wrote:

'It is not for me to tell the fascinating story of *The Bodley Head*; but no literary historian in the future can ever pass it by, because it was the Wonder House of those fermenting 'nineties whence sprang men of infinitely reaching influence in letters and art—the Wonder House created by the subtle and sympathetic genius of John Lane, Englishman through and through, and (as was his pride) Devonshire-yeoman bred.'[3]

---

[1] Reproduced in the *Yellow Book*, Vol. VI, July 1895.

[2] *The Bodleian* (publisher's house magazine, price 1d.), Vol. XII, No. 133.

[3] J. Lewis May, op. cit., p. 198.

II

When John Lane had first bought the lease of G.1 all was not well with Albany. The chambers were thought old-fashioned and were becoming more difficult to let. At the 627th Meeting of the Trustees, in March 1889, it was reported that a Miss Hubbard had applied to take rooms in Albany and after testimonials to her character had been read, consent was given for her to take the rooms I.6. (Leave was given to the owner to let them to a Major Trafford four months later, so evidently Miss Hubbard did not take advantage of their permission.)

This is the first time that the Trustees are recorded as giving their consent to a woman taking rooms in Albany with the intention of living there, though the widow of a previous owner, Mrs. Inez E. Crawley, may have lived in K.5 after her husband's death, when it was not sub-let, until she re-married; her second husband, Captain Pringle, being the tenant of K.6 for ten years from 1891. The Trustees were no longer in a position to turn down female applicants, though one can imagine the fury of some of the older tenants at seeing their masculine stronghold thus invaded. At the very next meeting a Mr. Beamish asked if there would be any objection to his purchasing the Chambers L.1 for himself and his wife to reside in them, and the Secretary was authorized to write 'that there was no rule against it'.

Many thought that Albany's days were numbered. The owners of two sets of chambers in the Mansion-house objected to paying the Trust Rate for the upkeep of Albany, and said that they thought the Trust should be ended. The Secretary explained that the Trust Deed of 1804 authorized the making of such a rate as often as it should be required. It had usually been found necessary to make a rate of 1s. in the pound every quarter, and that had been barely enough to meet the current expenses.

The tenants' protest reflected the general feeling that Albany was now out of date, antiquated and inconvenient. But its site was extremely valuable. The inevitable happened. At the end of that year (1889) a would-be purchaser appeared. The Trustees first thought of calling 'a General Meeting of the Proprietors upon the subject of the pending negotiations for the sale of Albany', then they had second thoughts and decided to send round a circular. The price suggested seems to have been £250,000, but negotiations were still dragging on after several months, because of the difficult position made by the Albany Trust. The Trustees seem to have wavered and been unable to decide what they should—or even could—do. In May 1890 they were talking of applying to Parliament for compulsory powers, if four-fifths of the Freehold Owners and holders of Leases of more than ten years should agree to the sale. In July negotiations broke down. In December the same would-be purchaser, Mr. Kirk, was making alterations in a draft Agreement. But nothing more was done.

For some years past there had been complaints of ceilings falling as the result of leaking roofs, of the bad condition of the North Lodge, of a bulge in the North wall of the Mansion, and of the gravel on both sides of the covered way being in a disgraceful condition. Now the tenant of B.6, Mr. Pagdon, voiced the feelings of many. He wrote to the Trustees that he could not let his chambers. 'I think the time has now arrived (May 1892) when all the Chambers should be converted for some other purpose . . . I feel rather disposed not to pay the Ground Rent much longer but to hand over the property to the Owners to deal with . . .' The Trustees, after discussing this letter, directed the Secretary to write to the Owners of Chambers inviting their co-operation, if the Trustees should apply to Parliament for powers either to sell

Albany or to alter the Trust, with the idea of converting the buildings to other uses.

Before any action had been taken a new tenant had appeared, whose coming was to affect Albany more lastingly than that of any man since Alexander Copland. At the 653rd Meeting of the Trustees, on 19 April 1893, after granting permission to Mr. H. H. de Burgh to have a call box of the District Messengers Company affixed to his rooms, B.6, they gave their consent to the Trustees of the Reverend J. A. Burrow for the sale of the rooms D.6 Albany to William Stone, Esq.

A year later nine proprietors, 'being dissatisfied with the present condition of the property, the existing arrangements for its management and the heavy and increasing rates which are levied on the proprietors without much apparent benefit to their property,' wrote that the time had come when an effort should be made to place the affairs of Albany on a more satisfactory footing, and asked that a General Meeting of Proprietors should be called without delay.

One of the principal grievances appeared to be that, contrary to the original Regulations, a number of the Trustees were not resident in Albany. Dissatisfied Proprietors now formed themselves into a Committee of Albany Proprietors and immediately demanded that three residents should be added to the number of Trustees. The Trustees countered with a reminder that the Trust Deed required that Trustees of Albany should not exceed the existing number of seven. Mr. H. W. Lyall of A.10, Hon. Secretary of the Committee, replied at once that their suggestion was that 'three of the present Trustees should offer to retire so as to enable the Proprietors in General Meeting assembled to elect . . . three proprietors resident in the Albany'.

The Trustees refused, but, presumably in deference to the complaints about the way in which Albany was being run, they considered at their meeting an estimate for 'a new ornamental cast iron glazed covered way, with mosaic paving, complete from the Mansion to Savile Row with lateral branches'. It was reported that this would cost over £1,400—the glass roof nine hundred, and the paving £534 14s. 0d. An estimate was then demanded for 'a wire wove roof', but that was found to cost even more. The Surveyor, John P. Seddon, reported that 'possibly a lighter slate roof might be substituted for the present covering if it be determined to preserve the present rustic character, but if a new covered way be decided upon it should be of a more modern description.'

This was in May 1895. At their next meeting the Trustees were confronted by another letter from the Committee, who had circularized all Proprietors and Tenants and 'in not one instance has the reply been hostile . . . Strongly supported as the Committee are, they desire courteously but decidedly to call your immediate attention to the facts, and to express their earnest hope that you will accede to their reasonable request that three resident Proprietors should be at once placed on the board of Trustees.' Two Trustees agreed to resign and the Committee nominated Mr. William Stone and Mr. Lyall, their Hon. Secretary, to fill the places.

The new Trustees began by considering whether Albany should be brought up to date or whether powers should be sought to sell such a valuable site. Counsel advised that it was doubtful whether the original Deeds of 1803 and 1804 had created a valid Trust, and recommended that an action should be brought, when it would be decided whether the Trusts of the Deeds were valid or not.

After more than a year it was decided to stop the pending proceedings in Chancery, and also to call a General Meeting of the Proprietors to consider the question of improvements to Albany. At this meeting, on 8 July 1897, at the French Room in the St. James's Hall Restaurant in Piccadilly, the Trustees said that their object in calling the Meeting was 'to invite the attention of their Fellow

Proprietors to the condition of the building and approaches of Albany and to ascertain their views and wishes as to contemplated repairs and improvements . . . Extensive repairs have been recently executed by the Trustees and further repairs . . . are necessary or desirable in the interest of the property.

'The roof pavement and iron railings of the long walk are much out of order while the entrance from Savile Row and the vacant spaces on each side of the walk including the ground adjoining the Mansion and the boundary walls present a mean and neglected appearance.

'Some repairs are absolutely necessary and the question on which the Trustees desire to consult their Fellow Proprietors is whether the repairs should be executed on the old lines and with a rigid regard to economy or whether an opportunity should now be taken of effecting permanent improvements which would do justice to the value and importance of the site.

'In this view it has been suggested:

(1) That the old wooden roof should be replaced by a light glass structure with suitable railings and iron supports.

(2) That the old stone pavement which is practically worn out should be relaid with some new and desirable material.

(3) That the Savile Row entrance should be reconstructed with an appropriate arch and new doors.

(4) That whether all or any of these improvements are effected or not the vacant spaces should so far as practicable be laid out by planting or otherwise on a uniform plan and maintained as ornamental grounds.

'The Trustees are of opinion, that the suggested improvements are such as would commend themselves to any prudent owner desirous of increasing the value of his estate, and that they would permanently raise the letting value of the property, and enable it to compete on favourable terms with properties in less favoured localities, which at present command higher rents, but they are reluctant especially in view of the recent abnormal expenditure on necessary structural repairs, to incur expenses for the proposed improvements without ascertaining the views of the other Proprietors.'

To the benefit of posterity the sense of the meeting was against making a new glass roof to the covered way. A proposal that the old stone pavement should be relaid was carried unanimously, as was a second that 'no architectural alterations be made' to the northern entrance. All this in 1897. What a narrow escape!

Saved for the moment from hideous renovations by the conservative prejudices of its inhabitants, Albany's future was still very uncertain. A complication was that when the estate had been purchased from the Duke of York and Albany and the Trust created in 1803, he had already granted Building Leases for 99 years from Lady Day 1803 of the four houses on Piccadilly. The Estate was bought subject to these Leases, and as they had been granted before the Trust was created, the houses had never been considered subject to Albany Rates. The question now arose as to what should happen at the end of the leases, on Lady Day 1902.

Mr. A. E. Copland-Griffiths, one of the Trustees and grandson of Alexander Copland, was the equitable proprietor of the four houses, and contended that at the end of the Lease they should be conveyed to him, free of the Trust. The opinion of one of the leaders of the Chancery Bar was sought, and he considered that the houses were included in the Albany Trust and subject to its Rules and Regulations, except as regards rating. The Trustees pointed out to Counsel that although 'the Albany Buildings are old, worn-out and not well suited to modern requirement, the Trust deeds contain no machinery for rebuilding or for selling the property.' He thought the best scheme would be to apply for a special Act of Parliament.

Meanwhile Copland-Griffiths gave notice in November 1900 that he intended to deal with the houses as absolute owner and without consulting the Trustees. The latter then began an action in the Court of Chancery to restrain him and to have the Trusts and duties of the Trustees decided by the Court. Copland-Griffiths immediately brought a counter-action against the Trustees. The two Chancery actions came on for trial simultaneously, but it was arranged in Court that the Counsels should meet and 'settle terms for a compromise and a plan for putting the Albany on a better legal footing under a Private Act of Parliament similar to that by which the freehold chambers in New Square, Lincoln's Inn are managed, and that this Act should enable Trustees, with the consent of Proprietors, to raise money by mortgage for the purpose of rebuilding, and also to sell the whole Estate if occasion should arise.'

Opinion at a General Meeting in December 1902 was not entirely favourable to the Trustees. A resolution was put that Proprietors regretted the course adopted by the Trustees in entering on serious and costly litigation without the knowledge and consent of the Proprietors as a body. But an amendment was carried that six Proprietors should be appointed to a Committee to confer with the Trustees. Mr. Copland-Griffiths died that month, and at another General Meeting in the following April the Chairman read a resolution 'that the Trustees of Albany, acting in conjunction with the Representatives of the late Mr. A. E. Copland-Griffiths, be authorized to take steps in the direction of a General Sale of the Albany Estate.'

After some discussion the Resolution was dropped, 'as the general opinion of the Meeting appeared to be that it was unnecessary.' More discussions about Private Acts of Parliament and the sale of Albany continued for some time, but gradually faded away with no action taken.

The houses standing in Piccadilly, on either side of the entrance to Albany, were later sold by the Copland-

Griffiths Trustees. The building on the west was eventually pulled down and rebuilt in 1926, and that on the east suffered the same fate eleven years later, but Holland's shop-fronts had already been much altered before their demolition.

CHAPTER IX

IN MODERN TIMES

I

IN 1912 Compton Mackenzie, then twenty-nine years old, had just had his first success with his book, *Carnival*. He was offered a long lease of E.1, the first chambers occupied by Macaulay, on the ground floor off the covered way, and was very tempted to take them. But the rent was £180 a year and after long thought he decided that it was too formidable a rent to be committed to on the strength of one book. '£180 a year!' he writes today. 'The only regrets I've had have been for my economies. However they have been very very few.'[1]

In his next book, published a year later, *Sinister Street*, that fascinating record of the generation who were young in the opening years of the century, he gave a brilliant impression of these chambers. For the purpose of his story he made them over to Prescott, the bachelor friend and fellow-officer of Michael Fane's dead father.

'On the night before he went up Michael dined with Prescott at his rooms in the Albany. He enjoyed the evening very much. He enjoyed the darkness of the room whose life seemed to radiate from the gleaming table in its centre. He enjoyed the ghostly motions of the soldier-servant and the half-obscured vision of stern old prints on the walls of the great square room, and he enjoyed the intense silence that brooded outside the heavily curtained windows. Here in Albany Michael was immeasurably aware of the life of London that was surging such a little

[1] Letter to the author.

distance away; but in this modish cloister he felt that the life he was aware of could never be dated, as if indeed were he to emerge into Piccadilly and behold suddenly crinolines or even powdered wigs they would not greatly surprise him. Albany seemed to have wrung the spirit from the noisy years that swept on their course outside, to have snatched from each its heart and in the museum of this decorous glass arcade to have preserved it immortally, exhibiting the frozen palpitations to a sensitive observer . . .

'The glass of champagne that owing to the attention of the soldier-servant was always brimming, the dark discreet room, and Albany's atmosphere of passion squeezed into the mould of contemporary decorum or bound up to stand in a row of Thackeray's books, all combined to affect Michael with the idea that his life had been lived.'[1]

II

On 26 April 1914, just over three months before the outbreak of the Great War, Edward Knoblock, a forty-year-old American playwright, signed the lease for the rooms G.2. His passion for the theatre, in which he had lately achieved two resounding successes, was equalled only by his delight in old furniture and interior decoration, which he intended to gratify in the arrangement of his chambers.

He had spent his schooldays in Europe and graduated at Harvard, where he determined to become a playwright. Paris was then the great centre of dramatic art, so to Paris he went, to study the theatre and to see a play every evening for the next ten months. He managed this on a very small income by becoming one of the *claque*. To be a member of this peculiarly French institution one had to wear a black coat, a good tie and a clean collar. They were seated together in the centre of the pit or the second

[1] Compton Mackenzie, *Sinister Street* (1949 ed.), pp. 444-6.

balcony, with the *chef de claque* in their midst. When he said '*Bravo*' they clapped; when he said '*Assez*' they stopped. In this way Knoblock saw all the good plays several times for nothing, and was paid one franc a night for his services.

He came to London from Paris just before the Queen's Diamond Jubilee. From the moment of his arrival he felt that this was the place where he would like to live and work. That Jubilee Summer was a revelation to him. 'In Bond Street frock-coated, top-hatted men and tight-waisted, flower-crowned ladies moved up and down sedately as if the whole street were one long corridor holding some formal reception.' The theatrical season was brilliant. He saw Henry Irving in *The Bells*, Cyril Maude in *Under the Red Robe* and Marie Tempest in *The Geisha*. But the part of London which enchanted him most was the Regency architecture. He seemed to feel at once an affinity with this period, which he never lost—'Regent Street set in its creamy, intimate façades of my beloved Regency. Regent's Park—more Regency!—shone in a green such as I had never seen, set off by graceful terraces of classic columns.'

After no less than fourteen years' persistent work at his chosen profession—in London, Paris and America—writing every kind of play, he was at last rewarded with a triumph, when the audience at the first night in London of his *Kismet*, based on Burton's *Arabian Nights*, shouted and cheered for ten minutes after the curtain had fallen. A few weeks afterwards he was introduced to Arnold Bennett, who was becoming famous as chronicler of life in the Five Towns. Bennett still looked a provincial, in spite of the carefully brushed quiff of hair, the immaculate, pleated evening shirts and the heavy gold fobs which were his gifts to the cartoonists. He had a jutting nose, drooping eyelids and a mouth apparently so full of teeth that it was usually half-open. He suffered from an impediment in his speech and affected a jaunty swagger with which to hide a sense of diffidence. In spite of his great success as a novelist, Bennett had so far failed as a playwright, a profession in which he was most anxious to shine. Three of his plays had been produced, but none had been successful, and many others had failed even to find a producer.

He proposed a collaboration with Knoblock, hoping to learn from him some of the subtle rules of the dramatist's craft which he felt himself to lack. Knoblock was flattered by the suggestion and agreed to visit Bennett at Fontainebleau, where he was living with his French wife, and there they wrote together the play, *Milestones*. This was a tremendous success. The difference in the characters of the collaborators was shown by the way in which each spoke of the other's share in the work. Bennett wrote of Knoblock in his journal, while they were working on the play, 'Whenever he adds a phrase of his own it is heavy and uncolloquial, and has to be altered. Still, he knows the stage, and his help is valuable. Also the original idea of the play was his, and the skeleton his. But nineteen-twentieths of the actual imagination and invention of the detail is mine. The thing would have been tremendously inferior if I had allowed him to do the draft. In getting half the kudos and the money, he is doing well for himself.'[1]

Knoblock's reaction was more generous. 'I might possibly have written the play by myself after finishing the scenario. But it would never have turned out to be a play of the same mellowness, the same dignity, the same restraint. All these qualities *Milestones* owes to Bennett.' Bennett was delighted with the success of the play, 'but,' Knoblock said, 'his Five Town-ishness won't let him say much.'

Bennett made £16,000 that year, largely out of *Milestones*. With this fortune he returned to England, and bought a country house and a yacht. Knoblock had already branched out. After his first success with *Kismet*, he had bought a charming apartment in Paris—in the Palais

[1] *A. Bennett's Journal*, 13 August 1911.

Royal—and was at last able to indulge his passion for collecting antique furniture.

'Money flowed in at a glorious rate' from his two plays and he now thought it would be an excellent idea to have another apartment in London, so that he could flit between France and England, unencumbered by luggage. He had always wanted to live in Albany, and when he saw that the apartment was to let which for years he had coveted— 'one with a huge eighteenth-century bow-window and balcony facing Vigo Street'—he bought the lease at once. Everyone else was still busily collecting English oak, or early eighteenth-century furniture. Knoblock took immense care to decorate and furnish his rooms in his favourite Regency style—one which at that time was completely unfashionable, but perfectly suited to the period when Holland's additions were made to Albany. Few inhabitants of Albany at any time can have taken as much trouble over the decoration of their chambers. He described them when he had finished.

'The principal room was very large and exceptionally lofty—about twenty feet high. I am not exaggerating, for adjacent to it were two small rooms one above the other, the upper being reached by a tiny winding staircase. The one below I made my bedroom—the one above a very small dining-room . . . The big room to which I have already referred had a smaller one off of it, by which it was connected with an archway. Here I had my books and did my writing. In the big room was a piano, a huge sofa in the bow-window, a Récamier couch and various cabinets—all, of course, of solemn Regency. The walls were marbled in a deep sienna and varnished, softly reflecting the light from the window at day-time, and the candle-light at night. As a border for the various panels into which the walls were cut up I found an old model in the hall of a Club, which had not been altered for a hundred years. It was a variation of the Greek key-pattern, very beautiful and intricate. I engaged a special artist to do this painting, which took him over two months to complete. Many years later when I had left Albany, I was one day introduced to a tenant that had succeeded me.

' "I've got your old rooms, you know," he said. "But, of course, I had them all repainted apple-green."

'I could have killed the vandal, for here I thought I had done something which others would respect. The varnish only mellowed the colour in time, and could easily have been washed down. There was no necessity of renewing the decoration because of London grime.

'But the taste of man is unaccountable and intensely personal. And perhaps this fool was right. He wanted the room to express his personality, just as I wanted it to express mine. And clearly his ego was an "arty" shade of apple-green.'[1]

War came and after a very short time Knoblock felt that his work in the theatre was out of place. He tried to join up, but was refused as an American citizen. Until the War he had never bothered about his nationality, but the sinking of the *Lusitania* decided him. America was apparently determined to remain neutral. Knoblock felt that he belonged to England. Before finally committing himself he called on Henry James, whom he had known for many years, and whose nephews had been at Harvard with him.

'You first discovered yourself in England, just as I did myself,' said James, 'and a self-discovery is always a rebirth . . . You will never go back to live in America. Go and do as I am doing.'—He was taking out naturalization papers—'You are right. Your first duty is to this country.'

Through an introduction from Somerset Maugham, Knoblock, now a subject of the King, found himself in an Intelligence Department, and after some travelling about was sent to Greece. Arnold Bennett, meanwhile, was in London most of the week, staying at the Royal Thames Yacht Club in Piccadilly. With the War there had come a

[1] E. Knoblock, *Round the Room*, pp. 195-7.

big drop in his earnings. He worked for several Government Departments and turned more and more to journalism. Living at a club, dining out in restaurants and hotels, and meeting people in the political and social world of London, he was rapidly becoming a man-about-town. By so doing he lost his strength—the strength which was drawn from the Five Towns, the Potteries, from the scenes and characters he had known in his childhood.

He planned a complete change of direction. He would write novels now about life in London. His relationship with his wife was worsening; he went to their home in the country only on Saturday and left early every Monday morning. He worked immensely hard, for he had never become accustomed to the luxuries of life, though he revelled in them all, and was haunted by fears of poverty, illness and old age. He slept badly and carried round with him a variety of patent medicines—tonics and tablets.

On the evening of the 26th of September 1917, Bennett was in Albany, perhaps using Knoblock's rooms, which were often offered to his friends. Bennett was working on a novel about the life of a French *cocotte* in war-time London. He wrote in his diary:

'Yacht Club.

I wrote a chapter of novel in the morning, a Sardonyx article in the afternoon. Began the day feeling perfectly rotten, and ended it feeling quite well. A raid began precisely at the moment I left the Yacht Club. The buses seemed to quicken, the streets appreciably emptied. Most people hurried; I did; but a few strolled along. I was glad when I got to the Albany. Firing when there nearer, and everything was faintly lit up with flashes. I found that the Albany alley had been covered with thick glass thrown over from an explosion or a hit on the Academy on the previous night.'[1]

[1] *Journal of Arnold Bennett*, p. 205.

This German bomb had dropped on the premises of the
Royal Academy, immediately behind Block C of Albany.
Several chimney stacks were damaged by the explosion,
but British anti-aircraft guns were responsible for the only
lasting scar. A piece of shrapnel fell on the roof of Albany's
covered way and made a hole through one of the old slates
which form its roof. It proved impossible to find a modern
slate of equal size, so the old one was patched and replaced
in position.

Knoblock returned on leave a few weeks later. He had
been invalided home from a hospital ship off the Turkish
coast. He found London much changed. Food regulations
were very strict, dancing was more popular, there were
few taxis and the streets at night were dimly-lit. Everyone was working for the war. 'When the wounded were
well enough, dowagers would drive them out in their cars
to visit whatever sights they cared to see. The men almost
invariably asked to be taken to Hilldrop Crescent, where
Crippen, the murderer, had lived and buried his wife's
body in quick-lime in the cellar.'

Knoblock was naturally plump, but though he had lost
a great deal of weight during his illness and still felt very
weak, his spirits rose at the sight of a Sale catalogue.
Soon after his return to England, still feeling very shaky,
he dragged himself down to the country for the sale at
Deepdene of the Hope collection. Thomas Hope had been
a designer, as well as a patron of arts, in Regency England,
and had spent much of his youth travelling through
Greece and the Levant, where he had soaked himself in
the classic tradition. His vast collection of statues, vases
and beautiful furniture was dispersed at the sale in 1917
where Knoblock sat, exhausted and ill, for the whole day,
bidding for interesting pieces. Those that he bought were
so fine—a huge book-case, a writing-table of faded
mahogany with a rich red leather top, console tables and a
dignified Regency sofa—that from that day he set himself
fresh standards and discarded many pieces of furniture

from his chambers, with which he had until then been perfectly satisfied. He felt that this was the turning-point in his convalescence.

That autumn there were many air-raids. The maroon would sound and a warning would shine out in red at the junctions of major streets—'Take Cover.' One evening, when the guns were firing and Knoblock was sitting in his rooms, Sir John Lavery and his beautiful wife suddenly appeared. They explained that they had been helping to arrange a small Rembrandt Exhibition at the Burlington Fine Arts Club, when the maroons had sounded and they had taken all the pictures to the cellar. They were supposed to be dining at the Ritz. Could they stay with him until then? Knoblock was delighted.

'We sat and talked,' he said, 'and Hazel was telling me of a string of pearls that John had promised her for Christmas. By this time the bombs of the aeroplanes had begun to fall. But this didn't put Hazel off in the least— so thrilled was she at the prospect of the promised present.

' "Now would you have large pearls of a less fine quality?" she asked me, "or——" and she stopped as a bomb crashed. "Listen! There's another one——" she added casually and then continued. "Or would you have a string of smaller pearls of——" She stopped again. "There's another bomb closer," she interrupted herself. "Or smaller pearls of the best quality—— There! That one nearly got us, didn't it? Now John says that big pearls are more becoming to me!"—Bang—bang—"But I think——"

'And so she went on chatting gaily till the old house began to shake rather badly and I finally suggested our going down into the cellar. We did so, my good servant carrying an electric torch to light the way.

'Down in the cellar we found John Lane, the publisher, who had his offices just beneath my rooms. He was clutching a bottle of brandy and a glass, out of which he drank large gulps.

' "I'm not doing this for myself," he stammered self-consciously. "I'm only thinking of all the people I employ."

'We stood there for a few minutes amongst the grime and cobwebs.

' "Do you always go in the cellar, James?" Hazel asked my servant.

' "Oh no, Madam," he said. "Never. We're only doing this because of you, Madam."

' "Oh, then do let's go upstairs again and be comfortable," she said. And up we went for the rest of the heavenly battle.

'The heavenly battle died down at about 7.30, when I walked with the Laverys as far as the Ritz. I was going on to the further end of Ebury Street to have dinner with Harold and Vita Nicolson. So after I left Hazel and John I started walking along Piccadilly. There were no taxis to be had. The streets were inky black. As I got to Ebury Street, which is a pretty long street as everybody knows, the bombs began to fall again. There wasn't a soul in the entire street. I walked on. All at once a bomb fell quite close—it turned out later to be by the Russian Embassy, not three hundred yards from where I was. Ebury Street began to seem very long indeed to me. But what re-assured me was the sight of a huge policeman standing in an area, his arms clasped about a cook, shouting "Take cover!" at the top of his voice. He certainly was taking cover. So on I walked heroically . . .'[1]

Arnold Bennett finished his novel in the New Year (1918) and called it *The Pretty Lady*. He said to Knoblock in his staccato way: 'I've put your flat in my new novel. D'you mind?' Knoblock said he was delighted that it should have served him as a model, but when he read the description he realized what a novelist can do with material, 'for he certainly "embroidered" bits of it in his own fashion.'

[1] Knoblock, op. cit., pp. 245–6.

This is Bennett's description of G.2, which he had made into the home of the bachelor hero of his novel:

'He had furnished his flat in the Regency style of the first decade of the nineteenth century, as matured by George Smith, "upholder extraordinary to His Royal Highness the Prince of Wales." The Pavilion at Brighton had given the original idea.

'His dome bed was yellow as to its upper works, with crimson valances above and yellow valances below. The yellow-lined crimson curtains (of course never closed) had green cords and tassels, and the counterpane was yellow. This bed was a modest sample of the careful and uncompromising reconstitutions of a period which he had everywhere carried out in his abode.

'The drawing-room, with its moulded ceiling and huge recessed window, had presented an admirable field for connoisseurship. Here the clash of rich primary colours, the perpendiculars which began with bronze girls' heads and ended with bronze girls' feet or animals' claws, the vast flat surfaces of furniture, the stiff curves of wood and of drapery, the morbid rage for solidity which would employ a candelabrum weighing five hundredweight to hold a single wax candle, produced a real and imposing effect of style; it was a style debased, a style which was shedding the last graces of French Empire in order soon to appeal to a Victoria determined to be utterly English and good; but it was a style . . . Even the pictures were hung with thick tasselled cords of the Regency. The drawing-room was a triumph.

'He went into the drawing-room, and there, by the fire and in front of a formidable blue chair whose arms developed into the grinning heads of bronze lions, stood the lacquered table consecrated to his breakfast tray; and his breakfast tray, with newspaper and correspondence, had been magically placed thereon as though by invisible hands. And on one arm of the easy-chair lay the rug which, because a dressing-gown does not button all the way down, he put over his knees while breakfasting in winter. Yes, he admitted with pleasure that he was "well served". Before eating he opened the piano—a modern instrument concealed in an ingeniously confected Regency case—and played with taste a Bach prelude and fugue.'[1]

The Pretty Lady had a *succès de scandale* and sold very well. With his newspaper articles and his enlarged acquaintance with important people, Bennett emerged from the war years as a successful journalist and a public figure, but with his reputation as a writer diminished.

Towards the end of the war Knoblock, on leave, fell in love with a house in Worthing—a perfect specimen of the best Regency period, but very dilapidated, overlooking the sea. He was seized with the idea of producing something which would be a perfect example of Regency days—a museum which he might ultimately give to the town. But his enthusiasm led him into far greater expense than he had anticipated and in the end it became a burden to him which he was glad to sell at a loss.

Hollywood claimed him for a time after the war, and soon he gave up his rooms in Albany in favour of a house and then a flat in Westminster, keeping for a time a small *pied-à-terre*—Regency of course—in Brighton, in which to write. Later he wanted to return to his bow-windowed room in Albany, but by that time its value had immensely increased and he had to content himself with his small Westminster flat.

His plays were now not so successful. But his hard-earned experience of the theatre was sought out by many younger dramatists, who learned their craft by collaboration with him. He wrote a few novels which had some good reviews but made little stir. He had friends of every class and profession—from society hostesses to taxi-drivers, and from actresses to keepers of china shops or stalls in the Caledonian market. He received them all alike in the flat where he was still surrounded by the furniture

[1] Arnold Bennett, *The Pretty Lady*, pp. 25–27.

that he loved so much. In fact there was little room for visitors. In his small sitting-room stood furniture of rosewood and satinwood and mahogany with bronze inlay and the carved feet of animals—furniture which had once caused G.2 to be known as the most beautiful of all the chambers in Albany.

III

Albany has in the past appeared as the *mise en scène* of innumerable romances. The convention—well known—of its being exclusively a bachelor community made it the perfect setting for a plot which involved a woman's honour. Alas for the writer—since Edwardian days and more decisively, since the Great War, women's new freedom has killed this age-old plot stone dead.

Let us imagine a bachelor establishment. A woman appears. Her presence is detected and scandal follows. The old situation is dead. Woman is no longer a social outcast because, often for the most trivial reasons, her 'honour' is questioned. No modern author can build the climax of a play or novel round the situation of a heroine being ruined, because she has been seen alone with a man who is neither husband nor brother. One of the plots most favoured by past generations has been put out of action, and with its collapse Albany is no longer a better back-cloth than anywhere else.

But there was one popular novel, partly set in Albany, which did not use this situation. The immortal 'Raffles', amateur burglar, lived in rooms in the mansion, facing the courtyard. Unfortunately his creator, W. W. Hornung, did not check his information sufficiently to convince anyone who knows anything about the place in which his hero was supposed to have lived. Raffles is made to escape from Albany 'with infinite resource', through a bedroom window on to the roof of a cab which was passing down a

narrow street at the side of Albany. His resource, if he did
so, has been very properly described by his creator, as
there is no such side street adjoining Albany.

Residents were also annoyed by talk of 'the manager',
and reference to 'clurks' showing would-be inhabitants
'the empties'. Those who wish to purchase chambers must
apply to the Secretary of Albany. There are no 'clurks' or
manager. Complete responsibility for all the buildings,
courtyard, covered way, in fact the entire property is
vested in the Trustees of Albany. The Secretary is in
charge of the administration and there are stalwart porters
at both entrances whose duty is to safeguard the inhabitants from the less attractive successors of the Raffles
tradition.

IV

It is now regarded as a solecism to speak of 'The Albany',
but it appears that it was not always so. Byron (in 1814)
wrote always of 'Albany' but Monk Lewis headed his
letters 'The Albany'. It will be seen from quotations in this
book that Lord Lytton (in 1836), Marmion Savage (in
1848), Lord Macaulay (in 1841 and 1845), and Compton
Mackenzie (in 1912) all used the prefix.

The Bar seem to have been divided in their opinions.
Counsel in 1854 spoke of 'Albany' and 'the Albany
Chambers', but the report on the legal proceedings of
1900 refers to 'the Albany'. When a circular was sent to
Proprietors in 1895 it referred to 'Chambers in the
Albany', but all documents relating to the abortive Bill in
1907 call it 'Albany'. The *cognoscenti* now never speak of it
in any other way. And they are right, for the first of the
Rules and Regulations drawn up in 1804 by the original
Proprietors and still binding on every modern inhabitant,
lays it down 'that the premises . . . shall be called
Albany'.

V

It seems almost a miracle that Albany was not destroyed in the second World War. In September 1940 the occupant of Macaulay's first set of rooms, E.1, was literally blown out of his bed by blast from the bomb which fell on Burlington Arcade where it emerges into Burlington Gardens. Mr. Clifford Bax, who was then occupying the rooms where Edward Knoblock had sat out the lesser raids of the First War—G.2—has left his account of that night.

'At ten o'clock on an evening in September the loud-wailer keened wildly from the roof of Savile Row police-station. Down in the dark street foot-steps quickened. An air-raid warden shouted something to a colleague. . . . Towards midnight the raid became savage. Our part of London was bellowing and bull-roaring all around us, and once or twice I thought I could distinguish the fuller and more self-satisfied detonation of a high-explosive bomb . . . At this moment I heard a gigantic tailor suddenly ripping two miles of calico. London shrieked. The German high-explosive bomb, bursting at the north end of Burlington Arcade—about seventy yards away—made a vaster noise than any which I had supposed to be producible. That bomb had instantly demolished five shops. . . . The guns were still pounding away, and I dared not make much use of a torch. I had, in fact, to feel my way round the rooms: it was obvious that most of the windows had been shattered and that some of the window-frames were sticking inward at odd uncanny angles, like dislocated fingers. . . . As soon as daylight did come, I explored the flat. Not much of the glass was left. Then I went on to the balcony in the cold grey dawn. Steel-hatted policemen were there at the junction of Savile Row and Vigo Street. Busy midgets were sweeping up masses of shattered glass and I noticed that Vigo Street had been roped off. . . . I dressed. I went out. I saw that "my" end of the Arcade was a Pompeian ruin. Dainty shoes and bright jewellery were scattered upon the pavement . . .'[1]

A week after these events several bombs fell in one night on Savile Row, and then an incendiary bomb fell on the south-east corner of the mansion and again what was not destroyed by fire was damaged by water, which afterwards led to dry rot. In October 1940 G block was almost entirely destroyed by an incendiary bomb. The chambers G.3 and G.2 collapsed and the ground floor—once John Lane's *Bodley Head* and now again a book-shop 'specializing in rare and limited editions'—was flooded and filled with rubble.[2]

In all, ten incendiary bombs fell on Albany, two of them through the slated roof of the covered way, skidding along the paving and burning themselves harmlessly out on the stone. St. James's Church in Piccadilly, where Lady Melbourne's favourite son, William, the future Prime Minister, had been christened, was destroyed by high explosives. A time bomb demolished houses in Sackville Street immediately to the east of the mansion. On all sides buildings were reduced to smouldering ruins. Flying-bombs took their toll. Every window in Albany was smashed. But it survived.

VI

Mr. William Stone, as we have seen, first came to live in Albany in 1893. He was elected a Trustee two years later, when Albany was in a state of disrepair and its future seemed very uncertain. He first took the Chair at a Trustees' Meeting in 1903, but in those days the Chairmanship was not continuous, a chairman being elected often for one Meeting only. For many years now the position has

---

[1] Clifford Bax, *Evenings in Albany* (1942), pp. 104–7.
[2] G block was rebuilt, to the original plans, in 1952.

been filled continuously by one man, and from 1909 until his ninety-fifth birthday in 1952 that man was William Stone.

Albany's position when he retired from the Chairmanship was very different from when he first became one of those responsible for its administration. It has long been restored to its original elegance, and to own chambers in Albany is a distinction which many seek. Mr. Stone's share in its rehabilitation has been large, and he confesses that to help in preserving one of London's landmarks has been his hobby.

Botany, travel and Arab horses have been the other interests in his long life, though as a young man of twenty-nine he stood for Parliament in the great Home Rule Election, as a supporter of the Fourth Party, the Tory Democrats led by Lord Randolph Churchill. Having achieved a 1st Class in the Natural History Tripos at Cambridge in 1878, when he was twenty-one, he set about easing his 'travelling itch'. He visited India, Ceylon and Java, travelled by camel across 250 miles of Egyptian desert, rode broncos in Texas and collected butterflies on the Great Wall of China. The heads of game in the hall of his chambers, A.1, once the home of Beerbohm Tree, who was his tenant, show his prowess with a rifle. In the hall, too, you will see those pathetic relics of old friends—hoofs, polished and mounted—last reminders of some of the Arab horses which he once owned.

Almost every morning when in London he could be seen in Rotten Row mounted on a fine Arab. But how different was the Row seventy, sixty, even fifty years ago. Then it was a social meeting-place. For hours on end it would be crowded with riders, not the anonymous few of the present day, but a throng of the most important and fashionable people in London. The men wore blue whip-cord trousers with a black stripe down the seam, tightly strapped over patent leather boots, buttoned frock-coats with a flower in the button-hole, and tall silk hats. The ladies, if not with a gentleman, were attended by grooms, and of course rode side-saddle. Society women, famous actresses and notorious courtesans could all be seen riding in the Row. Members of Parliament, officers, judges, actors and men-about-town moved in the throng. The Prince of Wales rode regularly, so did Mr. Gladstone. And when the reigning beauty, Mrs. Langtry, rode by, the people parading on foot climbed on the chairs to see her pass.

Herbert Beerbohm Tree, who lived in A.1 as Mr. Stone's tenant, 'was often to be seen galloping hard, reflecting absently on his theatre . . . and totally oblivious of his little daughter Viola, riding her pony at his heels and hanging on to the saddle for all she was worth.' Henry Arthur Jones, the dramatist and critic, who kept an apartment in Albany because the size of his family prevented him working at home,[1] could be seen 'with all his fair young daughters in a row'.[2] Jones had given William Morris *carte blanche* to decorate his chambers as he liked and the bill was said to be enormous. The rooms were those on which Knoblock afterwards lavished such pains.

Many residents rode from Albany to join the fashionable morning cavalcade in Hyde Park. As they clattered out of the courtyard into Piccadilly, Mr. Stone on his Arab, with the tails of his frock coat spread over its flanks, and a pink carnation in his buttonhole, the coachmen of the horse buses would pull up to make way for them, giving them the courtesy of the road. At the end of their ride those who were Members of the Oxford and Cambridge Club could go there and drink as much beer as they wanted free of charge. Cecil Rhodes, who kept a suite of rooms in the Burlington Hotel in Cork Street, thought of buying chambers in Albany at this time. 'I like this place,' he said. 'It's the silence that falls on you.' But he never became a resident.

As their Chairman from 1909 until 1952 Mr. Stone

---

[1] Henry Baerlein, *Squire of Piccadilly, Memories of William Stone*, p. 29.

[2] Harry Furniss, *The Two Pins Club*, p. 12.

has presided over the deliberations of the Trustees of Albany in two World Wars. During the first a General Meeting of the Proprietors passed a vote of thanks to him, which 'drew particular attention to the great benefits each proprietor had enjoyed in consequence of Mr. Stone's untiring efforts to retain Albany as a high-class residence for Gentlemen'.

These efforts he has continued, supporting Albany when times were bad, until the present day, when he has celebrated his hundredth birthday and is now proprietor of more than thirty sets of chambers.

Mr. Stone is the inheritor of a proud tradition. Trustees of Albany, the elected representatives of the inhabitants of this town within a town, have cherished for more than a hundred and fifty years the unique institution in their charge. The connection with the Copland family has been continuous, and today a great-grandson of Alexander Copland, Brigadier F. A. V. Copland-Griffiths, is a Trustee, as were his father and two elder brothers before him.

I like to imagine the changing appearance of these Trustees through the years. At that first meeting in 1803 they must have worn beaver hats and coloured cloth coats, with frilled shirts and voluminous white neck-cloths tied under their chins. Some would still have worn breeches, others skin-tight pantaloons with boots over them, and their hair would have been brushed forward in curls on to their foreheads. As the years went by they would all wear trousers, looser now and strapped under their boots. Then would come the age of the hairy face, until for a time only nose and eyes were visible in it—vast, patriarchal beards concealed all else.

The age of individual taste in dress was ending. When the Trustees first assembled a man could wear any colour that he liked, but within forty years their clothes were becoming increasingly drab and the meetings must have shown the age of uniformity in dress which had everywhere begun for men. Black became *de rigueur*, the top hat, frock-coat and heavy gold watch-chain a uniform. One can only be thankful that their wearers were soon shorn of excessive hair, contenting themselves with whiskers and moustache. Soon bowler-hats must have made their appearance, and gradually the Trustees' dress at their meetings must have become less formal and more comfortable. But how much gayer those first Trustees must have looked in their coloured coats and frilly linen.

Many of these Trustees have been distinguished men. All of them have served Albany without recompense. It is due to them that this extraordinary organization thrives in the centre of West London, where the value of the ground it covers is immense. It is due to them that the mansion of Lady Melbourne's fancy and the buildings and covered way designed by Henry Holland are still today as they looked two years before the Battle of Trafalgar.

Piccadilly has changed almost beyond recognition since our walk from Hyde Park Corner in 1771. The great private houses have been demolished or turned into clubs. The Tyburn stream is piped ignominiously underground. Even Devonshire House has vanished. But Albany remains, a reminder of eighteenth-century elegance, a hermitage; quiet as a lagoon, secluded from the roar of Piccadilly.

The Rope Walk still stretches its stone-paved length, unchanged, from the Mansion to the northern entrance. The same lanterns, once lit by oil and then by gas, still light the way, though now by electricity. Those who live in Albany can still enjoy its cloistral calm amid the tumult of a great city.

And if they listen in the frosty, foggy London evening they may hear the footsteps of those who passed this way before them.

BIBLIOGRAPHY

Minutes of Meetings of the Trustees of Albany
Minutes of the General Meetings of the Proprietors of Albany
The Albany Register
Documents in the possession of the Trustees
Documents in the archives of Messrs. Coutts & Co.
Piccadilly, Leicester Square and Soho by C. L. Kingsford. [1925]
Round About Piccadilly by H. B. Wheatley. [1870]
Piccadilly by A. I. Dasent. [1920]
Old and New London by Edward Walford. [1878]
Georgian London by John Summerson. [1945]
The Private Palaces of London by Beresford Chancellor. [1908]
The Story of the London Parks by Jacob Larwood
London and Paris by the Marquis de Vermont and Sir Charles Darnley,
   Bart. [1823]
Memoirs of Viscount Melbourne by W. M. Torrens. [1878]
Lord Melbourne by Henry Dunckley. [1878]
Letters of Horace Walpole
Historical and Posthumous Memoirs of Sir N. W. Wraxall. [1884]
Journal of Lady Mary Coke
Life and Letters of Lady Sarah Lennox edited by the Countess of
   Ilchester and Lord Stavordale. [1901]
In Whig Society by Mabell Countess of Airlie. [1921]
Life of Sheridan by Walter Sichel. [1909]
Memoirs of Mrs. Sophia Baddeley. [1787]
The Young Melbourne by Lord David Cecil. [1939]
MS. Correspondence of Sir William Chambers at the Royal Institute
   of British Architects
Biographical Dictionary of English Architects by H. M. Colvin
Georgiana edited by the Earl of Bessborough. [1955]
Dearest Bess by Dorothy M. Stuart. [1955]
The Two Duchesses by Vere Foster. [1898]
The Face Without a Frown by Iris Leveson-Gower. [1944]
Lady Bessborough and Her Family Circle, edited by the Earl of Bess-
   borough. [1940]

241

The Noble Duke of York by Lieut-Colonel Alfred H. Burne. [1949]
Frederick Duke of York by J. Watkins. [1827]
The Rival Princes by Mrs. Clarke. [1809]
Life of Mrs. Mary Anne Clarke by W. Clarke. [1809]
Authentic Memoirs of Mrs. Mary Anne Clarke by Elizabeth Taylor. [1809]
Royal Dukes by Roger Fulford. [1933]
Life and Letters of Sir G. Eliot. [1859]
The Home of the Hollands by the Earl of Ilchester. [1937]
In the Time of Queen Charlotte, Journals of Mrs. Papendiek. [1887]
Henry Holland by Dorothy Stroud. [1950]
A History of Albany (pamphlet) by 'Civis' (Leopold Stewart)
Paradise in Piccadilly by Harry Furniss. [1925]
James Wyatt by Antony Dale. [1956]
The Farington Diary
Reminiscences and Recollections of Captain Gronow. [1892]
Jane Austen's Letters edited R. W. Chapman. [1952]
A Memoir of Jane Austen by J. E. Austen-Leigh. [1871]
Life and Letters of Jane Austen by W. and R. A. Austen-Leigh. [1913]
The Monk by M. G. Lewis. [1795]
Journal of a West Indian Proprietor by M. G. Lewis. [1834]
Life and Correspondence of Matthew Gregory Lewis. [1839]
Life, Letters and Journals of Lord Byron edited Thomas Moore. [1838]
Memoirs, Journal and Correspondence of Thomas Moore edited Lord John Russell. [1860]
Byron, the Years of Fame by Peter Quennell. [1935]
Byron, the Last Journey by Harold Nicolson. [1924]
Lord Byron's Correspondence edited John Murray. [1922]
Conversations with Lord Byron by Lady Blessington. [1834]
Reminiscences of Henry Angelo. [1830]
The Age of Elegance by Arthur Bryant. [1950]
The Greville Memoirs edited Lytton Strachey and Roger Fulford. [1938]
The Creevey Papers
Life and Letters of Lord Macaulay by Sir G. O. Trevelyan, Bart. [1893 edition]
Macaulay by Arthur Bryant. [1932]
Literary Studies by Walter Bagehot. [1879]
Sketches in Ninteenth Century Biography by Keith Feiling. [1930]
Sir George Otto Trevelyan by G. M. Trevelyan. [1932]

Hours in a Library by Leslie Stephen. [1892]

Gleanings from Past Years by W. E. Gladstone. [1879]

William Ewart Gladstone by John Morley. [1903]

Mrs. Gladstone by Georgina Battiscombe. [1956]

Life, Letters and Literary Remains of Edward Bulwer, Lord Lytton by his Son. [1883]

Life of Edward Bulwer, 1st Lord Lytton by his Grandson. [1913]

Life of Rosina, Lady Lytton by Louisa Devey. [1887]

Unpublished letters of Lady Bulwer Lytton to A. E. Chalon. [1914]

Bulwer Lytton by A. W. Frost. [1913]

Bulwer: A Panorama by Michael Sadleir. [1931]

Retrospect of a Long Life by S. C. Hall. [1883]

Life of Sir J. F. Stephen by Leslie Stephen. [1895]

John Lane and the '90s by J. Lewis May. [1936]

The Romantic '90s by Richard le Gallienne. [1926]

The Aesthetic Adventure by William Gaunt. [1945]

The Bodleian (Bodley Head house magazine)

The Yellow Book

Sinister Street by Compton Mackenzie. [1914 edition]

Arnold Bennett's Journal edited N. Flower. [1933]

Life of Arnold Bennett by Walter Allen. [1948]

My Arnold Bennett by M. Bennett. [1931]

The Pretty Lady by Arnold Bennett. [1916]

Round the Room by Edward Knoblock. [1939]

Evenings in Albany by Clifford Bax. [1942]

Squire of Piccadilly by Henry Baerlein. [1951]

The Two Pins Club by Harry Furniss. [1925]

INDEX

Adam, Robert, 5–6, 55
Adams, Captain Charles, xiii
Ainger, Canon, 198
Albany, apartments:
  2 (Lord Byron's), 86–98, 123, 140–7
  A.1, 237–8
  A.3, 191
  A.4, 115, 189
  A.6, 191
  A.10, 215
  A.14, 66, 147–50, 190–1
  B.2, 190
  B.6, 214
  D. block, 186
  D.6, 215
  E. block, 186
  E.1, 151–2, 157, 161–9, 221, 235
  E.6, 190–1
  F. block, 186
  F.3, 151 and n., 152, 169–84
  G.1, 187–9, 196–213
  G.2, 190, 222–33, 235–6
  G.3, 236
  H.6, 191
  I.6, 213
  K.1, 67–68, 69 n., 80–82, 84–85, 103,
    108
  K.5, 191, 213
  K.6, 213
  L.1, 213
  L.2, 116–23, 190
  as Melbourne House and York House,
    see under; Rope Walk, *see under*
Albert, Prince Consort, 177
Alexander I, Tsar of Russia, 93, 110
Althorpe, Viscount, 87
Angelo, Henry, 54–56, 89–90
Argyll, Duke of, 73 n., 79
Arlington Street, 2
Austen, Cassandra, 57, 59–60, 62 n.,
  111 n.
Austen, Edward, 60
Austen, Reverend George, 56–57
Austen, Mrs. George, 56–57, 59–60
Austen, Reverend Henry, xii, 56–64,
  111 and n.

Austen, Mrs. Henry, 57–61
Austen, Jane, xii, 56–64, 111 and n.,
  155, 180

Baddeley, Mrs., 7–9
Bagehot, Walter, 165, 174, 187
Baker, Mr., 190
Baldwin, Major, 190
Bancroft, Squire, 205
Barrymore, Countess of, 16–17
Bath House, 2
Bax, Clifford, 235–6
Beamish, Mr. and Mrs., 213
Beardsley, Aubrey, xii, 197–8, 200–5,
  211
Beerbohm, Max, 202, 211
Benger, Miss, 128, 129
Bennett, Arnold, 223–4, 226–7, 230–2
Benson, Mr., 190
Benson, Miss Sarah, 190
Blücher, Field-Marshal, 110–11
Bodley Head, The, xii, 192–212, 236
Bond Street, 3, 198, 223
Brighton, 32, 232; Pavilion, 50, 231
Bristol Hotel, Burlington Gardens, 190
Broadhead, Theodore Henry, 29, 31
Brocket, Lord, xiii
Brocket Hall, 9–10, 24, 29, 124–6, 130–
  131
Brook-Caws, R., xiii
Brooks's Club, 31 n., 50
Brown, Kennish, xiii
Brownlow, Reverend Francis, 116
Bulwer, Edward, and Mrs., *see* Lytton
Bulwer, General, 124
Bulwer, Henry, 109
Bulwer, Mrs. (mother of Edward
  Bulwer Lord Lytton), 124, 126,
  128–35, 138, 147
Burlington Arcade, 113–14, 235
Burlington Gardens, 150, 184–5, 191,
  235
Burlington House, 3, 5, 43, 110–12,
  113–14, 184–5
Burrow, Reverend J. A., 215
Byron, George Gordon Lord, xi, xii,